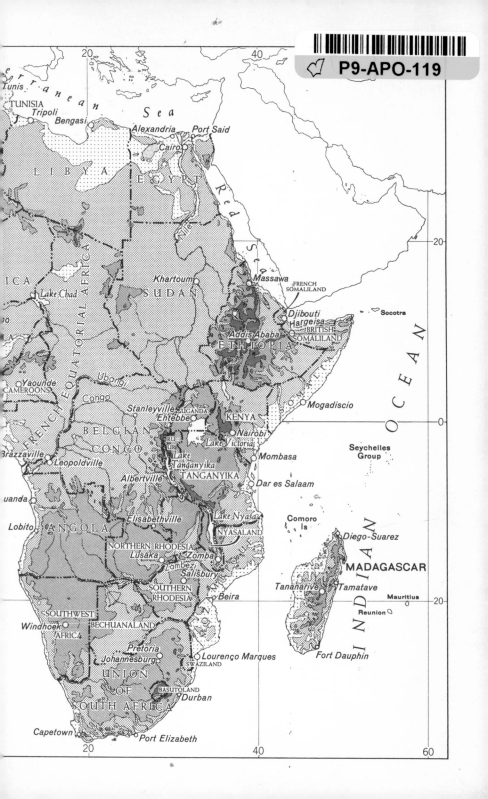

AFRICAN ECONOMIC
DEVELOPMENT

AFRICAN
ECONOMIC
DEVELOPMENT

by

WILLIAM A. HANCE

Published for the
COUNCIL ON FOREIGN RELATIONS
by
HARPER & BROTHERS
New York
1958

The Council on Foreign Relations is a non-profit institution devoted to study of the international aspects of
American political, economic and strategic problems. It
takes no stand, expressed or implied, on American policy.
The authors of books published under the auspices of
the Council are responsible for their statements of fact and
expressions of opinion. The Council is responsible only for
determining that they should be presented to the public.

330.96
H19

Published in Great Britain and the British
Commonwealth, excluding Canada, by
London: Oxford University Press

COUNCIL ON FOREIGN RELATIONS

PREFACE

MOST of the chapters of this book originated as research papers for the Council on Foreign Relations' Discussion Group on Economic Development in Africa, which met from 1955 to 1957. They are based in part upon field work in Africa in 1952 and 1956 and in part on library research in this country, Europe, and Africa. A glance at the table of contents will reveal that the book is neither intended to be an exhaustive description of the economic position of Africa nor a systematic exposition and analysis of factors in the development of an underdeveloped area. It is, rather, a series of studies whose common theme is economic development in Africa south of the Sahara. These studies include cases in agricultural and industrial development, an analysis of transport problems in tropical Africa, and papers concerned with individual African areas such as Liberia, Central Africa, and Madagascar.

Chapters first prepared as background for discussion meetings have been revised and brought up to date. This revision has benefited greatly from the material presented by discussion leaders and from the often stimulating exchanges among members of the group. The responsibility for the contents of the book, however, is fully mine. Particular appreciation goes to the chairman of the discussion group, Dana T. Bartholomew, who judiciously combined leadership and freedom of expression. The other regular members of the group were: Robert R. Barker, Robert P. Bass, Jr., Norman S. Buchanan, Thomas W. Childs, Lansdell K. Christie, the Reverend John J. Considine, Frank Cooper, L. Gray Cowan, William Diebold, Jr., Thomas L. Farmer, J. Wayne Fredericks, Lloyd K. Garrison, Heman Greenwood, Fred L. Hadsel, Harry L. Heintzen, Harold K. Hochschild, Walter Hochschild, Andrew M. Kamarck,

L. Wade Lathram, John C. Leslie, Vernon McKay, John E. Masten, William Moran, Edwin S. Munger, Charles Phelps Noyes, 2nd, Leslie Paffrath, C. Brooks Peters, Alan Pifer, Judd Polk, the Reverend Emory Ross, Roger Ross, W. Clifford Shields, Blackwell Smith, Isaac N. P. Stokes, Rear Admiral George Wauchope, Robert West, H. A. Wieschhoff, and Walter B. Wriston. Frank Conant and Egon E. Weck served as rapporteurs for the meetings of the group.

The following persons served as discussion leaders at individual meetings: John H. Adler, Edmund de S. Brunner, Nathanael V. Davis, Bernard Frazier, Roger Vaurs, and Frederick J. van Wyk, and, from the group, Messrs. Christie, Fredericks, Hance, Kamarck, Wauchope, and Wriston.

I am deeply indebted to numerous people for direct and indirect assistance in the preparation of this book, including many in this country, England, France, and Africa, who made my research task both stimulating and pleasant. I should like particularly to express my sincere thanks to William Diebold, Jr., Director of Economic Studies of the Council on Foreign Relations, who is in considerable part responsible for the inception and furtherance of the whole project. The Reverend Emory Ross and Mr. Lansdell K. Christie graciously supplied material helpful in preparing the chapter on Liberia. Mrs. Jean Pearce, Miss Jean Gunther, and Richard J. Peterec have my appreciation for their assistance in preparation and proofing of the manuscript. Lastly, a full measure of gratitude to my wife for her typing, proofing, and abiding patience.

WILLIAM A. HANCE

CONTENTS

TABLES

MAPS

AFRICAN ECONOMIC
DEVELOPMENT

Chapter 1

ECONOMIC DEVELOPMENT IN TROPICAL AFRICA [1]

THE WEST TODAY faces the tremendously challenging problem of assisting the peoples of the world's second greatest continent to bring their economic, social, and political status closer to the levels prevailing in the rest of the world. The successful outcome of these efforts is of great import not only to this largely undeveloped area, but to underdeveloped areas elsewhere, and to the more advanced Western nations themselves. The willing adherence of African nations to the free world when they achieve self-government will depend in considerable measure on the work that is being done today and that will be done in the next few decades. A brief examination of the state of present economic development, of the potentialities of advance, and of some of the obstacles, will reveal the multitude of ways in which physical and social scientists, commercial and financial organizations, governments, and others may help in this staggering and exciting task.

Although common denominators may be found in all the countries of Africa, Mediterranean Africa and the Union are sufficiently different from the rest of the continent to justify their exclusion from the present discussion, which focuses on the remaining great, tropical, underdeveloped area. This region of eight and one-quarter million square miles covers about 70 per cent of Africa. Madagascar, with an area of 227,736 square miles, may be added to this area, as it, too, is entirely tropical. Except for Liberia, the Federation of Ethiopia and Eritrea, Ghana, and the

[1] This chapter revises and brings up to date a paper by the author read before the American Economic Association, December 1955, and printed in *The American Economic Review*, v. 46 (May 1956), pp. 441-451.

Sudan, tropical Africa is composed of non-self-governing territories, though Nigeria and Somaliland are rapidly approaching independence, and the Central African Federation may not be far behind.

Tremendous cultural, physical, economic, and political variation and contrast exist within tropical Africa. The variety is greater than on any continent but Asia. Generalizations must be accepted with this caution constantly in mind.

PRESENT STATUS OF ECONOMIC DEVELOPMENT

Tropical Africa is in transition from a subsistence to an exchange economy. There are relatively few areas and peoples who have not been affected in some way by the march of economic penetration. Most of the area, however, remains scientifically unknown. Base topographic maps, geological and soil surveys, meteorological studies, censuses of population, and other statistical compilations are woefully inadequate, though great progress is now being made in improving this situation.

We do know that traditional systems of cultivation and grazing, characterized by low production per man and low productivity per acre, prevail over the larger part of the tropics. The rates of illiteracy, incidence of disease, infant mortality, and death are pitifully high. The continent stands out with glaring prominence on the American Geographical Society's maps depicting distribution of disease and areas of human starvation.

Average incomes for most countries in 1954–1955 ranged from $50 to $60 per capita per year, with the Gold Coast having a per capita income of $156 in 1955, probably the highest in tropical Africa.[2] It is estimated that 69 per cent of the total cultivated area is devoted to subsistence production which occupies about 60 per cent of the male pop-

[2] *Statistics of National Income and Expenditure,* UN Doc., 1957.XVII.4 (New York, January 1957), pp. 21, 103, 165, 231, 250, 278.

ulation over 15 years of age.[3] In 1956, tropical Africa accounted for only about 3.3 per cent of the value of free-world imports and 3.4 per cent of free-world exports.[4]

There is, however, considerable evidence of growth. Before the war, the area accounted for only 2.4 per cent of free-world exports, so the 1956 figure represents a 42 per cent improvement in this regard. The value of exports increased from about $429 million in 1938 to $1,709 million in 1948, $2,550 million in 1951, and over $3,200 million in 1956.[5] Imports increased in value from about $427 million in 1938 to over $3,100 million in 1956, reflecting, with allowance for inflated prices, both higher consumption levels and a greatly enlarged investment in developmental programs. Intra-tropical exchange has also increased, notably in the supply of food to the deficit rainforest areas.

A substantial part of the improvement in exports stems from the higher value of raw materials. The volume of the export trade of each territory has typically increased by from one-fourth to two and one-fourth times the prewar level. Exports which have increased significantly in volume include, in the agricultural sector, peanuts, cotton, palm oil and kernels, coffee, tobacco, and rubber, and among the minerals, where more spectacular increases are seen, industrial diamonds, cobalt, manganese, bauxite, copper, chrome, iron ore, tin, columbite, and uranium ore. The Congo, which is estimated to have produced 57.8 per cent of the free-world output of uranium ore in 1953, was still among the leading producers in 1957.

In agriculture, output is estimated to have increased by about 54 per cent from prewar years to 1956–1957, considerably above the estimated increase for the world of 37 per cent.[6]

[3] *Enlargement of the Exchange Economy in Tropical Africa*, UN Doc., 1954.II.C.4 (New York, 1954), pp. 14, 17.
[4] *Monthly Bulletin of Statistics* (UN), v. 12 (January, 1958), pp. 96-99.
[5] Same. See also *Review of Economic Activity in Africa, 1950 to 1954*, UN Doc., 1955.II.C.3 (New York, 1955), p. 68.
[6] Food and Agriculture Organization, *The State of Food and Agriculture, 1957* (Rome, 1957), p. 12.

A considerable expansion in industrial output may also be noted, though percentage figures are misleading in view of the low level of development. Consumption of energy increased three to six times from 1937 to 1955 in the tropical African countries reporting to the United Nations,[7] but per capita consumption of energy is still usually only 2 to 7 per cent of the free-world average. Only Kenya and the Federation of Rhodesia and Nyasaland stand out with 11 and 36 per cent, respectively, of the average per capita consumption.

In industry, Southern Rhodesia and the Belgian Congo have made the most significant advances. Southern Rhodesia has attained some development in all major categories of industry, including the basic production of iron and steel. There are now over 10,000 Europeans and 60,000 indigenous workers employed in manufacturing industries in Southern Rhodesia. In 1953, the latest year for which summary data are available, there were 714 manufacturing establishments in that country and the gross value of production was $173 million.[8] Industrial production in the Congo increased from 1947–1949 to 1955 by 315 per cent. The food industry occupies a predominant position in Congo manufacturing, though output of textiles, chemicals, and construction materials has expanded greatly.

Most manufacturing in tropical Africa is concerned with the primary processing of agricultural, forestry, and mineral raw materials. Industries catering to the domestic market are poorly represented and widely scattered. They include, especially, establishments producing high-bulk, low-value items such as cement and bricks, beer and carbonated beverages, steel windows, furniture, and metal drums. Textile and clothing plants, based upon low-wage labor and protection against imports, are found in many territories.

One of the striking results of development in Africa is the very rapid growth of urban centers, a growth accom-

[7] *Statistical Yearbook 1956*, UN Doc., 1956.XVII.5 (New York, 1956), p. 308.
[8] Same, p. 180. See Section 5 for a discussion of industry in the Federation of Rhodesia and Nyasaland.

panied by many economic and social problems to which inadequate attention has thus far been given.[9] Greatly increased governmental activity, growing trade, and expanded industry are largely responsible for rising urban populations, although an indeterminate number of Africans have been attracted to cities by the same intangible factors that have contributed to urbanization elsewhere.

There are striking contrasts in the rate of economic advance from territory to territory and within individual nations. There is no continuous frontier, but rather a series of economic "islands" in which the bulk of the economic output is rather highly concentrated. These islands are often separated by great spaces where an exchange economy is poorly developed. Almost all of them may be classified under three headings: the littoral or peripheral areas, which owe their importance in considerable part to ease of access and proximity of shipping points; the highland areas, where superior soil and climatic conditions are attractive, and which include the areas of European farming; and thirdly, the mining centers or regions.

These distinct and separate economic islands combined make up perhaps 4 per cent of the area of tropical Africa, but probably account for at least 85 per cent of the value of produce entering world trade. Although this suggests that there are tremendous opportunities for increased production simply by enlarging the present areas of concentration to embrace adjacent areas with similar physical attributes, it should not be taken to imply that there are large areas of high quality only waiting to be opened up. I would hazard a guess that the economic map of Africa fifty years from now would continue to display this same islandic pattern.

In assessing the developments under way in tropical Africa it is well to note the changing relative position of the continent in the world. For centuries Africa was more

[9] See *Social Implications of Industrialization and Urbanization in Africa South of the Sahara,* prepared by the International African Institute, London, UNESCO Tensions and Technology Series (Paris, 1956).

important as an impediment on the route to Asia than as an area of economic interest. Opportunities seemed far more attractive in other parts of the world, and even after partition of the continent economic penetration remained meager for several decades. Two world wars and a world-wide depression further delayed progress. After the second World War, however, Africa looked entirely different, particularly to the metropolitan powers of Europe. To a high degree it became the focus of their interests. Its strategic, political, and economic importance appeared to have burst forth rather suddenly and even ominously. Contributing to the formation of new concepts regarding the continent—in addition to the loss of former territories in Asia and the rise of nationalism in the third great tropical area of Latin America—were the growing needs for food and for agricultural and mineral products, the desire to develop "dollar-savers" and "dollar-earners" within each nation's monetary bloc, the effort to offset the threat of anti-colonialism, and the changing attitudes toward underdeveloped peoples, attitudes which were earlier applied to depressed areas in the domestic scene and which call for the state to assist more actively in their development.

The awakening will of Africans themselves is a factor of rapidly increasing significance. Though relatively few areas may now be said to have reached the "self-starting" stage, the marked expansion in educational facilities, coupled with the great demand for learning, reaching almost pathological levels in certain areas, suggest that the African will be contributing to his advance far more effectively than in the past. He will also be assuming much more of the direction of it.

POTENTIALITIES OF DEVELOPMENT IN TROPICAL AFRICA

In briefly analyzing the potentialities of economic development in Africa, the focus in this chapter is primarily upon the physical attributes and limitations of the area. At least for many years, physical factors will largely condition the possibilities for development; cultural, social, economic, and political circumstances are of greater significance in determining the speed with which the potentialities may be realized.

There is a very great deal to be learned about the physical environment of middle Africa. As additional knowledge becomes available and new technological advances are made, continuing re-evaluation will be required. Only the more important points can be noted in the following analysis; detailed, rigorous studies of individual regions would reveal the many nuances and exceptions to the broad generalizations made here.

Topographically, Africa is the "plateau continent." The scarp zones which lie behind the narrow coastal plains have presented a formidable barrier to penetration. Streams which are characterized by high seasonal variation of flow, by the presence of rapids in their lower courses, and by mouths where entry is impeded by shifting river and offshore bars, have further contributed to the problem of gaining access to interior areas. Away from the coasts, movement overland is often further obstructed by scarps and, in East Africa, the two great rift zones are barriers of immense proportions.

The landform disadvantages should not be exaggerated, however. They were more significant as obstructive forces in early penetration. There is now an increasing number of good-to-excellent ports on both coasts. Along the West African bulge, where surf and lighterage ports were formerly so important, there is an impressive list of modern establishments: Dakar, Conakry, and the postwar lagoon-harbor of Abidjan in French West Africa; Bathurst in Gambia; Freetown in Sierra Leone; Monrovia in Liberia; Takoradi and the building port of Tema in Ghana; and Lagos and Port Harcourt in Nigeria. Proceeding down the Atlantic, Douala, Pointe Noire, Matadi, Luanda, and Lobito are first-class ports, though the Congo's Matadi has access problems and has often been highly congested in postwar years. On the shorter Indian Ocean front, Lourenço

Marques, Beira, and Nacala in Mozambique, and Mtwara, Dar es Salaam, and Mombasa in British East Africa are fairly well spaced, although, again, port facilities have not always kept up with the rapidly increasing traffic. Madagascar has only one really modern port, Tamatave, and it has been overworked in postwar years. Road building and railway construction in tropical Africa is an expensive business, but it is not only the topography that makes it so. Lastly, it is easier in the long run to overcome the landform handicaps than it is to meet the problems occasioned by other physical conditions. New roads and rail lines and improved port facilities reduce to a very considerable degree the dimensions of the topographic problems.

Among the physical elements, climate probably has the greatest influence in retarding economic advance. About two-fifths of tropical Africa is steppe or desert where inadequate or unreliable precipitation condemns the area to low productivity. At least a third is savanna country with adequate rainfall in the high-sun period but with violent seasonality and, again, undependability.

Thus far man has had very little success in controlling climate and, as near as we can tell, these vast areas will remain regionally poor for many years to come. However, there are notable possibilities for some relatively large-scale control efforts and for a multitude of smaller efforts. As examples of large-scale irrigation works, one can cite the Niger Office on the interior delta of the Niger River, and the Gezira Scheme in the Sudan, both of which can be greatly extended. Other projects can be placed along the Gambia, Senegal, Tana, Rufiji, and Zambesi Rivers and in the Lake Chad basin. Lesser projects would include control of flow in smaller streams and wadis, the digging of "hafirs" or shallow surface reservoirs, the further tapping of underground aquifers, and the bunding of vast flattish areas to reduce run-off and increase soak-in in the rainy season. High-powered earth-moving equipment makes many transformations feasible today that were impractical a few years ago, and technological improvements may be expected to bring other control schemes within the realm of economic possibility.

New farming systems will further increase the potentialities of steppe and savanna areas. "Harig" cultivation is an example. This involves the saving of old grass and stubble for burning shortly following the new rains; the burning kills off new shoots and the desired grain is planted thereafter. This grain may then be left until harvest time while livestock owners graze their beasts in other areas. This, or some other type of farming which would make provision for storage of dry-season fodder, would greatly improve the capacity of large, seasonally dry areas.

Some fairly extensive areas of savanna and steppe are now covered with swamps, and the excess of water invites an effort to bring them under control. Much investigation will be required before their proper utilization can be known, but vast areas such as the Bahr el Ghazal region of the Upper Nile, the Bangweulu, and the Okovango Swamps, may one day be important agricultural areas. In Northern Rhodesia alone, the six largest swamps total 13,754 square miles, or 6 per cent of the country, while numerous "dambos" and "vleis," smaller areas of impeded drainage, are found throughout the area. The potentialities that would arise from low-cost de-salting of sea water and low-cost power to pump the sweet water onto the land stagger the imagination.

Possibly 12 per cent of tropical Africa is troubled by excessive precipitation, though the indirect effects of heavy rainfall are probably more disadvantageous than the amount itself. In the rainforest areas, possible advances include the use of mechanical trench-diggers for improving drainage and the use of other equipment for cutting out mangrove trees and bunding the resultant fields for cultivation of rice. Efforts are being made along this line in Sierra Leone.

The areas where climate, taken alone, may be said to be relatively favorable under present techniques may total only 12 to 15 per cent of tropical Africa, but this is an area about a third the size of the United States.

The picture with regard to soils is less encouraging. One of the greatest problems facing Africa is how to preserve the fertility of the poorly structured and leached lateritic soils which cover most of the rainforest and savanna areas. Indigenous systems of shifting cultivation may represent an excellent adaptation to soil conditions when there is adequate land but become precarious and destructive when population pressure forces a shortening of the fallow period. Palliatives include composting, litter-farming, cover-cropping, green manuring, application of artificial fertilizers, emphasis upon tree crops, and the use of deep-rooted bushes which coppice rapidly. The deep roots bring needed minerals to the surface, while the bushes may be burned to supply ash in what is essentially a modification of the usual forest-fallow system.

The best solution to this problem of soil degradation may be the development of a mixed agriculture, in which animals would supply the restorative manures. But many of the physical problems besetting Africa are intimately interconnected, and this one must await the solution of others, particularly control of the tsetse fly which carries trypanosomiasis and precludes keeping cattle in most rainforest and savanna areas.

The soils of the semi-arid regions of Africa also present problems, and cannot be compared in quality with soils of comparable regions in the middle latitudes. Another great disadvantage is the generally meager distribution of rich azonal soils, while soil erosion is a problem of immense proportions in many regions.

Certain features pertaining to the natural vegetation are frequently listed as deterrents to development. The native grasses are often highly silaceous, harsh, and unpalatable to quality animals. Improvement may be expected, however, by the introduction of better grasses and by gradual bettering of existing species. Elimination of uncontrolled and poorly timed grass burning and adoption of proper stocking practices are important programs for grassland regeneration.

The forests of tropical rainy areas which have been considered more of an economic liability than an asset now promise to be much more valuable. At least thirty species of trees are now regularly accepted in the world market, while mahogany has declined sharply in relative importance. Really significant strides are made possible by new developments permitting the pulping of mixed tropical woods. Successful operations in the pilot pulp and paper mill near Abidjan in the Ivory Coast suggest that tropical rainforest areas may become a major source of these products in the future. The increased use of tropical woods for plywood or pressedwood may also be expected.

Health and disease problems reach tremendous proportions in tropical Africa, affecting man, plants, and animals in sometimes direct but often complex ways.[10] It is impossible adequately to summarize the situation here, but it can be said that great progress has already been made and that even greater progress may confidently be expected in attacking these enormous problems. More sanitary living conditions, better dietary standards, widespread spraying, and development of preventative inoculations, are likely to mean that the major problem will be improving the fertility of the soil as rapidly as the fertility of man.

Most of the physical factors thus far outlined have more important bearing on agricultural potentialities than upon development of mining and industry. A brief survey of the power and mineral resources of middle Africa will be helpful in evaluating potentialities in these fields.

The outstanding facts about power resources are the relative poverty of good-grade coal and of petroleum, and the wealth of water power and fissionable or fusionable raw materials.

There is some coal of coking quality now mined at Wankie in Southern Rhodesia (produced at the rate of 4.5 million tons in 1957), and low-grade coal is mined in Nigeria, the Belgian Congo, and Mozambique. Coal deposits are

[10] See D. H. K. Lee, *Climate and Economic Development in the Tropics* (New York: Harper, for the Council on Foreign Relations, 1956).

also known in Tanganyika, Northern Rhodesia, Madagascar, and Nyasaland, but the general shortage of coal must be listed as a major handicap to transportation and to industrialization.

Oil has been discovered in the Sahara, the Niger basin in Nigeria, the Gabon basin in French Equatorial Africa, and on the littoral shelf of Angola near Luanda. Of these, only the Sahara find is likely to be a major one. Further prospecting is going on in these areas and in Ghana, Somaliland, Ethiopia, Zanzibar, Tanganyika, Mozambique, and Madagascar. Recently, a methane gas deposit with heat-producing potential equal to 50 million metric tons of coal was reported beneath Lake Kivu in Belgian Africa. But most of the continent is composed of basement rock where petroleum and natural gas will not be found. Interest has been expressed in extracting oil from coal in the Federation and from the bituminous schists near Stanleyville in the Belgian Congo, to reduce the expenditure of foreign exchange on petroleum products. But liquid fuels are likely to be a major import in most African territories for many years. The high cost of delivery to inland centers is a considerable charge on their economies. Great progress has been made in postwar years in the distribution of petroleum products. Improved port facilities, including underwater pipelines at several points and a new pipeline from Matadi to Léopoldville in the Congo, have been constructed; inland depots have been expanded and modernized, and oil barge traffic has been improved on the Niger and Congo waterways.

One of the redeeming features with regard to energy is Africa's possession of the greatest water power potential in the world. Tropical Africa is estimated to have about three-eighths of the total world potential at ordinary minimum flow, or as much as Europe, the Americas, and Australia combined. The Belgian Congo alone has 21.6 per cent of the world total. At present, there are very few hydroelectric developments, the installed capacity being less than 1 per cent of the world total. In French tropical Africa there are installations on the Konkouré in Guinea, the Sanaga at Edea in Cameroun, the Djoué near Brazzaville, and at Boali near Bangui in Equatorial Africa. In the Belgian Congo, where 95 per cent of electric energy is supplied by hydro sources, the major developments are on the Lufira and Lualaba Rivers in the province of Katanga, where they serve the great mining industry, and on the Inkisi near Léopoldville. In Portuguese territories there are locally important projects on the Dande, Catumbela, and Kunene Rivers in Angola and on the Revue River near Vila Pery in Mozambique. British Africa has the important Owen Falls Dam near the outlet of Lake Victoria and lesser installations serving Nairobi in Kenya, and Broken Hill and Livingstone-Victoria Falls in the Rhodesias.

The largest hydroelectric project under construction is at the Kariba Gorge on the Zambesi in the Central African Federation. Other developments that are being studied more or less intensively include additional projects on the Konkouré, a large scheme on the Kouilou in French Equatorial Africa, the Volta Scheme in Ghana, and the Inga Falls project on the lower Congo, which might have an installed capacity of no less than 20 million kilowatts, far larger than any other project in the world. The tremendous reserves of hydro power in tropical Africa are bound to stimulate the introduction of industries using electrical processes, particularly the production of aluminum from either domestic or imported bauxite and alumina. They may also attract the pulp and paper industry and lead to the electrification of the railways in favored areas.

Possession of some of the world's greatest known reserves of uranium ore may give significant leverage in decades ahead to assure a relatively early introduction of nuclear-electric plants. In addition to the tremendous deposit at Shinkolobwe, Belgian Congo, there are known reserves of fissionable raw materials in many tropical African countries including Nigeria, French Equatorial Africa, the Federation of Rhodesia and Nyasaland, Mozambique, Madagascar, British East Africa, and Ethiopia.

The energy position, then, shows exciting possibilities, but the great variation from place to place, the unfortunate location of many of the reserves, and the shortage of coal and oil are restrictive factors. The general absence of coking coal will inhibit the introduction of the iron and steel industry, which is still the foundation of a modern, integrated, industrial complex.

Iron ore, the second major raw material for iron and steel, is mined in tropical Africa at Que Que, Southern Rhodesia, in Liberia, French Guinea, and Sierra Leone. Except for Que Que, the ores are exported and are not well situated with regard to coal. Other iron ore deposits are known, and those in Tanganyika and Mozambique are close to low-grade coal.

Tropical Africa has a wealth of other mineral resources. Among the non-ferrous metals, it may soon become the chief producer of copper, and there are good-to-excellent reserves of lead, zinc, tin, bauxite, asbestos, and gold. In ferro-alloys, it is an important producer of manganese, cobalt, chromium, vanadium, and columbium ores. Prospects for the future appear bright, because much of the area remains to be thoroughly surveyed, and because large reserves remain in the existent bodies, while some sizable bodies are known that have not yet been opened up. However, greater significance probably attaches to the sale of these ores and metals to provide funds for development than as raw materials for African industry. Smelting and refining are important segments of manufacturing in many territories but there are few examples of metal-fabricating industries and there are not likely to be many for years to come.

In concluding this section, four points should perhaps be stressed: (1) the great force of the physical environment in Africa, which impresses students from all disciplines who examine the continent; (2) the great need for intensified research; (3) the fact that solution of many non-physical problems must await the solution of these basic scientific difficulties; and (4) the fact that it will take time, perhaps a long time, to find solutions to many of the problems noted. Here is one of the great dilemmas of the African scene: political and population pressures often call for speed, the physical environment and the need for time for adequate scientific research impede it. Nonetheless, it is quite obvious that an output far in excess of the present level is possible, and indeed practicable with known techniques.

SOME OBSTACLES TO ECONOMIC DEVELOPMENT

With a broad conception of the potentialities in mind, it is possible to focus very briefly upon certain of the problems and obstacles in the path of African advancement. Some of the obstacles have already been touched upon, including those associated with the physical environment, the absence of well-developed transport and distributive systems, and inadequate production of power. Other important deficiencies are: the inadequacy of statistical, economic, and social information; the shortage of investment capital; quantitative and qualitative labor shortages; and the whole broad range of problems in the social, cultural, and political fields, which are closely interwoven with the more directly physical problems. The human problems include some that are probably far more difficult to solve than the economic and physical ones. Many of these problems will be encountered in the context of a specific topic or area in the chapters that follow. But two great problems may be singled out for final brief discussion in this introductory analysis: the imbalance between population and resources in many African areas, and the imbalance in the rate of agricultural advance as compared with other occupations.

The population of tropical Africa is about 165 to 175 million, making an over-all density of only 20 to 21 per square mile. But these density figures are meaningless in view of the great variations in actual densities and the capacity of areas to support people. It is all too often assumed that Africa suffers from lack of population when in reality very considerable areas are overpopulated. Most of the desert, discontinuous belts in the Sudan of West Africa and in the humid tropical regions along the Guinea Coast, the Victoria plateau and many of the highlands of East Africa, Ruanda-Urundi and adjacent parts of the Belgian Congo, and Nyasaland show evidences of strain. Increasing rates of natural growth threaten to place other areas in the same category. These densely populated regions contain some of the most serious actual and potential problem centers of Africa. They may appear to cover a relatively small part of the total area, but the numbers of people involved are a far higher percentage of the total population.

On the other hand, areas such as the two Rhodesias, the Congo Basin, and French Equatorial Africa could probably develop more rapidly if they had larger populations. In these areas, a low density has necessitated a wasteful system of migrant labor, limited the development of a domestic market, made more difficult the construction of transport and public utilities, and led to serious problems occasioned by excessive migration of able-bodied males from the farming communities.

There are, however, certain real advantages in a relatively low population. When labor is plentiful and cheap, the temptation is strong to use it poorly. One sees Africans in these areas cutting grass lawns with knives, mining with pick axes, and building roads by hand. Where labor is scarce, more attention is given to the productivity of the individual African, labor-saving equipment is employed, and there is greater possibility of eventually achieving a standard well above the peasant level. Certainly it is far easier to set ambitious goals in areas like the Congo than it is in southern Nigeria, where an increasing population constantly presses against the available resources.

The second broad problem of imbalance is the slow advance of agriculture in relation to other pursuits. The output of food in Africa is not adequate to meet the needs of the present population; the rate of expansion of food production in the postwar years has not been adequate; large areas that should and could be surplus food producers are becoming more important deficit areas. Unless agricultural supplies expand more rapidly, advances in other fields will be increasingly impeded, as will the organic growth of the economies involved.

Contributing to the serious dimensions of this problem, in addition to all the physical difficulties and the pressure of population on the land already noted, have been an overemphasis on cash cropping in some areas and an excessive migration of men from tribal areas in others. In the Rhodesias, for example, from 40 to 70 per cent of the males are absent from many rural areas, resulting in a deterioration in the systems of cultivation, an unbalanced diet in the home community, and an inadequate supply of domestically produced food in the mining centers. Greater attention must be given almost everywhere to indigenous agricultural development.

Clearly, the obstacles to economic development in tropical Africa are impressive in their number, variety, and seriousness. But the potentialities of Africa make it realistic to aim toward far higher standards than prevail today. Each of the following chapters analyzes some aspect of economic development. The first two are devoted to case studies in agricultural and industrial development. Chapter 4 examines transportation, illuminating the pervasive and basic influence of this factor on the economies of tropical Africa. The succeeding chapters examine the economic potentials of specific areas: Central Africa, East Africa, Liberia, and Madagascar, though in each case from a somewhat different approach. In these studies, many of the elements and problems that have been mentioned in this introductory chapter are further developed, or are highlighted in the setting of a specific area or activity. Each chapter, it is hoped, will contribute to an understanding of the imperative challenge that is posed by the difficulties and by the potentialities of tropical Africa.

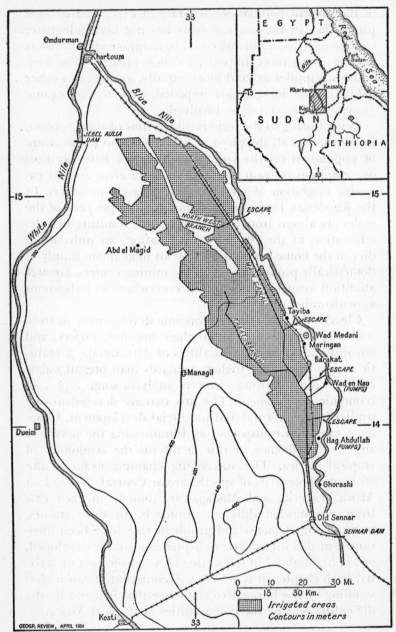

Map 1. The Gezira Scheme

Chapter 2

THE GEZIRA SCHEME, A STUDY IN AGRICULTURAL DEVELOPMENT

RAPID, even spectacular, progress has been made in the agricultural development of specific African areas in post-war years. But if these areas were entered on a map, they would appear as tiny oases in a largely self-sufficient, traditional, low-productive, agricultural desert. Throughout most of tropical Africa the peasants and pastoralists are still economically enslaved by archaic techniques and primitive systems. These systems no longer provide an adequate basis for the growing needs of Africa and of the world.

Many factors contribute to the urgency of tropical Africa's agricultural situation. Among the more important are the following:

1. In many areas, misuse of the land—the continent's most valuable resource—threatens permanent loss, or will saddle future generations with enormous costs for regeneration. Over-grazing, destruction of vegetation by fire, over-cropping, and improper rotational practices, including emphasis on a single crop, are important examples of misuse. Degradation of the soil and vegetation, outright erosion, and reduction of available water, are the consequences.
2. The ravages of plant and animal pests and diseases plague many areas, while human disease takes a terrible toll in life and energy.
3. Even areas with non-destructive practices require agricultural improvement, because most Africans have an improperly balanced, if not inadequate, diet. The Afri-

can continent stands out with undesirable prominence on the maps depicting areas of human starvation.[1]

4. In large areas, the population is growing with such rapidity, or has already reached such densities, that the land is, or soon will be, incapable of supporting it. As medical knowledge improves, the fear arises that population growth will outstrip the development and adoption of improved agricultural techniques, so that the fertility of man will surpass the fertility of the soil.

5. In some regions, excessive migration of men to seek employment in mining, agriculture, and industry has led to deterioration in farming practices and in dietary standards in the home communities, while at the same time creating food-supply problems in the mining and industrial centers.

6. Overemphasis on cash crops has been carried to extremes in some areas. This is not only harmful to the food supply, but causes more rapid soil deterioration.

7. No effective economic advance is likely to be achieved in any country unless greater output per worker is achieved. In some territories increased productivity may be achieved by building up mining and industry. But opportunities along these lines are quite limited in many regions, and any improvement in the economic standard must come primarily in agriculture, whether grazing or tillage.

8. The continent's ability to export, to meet the demands of other areas, and to pay for the imports it requires, is obviously reduced by many of these factors.

Unfortunately, agricultural problems are often more intransigent than others. Solutions to many of the physical problems will require long periods and heavy expenditure on research. We do not know, for example, how to maintain the fertility of tropical latasols (the poorly structured and leached soils characteristic of the humid tropics);

1 Jacques M. May, "The Mapping of Human Starvation," *The Geographical Review*, v. 43 (July 1953), pp. 253-255; "Human Starvation," *Focus*, v. 4 (May 1954), 6 p.

cattle cannot be kept in tsetse-ridden regions, and hence
the soil is deprived of restorative manures that would be
supplied in a mixed agriculture; we have only partial
answers to control of disease and insects. Similarly, investment in agriculture is usually less attractive than in mining,
commerce, or industry, and is more likely to raise suspi-
cions in nationalistically minded Africans. The human and
social problems compound the difficulties.

Yet it is probably no exaggeration to say that most other
forms of progress in underdeveloped territories ultimately
depend on substantially raising agricultural production
and productivity.

Granted the urgent need for increased agricultural production and productivity, the question becomes: How
can these goals best be achieved? Many interested persons
feel that the objectives will not be met in the African
milieu unless some greater organization and direction are
applied than in the past. There is no agreement regarding
the right form and degree of organization and direction,
but their importance is recognized in numerous development projects and in such large-scale programs as the
paysannat indigène system of the Congo, the agricultural
development program of Kenya (the Swynnerton Plan),
and the reserve development program in Southern
Rhodesia.

The Gezira Scheme in the Sudan is an important example of an agricultural project which contains strong
elements of direction and organization. It is often considered a classic example of the technique of developing
underdeveloped areas. Of interest to anyone concerned
with the advancement of African agriculture, it has already served as prototype for several more recent experiments in widely separated areas of the continent.

PHYSICAL ENVIRONMENT OF THE GEZIRA SCHEME

The Gezira Scheme, started in the 1920s, is almost a
grandfather among African development projects. It took

its name from "the Gezira," or "island," a five-million-acre clay plain stretching between the Blue Nile and the White Nile south of Khartoum, capital of the Sudan (Map 1).

Before the scheme was begun the semi-pastoral population of the area lived a traditional life, still enslaved by the requirements of a capricious climate. Average annual precipitation in this steppe area varied from about 7 inches in the north to about 18 inches in the south, with a pronounced maximum in July and August and at least five winter months of absolute aridity. The rainfall permitted the planting of drought-tolerant grain, but at least two years in five produced poor crops. In the winter, the pastoralist-cultivators were forced to migrate southward to better grazing areas. The livestock in these days were mainly goats, which browsed on the sparse thorn-bush of the plain. Water for man and beast had to be hauled night and day from 120-foot-deep, hand-dug wells.

Today about one million acres, or one-fifth of the area, have been brought into the scheme and about half of them are irrigated each year. Cotton is the economic mainstay of the operation but there is also an assured production of food and fodder. A highly organized, highly productive irrigation system has replaced a low-productive, precarious semi-pastoralism. The ability to support people has been enormously increased.

Despite certain problems associated with environment, there can be no doubt that the Gezira has important physical advantages.[2] Topographically, the gentle downward slope from south to north and from the Blue Nile to the White practically eliminated expenses of leveling and permitted gravity irrigation, while the banks of the Blue Nile were sufficiently high above Sennar to make practicable the Sennar control and storage dam.

Climatically, the prolonged winter aridity permitted a far more effective control of plant pests and diseases than

[2] Much of the material on the physical aspects of the scheme is based upon a previous article by the author: "The Gezira: an Example in Development," *The Geographical Review*, v. 44 (April 1954), pp. 253-270.

would have existed otherwise. During the dry period strenuous efforts are made to uproot and destroy all cotton plants, the efficiency of the clean-up permitted by this period being considered a major factor in the success of the scheme. The dry period also causes the soil to crack, so that greater permeation of water and air is possible. The clay soil is so heavy, in fact, that continuous cultivation might have proved impossible without this annual cracking.

The soil, despite certain limitations, is also one of the favorable physical elements. It was deposited many years ago in great depth when the Blue Nile flooded annually across the Gezira plain. The soil is high in minerals, containing adequate amounts of all plant foods except nitrogen. Its quality is demonstrated by the fact that one experimental plot has yielded good returns after 37 years of successive planting to cotton. The impermeable character of the soil has had advantages in preventing the effects of a rising water table and, more important, in permitting negligible loss by seepage from canals, even when they flow above the general level of the fields. The expense of lining the many hundreds of miles of major and minor canals was thereby obviated.

There have been, however, and there continue to be, problems associated with the physical environment. The amount and distribution of summer precipitation is one factor that causes difficulties. High rainfall on the fields that are fallow the year preceding a cotton crop results in lower yields, probably because it leads to heavy weed growth, thus increasing the hosts for insects and disease. Similarly, the greater prevalence of black-arm disease in the wetter, southern Gezira necessitates the planting of X1730A cotton, with better recuperative abilities, in place of the somewhat superior Sakel grown in the north.

The exceptional heaviness of the clay soils, probably unique among irrigated soils, also has undesirable effects. The impermeability of the soil is so great that no through drainage occurs. It was thought at one time that this might

require the tremendous expense of laying underground
drains, but research revealed that they would be useless and
that a very occasional planting to saltbush would prevent
excessive saline accumulation. Waterlogging, which is inevitable in such impermeable soil, is a deterrent to plant
growth, though its effect is reduced by the deep cracking in
the arid season.

IRRIGATION OF THE GEZIRA

The principal engineering feature of the project is the
Sennar Dam, situated on the Blue Nile about 18 miles
above the irrigated area. About two miles long, the dam
is capable of passing through its sluices a peak flow 25 per
cent greater than the record 1946 flood. It functions partly
as a barrage, raising the water to the level of the main
canal, and partly as a storage dam; 448 million cubic
meters are stored for the Gezira after the Blue Nile flood
has passed. The Nile Waters Agreement of 1929 between
Egypt and the United Kingdom prescribes the amount of
water available to the Gezira: the full canal flow for six
months, decreasing amounts for three months thereafter,
and only sufficient water for domestic purposes from mid-
April to mid-July. Since an area six times the present total
irrigated area is considered irrigable, water, not land, is
the vital limitation to the size of the scheme.

The total area so far brought under the Gezira Scheme is
about one million acres, of which about half is irrigated
each year. Flow of water is continuous during the irrigation season in the main and branch canals and major distributaries, which total 600 miles in length. The canal
system commands almost the entire area by gravity flow,
but low-level pumps are necessary in the south. In the
minor distributary canals, spaced about every 1,500 yards
and totaling some 2,000 miles in length, a unique system
of "night storage" is employed by which regulators close
and fill the canals at night so that water is applied to the
fields by day only. This system assures easy gravity flow,

greatly simplifies supervision, and prevents wastage of water. Its disadvantages are increased silting and weed growth in the major canals, which have required mechanical cutting and cleaning and the application of hormone weed killers. In half of the 100,000-acre northwestern extension of the Gezira, continuous watering is being applied to determine its practicability from the administrative and farmers' viewpoints and its effect on the crop.

From the minor canals, distributing channels feed the individual fields. The standard watercourse feeds nine standard, 10.38-acre, cultivation plots, called "numbers." Each number is treated uniformly every year. Numbers under each type of crop are grouped in pairs, each pair drawing its water from the same minor canal, one part watering while the other is closed off. This arrangement greatly simplifies the watering schedule and maintains an even draft on the canal.

To counter the danger of excess water, four large discharge canals lead back from the main canal to the river, and drainage channels have been provided within the fields, particularly in the wetter southern section. The total length of discharge canals and drainage channels is now about 480 miles.

Careful attention is paid to every aspect of water utilization. Requirements for water vary with the amount of precipitation, the rate of evaporation, the percentage of the area being planted, and the kind of crop grown. Experiments showed that there was no loss of crop when watering was discontinued six weeks earlier than usual, and that stopping it as much as two and a half months earlier reduced yields by only 7 per cent.

The Sudanese have recently begun work on a major addition to the scheme, the Managil extension. This will eventually add about 830,000 acres to the area commanded by the irrigation system, at a cost of about $100 million. Completion of the first 200,000-acre section is scheduled for 1958. The Managil extension will require widening the main canal for 34 miles below Sennar and constructing a 46-mile branch canal to the new area.

In the long run, the success of the greatly enlarged Gezira Scheme will depend on building a dam at Roseires on the Blue Nile near the Ethiopian border. Any large increase in extraction of water from the Blue Nile would involve a change in the Nile Waters Agreement. Before the Sudan became independent on January 1, 1956, the Egyptians agreed to allow increased quantities to be taken. But the amount suggested by them in subsequent negotiations was considered so unreasonably small that discussions were peremptorily suspended by the Sudanese. Since the Sudanese, with a growing population, have pretensions and needs for an expanding economy, and since the Nile Waters Agreement was concluded when the Sudan did not have an independent voice, it is obvious that there are dangerous grounds for dispute between the two countries. The "unity of the Nile," which Egypt promoted as a base for political association with the Sudan, threatens to be the greatest factor making for dissension.

CROP PRODUCTION

About one-quarter of the area now in the Gezira Scheme is devoted annually to long-staple, Egyptian-type cotton, and about one-fifth to other crops, chiefly dura and lubia, plus a small acreage of wheat, peanuts, and vegetables. Dura, a sorghum-millet, is the chief food crop. Lubia, a leguminous plant, is the main fodder crop for the several hundred thousand animals maintained in the Gezira. Dura is hardy, easily grown and stored, but lubia requires a lot of attention. Some of the tenants are considered incompetent to manage it, while others renounce their rights to produce it because their lubia allotments are too far distant from their other fields.

All of the cotton grown in the Gezira is of the Egyptian type; 45 per cent is long-staple Sakel, the remainder its derivative X1730A. The economic success of the Gezira may be attributed in considerable part to the ecological suitability of these high-value cottons and their small range outside the Nile Basin. Yields averaged about 430 pounds per acre from 1941 to 1952, and 464 pounds per acre from 1953–1954 to 1956–1957.[3] Cotton yields have varied sharply in the past, considering the degree of control that has been applied to production. The variance may be attributed partly to precipitation differences, but mainly to pests and diseases. The fight against the chief diseases, black-arm and leaf-curl, and against the most damaging insect pest, the jassid, has been one of the most interesting and successful phases of the Gezira operation.

The "open" rotation system now followed in the Gezira includes four fallow years in an eight-year course. This represents the best known adaptation to the conditions of climate and water supply, because fallowing is an inexpensive and simple way of maintaining yields, and because it permits cleaning the land quite thoroughly between cotton crops. Additional quantities of water, application of fertilizer, and better control of diseases and pests, would permit a shorter period of rotation with consequent higher yields per unit of area.

The requirements of providing about the same acreage for each tenant each year, for following the fairly complex rotation system, and for maximizing the possibilities of mechanization, combined with the details of a rigid watering schedule, make a high degree of organization necessary. This, in turn, justifies the rather unusual amount of direction characteristic of the scheme, a factor in its success which will be discussed later.

Some of the farming processes in the Gezira are now mechanized, including most of the cultivation of cotton fields, the spraying of cotton from the ground and from the air, and the digging of field irrigation channels. Most of the work, however, is done by hand with the use of relatively primitive equipment, such as the *seluka,* or sow-

[3] Republic of the Sudan, *Foreign Trade and Internal Statistics* (Khartoum, February 1957), p. 45.

ing stick, and the hoe. There are tremendous possibilities for further mechanization, especially in weeding, root-pulling, ridging for all crops, threshing of grain, and transport of crops, not to mention the picking of cotton which uses a large amount of labor.

The cotton is ginned in factories run by the Sudan Gezira Board, which has the largest ginning enterprise under single management in the world. Annual production averaged 41,625 metric tons from 1941 to 1952 and 51,930 metric tons in the four seasons to 1956–1957.[4] The ginned cotton and most of the cottonseed are exported via Port Sudan, with the United Kingdom and India being the major markets.

This brief description of the physical environment, the irrigation system, and the crops produced, is important in understanding the lessons to be learned from the scheme. However, the physical assets of the area suggest that caution must be exercised in translating the experiences of the Gezira to less-favored sites. There are areas, such as the interior delta of the Niger River in French West Africa and lowlands along other rivers, where projects closely comparable in all regards to the Gezira might be installed. But such sites are relatively few; hence it is the other features of the Gezira Scheme which are of greater interest in suggesting techniques that might be used in development projects elsewhere.

TENURIAL AND PARTNERSHIP ARRANGEMENTS

Two of the most important and most closely studied features of the Gezira Scheme are the tenurial arrange-ments and the tri-partite partnership under which it has operated. As Arthur Gaitskell, former manager of the Sudan Gezira Board, phrases it: "The question of what sort of links between government and people, and between one nation and another, are really true as a basis for stable, contented, and competent development has be-

4 Same.

come so important to production in underdeveloped areas of the world that some of our experience may have a world-wide interest." [5]

The tenurial arrangements are said to have been first proposed by Lord Kitchener, who was unfavorably impressed by the inequitable results of irrigation development in Egypt. At the inception of the scheme, the government nationalized the use, but not the ownership, of the land. The owners were paid a rent equivalent to the highest market rate before the scheme started, and were given priority for themselves and their relatives in the allotment of tenancies. The purchase of land in the Gezira by persons other than local inhabitants or the government was prohibited. The government has, by purchase in the open market, gradually acquired ownership over about one-third of the lands in the scheme, which are held in trusteeship for the nation. This was possible because the tenants' real returns come from their share as workers, not through receipts for ground rent of the land. Security of tenure is assured so long as the tenant keeps his practices up to prevailing standards.

These tenurial arrangements have obvious advantages: they permit the direction of land-use in the best interests of the area as a whole; they prevent land speculation, the concentration of land in the hands of a few, and the excessive subdivision of land among inheritors; and they provide security of tenure while discouraging absentee ownership. It would be erroneous to conclude, however, that no problems exist in this sector. Although the listed tenants are now limited to about 29,000, it is believed that there are about 90,000 adult males residing in the area. The total population of the scheme is probably 500,000, with an additional 150,000 entering the area during the picking season. The division of profits looks far less attractive when so large a group shares in it, though

[5] Arthur Gaitskell, "The Sudan Gezira Scheme," an address before a joint meeting of The Royal African and The Royal Empire Societies, July 25, 1952 (mimeographed).

it does have the advantage of spreading the wealth more evenly. Perhaps the dispersion of wealth by the social, cultural, and economic interrelations that exist has prevented the formation of a class of rich peasants that would excite the envy of the less fortunate. But a continued growth of population dependent on the area might gradually lower the tenants to the status of the Egyptian fellaheen.

The second important feature involving relationships between the developing authorities and the peasants is the three-way partnership of the tenants, the government, and the managing board.

The first of the three partners, the tenants, of whom there were 29,216, in 1954, have a 40 per cent share in the cotton crop, plus full, tax-free right to the other crops. Their responsibilities are to provide the labor for producing the crops, for cleaning the cotton fields, and for maintaining the minor watering channels. They must also share the expenses of certain agricultural operations carried out by the managing board on their behalf. Lastly, they contributed to the Tenants Reserve Fund, designed to permit cushioning the impact of unsuccessful years, until the statutory maximum of £3 million was reached.[6]

The second partner, the government, also has a 40 per cent share in the cotton crop. The government undertook the responsibility for building and maintaining the Sennar Dam and the major canals. Its share in the returns have been used to amortize the original investments, to pay ground rent on the area still held by individual owners, and, in recent years, to finance economic and social development in the Gezira and other parts of the Sudan.

The third partner, which has a 20 per cent share in the cotton crop, is the manager of the scheme. Two private companies, the Sudan Plantations Syndicate Ltd. and the Kassala Cotton Company Ltd., managed the scheme until

[6] Originally Egyptian pounds. In 1957 the Sudanese introduced their own monetary unit. For simplicity, this chapter makes no distinctions between these units and pounds sterling, with which they are normally at parity.

1950, when their concession expired and they were replaced by a public utility, the Sudan Gezira Board. The responsibilities of the Board include general supervision of the scheme, maintenance of the minor canals, provision of the seed, support for part of the research, advancing loans to enable the tenants to hire extra labor, and financing the transport, ginning, and marketing of the cotton crop. Beginning in 1950, the Board has been required to give one-tenth of its proceeds—up to a maximum of £250,000 —to the Social Development Fund. If its share in the profits exceeds a certain amount, determined by an elaborate sliding scale, the remainder goes to a reserve fund.

In the accounting before the division of net proceeds among the three partners, the returns from the sale of lint and seed are credited to a Joint Account. The costs incurred after delivery of cotton to the local collecting stations and before its final disposal are debited to this account. These costs, which include the provision of sacks, transport, ginning, insurance, and marketing, are thus borne jointly by all three partners.

Several features pertaining to the allocation of proceeds to the tenants are important. This "allocation is based upon a compromise between the reward of individual effort and the spreading of certain costs on a communal basis for the good of the tenants as a whole and for the stability of the Scheme." [7]

Individual effort is rewarded by crediting the tenant with the exact quantity of cotton he delivers to the collecting station and by allowing for the quality of the cotton he produces.

The communal principle is followed in allocating evenly the costs of fertilization, cleaning foul land, crop spraying, and plowing. Some injustice results from sharing these costs equally, for all tenants do not necessarily benefit equally. For example, some areas require more

[7] B. W. B. Sharpe, "Finance of the Gezira Scheme," in The Sudan Government, *The Gezira from Within* (Khartoum: Government Printer, 1954), p. 45.

heavy fertilization than others, insect attack varies widely throughout the area, and the heaviest lands require deep plowing and ridging, while the lighter, cleaner soils may be plowed by light tractors. To some extent, bearing these costs equally may be considered a kind of insurance each tenant pays against the contingencies of nut-grass infestation, of salinization of the land, or of unusual attack from plant insects and diseases. It has also resulted in a wider and more even spread of prosperity, reduced the danger of serious indebtedness, and minimized distress in the less favored areas.

ASSESSMENT OF THE PARTNERSHIP ARRANGEMENTS

What, then, are the advantages and disadvantages of this partnership arrangement? How have each of the partners benefited or been injured? Basically, the advantages of the original partnership arrangement were that it protected the interests of the indigenous people, permitted the long-term financing of capital expenditures, and secured the services, for a specific period, of an outside, independent, commercial organization that provided managerial experience and ability for a return sufficient to assure its interest.

The government got about 25 per cent of its revenues from the scheme before the war and in recent years more than half. The government, furthermore, did not have to enter into the direct management of the operation, which might have entailed the undesirable intrusion of political considerations into an essentially commercial operation. Some fear has been expressed that the present government will be unable to resist the temptation of meddling in the operation of the scheme and that nepotism will reduce the quality of the officials most closely concerned with it.

The facts that the Sudan government received a large share of the proceeds and that there was a definite termination date set at the beginning for the commercial managing company, undoubtedly spared the government many complaints that the Gezira was run primarily for the benefit of foreign imperialists and colonial exploiters. It is an unfortunate fact that criticism of this nature is far more likely to be directed toward enterprises producing from the land than toward those investing in other types of activity. This means that investment is often most difficult just where it is most needed. Insofar as it meets this criticism, the Gezira partnership arrangement suggests one possible answer to a very serious dilemma.

The inclusion of independent, outside managing companies in the partnership was probably one of the more important factors in the success of the operation. Specifically, it had the following advantages: the prior experience of the companies in cotton growing was applied to the Gezira; their managerial skill was of inestimable benefit in meeting many problems; and their concern that the scheme be a profitable commercial enterprise assured a more practical approach than might otherwise have existed. The insistence upon a scientific approach, which has characterized the scheme from its inception, may in considerable part be attributed to the managing boards. The largely successful fight against cotton diseases and insect pests may be cited as an example. Although a variety of techniques has been employed to combat disease, the greatest advance has probably come from the development in the Gezira of new varieties that have true genetic resistance to the major diseases. The Wad Medani Research Farm is recognized as an outstanding tropical research institution. Its work and that of other research units in the Sudan have undoubtedly added millions of pounds sterling to the value of output, not only by control of pests and diseases, but by positive improvement of agricultural practices. Now that the Sudan is independent, some fear exists that this fine work will suffer from excessively rapid Sudanization. Certainly there are no adequately trained Sudanese to carry on the work of the geneticists, agronomists, and other research scientists at Wad Medani, and it takes more than a few years to train such experts.

The Sudan might well study the more moderate approach toward employment of Europeans that has been adopted in Ghana, which has a far greater number of educated citizens than the Sudan.

The directive powers of the management companies also go far to explain the success of the scheme. The change from a self-sufficient semi-pastoralism to an organized, commercial, irrigation agriculture was almost a cataclysmic one. Yet the supervising and managing prerogatives of the companies permitted the rapid introduction throughout the scheme of the latest scientific advances and the best available techniques. The maintenance of fertility and quality, the control of diseases and insects, and the introduction of improved rotation, cultivation, and cleaning methods, would not have been possible without this direction. Its importance may be better appreciated by comparing the Gezira tenants with other peasant producers of commercial crops, such as the cacao, oil palm, and peanut farmers of West Africa, where methods are primitive and scientific application has been retarded. The increase in wealth of these other peasants has not been matched by a comparable improvement in techniques.

The concession companies were, naturally, subject to criticism. There were rumblings against their "imperialistic" character in the latter years of the concession and local strikes occurred in 1946. More serious was the accusation that they were too slow in preparing Sudanese for positions of responsibility. Few people, of course, foresaw the rapidity with which the Sudan would become independent.

An additional criticism is that farmers were not permitted to develop initiative and independence. Arthur Gaitskell writes: "When I first went there, the British administration was blissfully direct. We were the 'Nannies' and the people were the children in the nursery." [8] Dr. Hugh Ferguson, formerly of the Wad Medani Research Farm, wrote in 1952 that the peasants had become expert cotton growers but

[8] "The Sudan Gezira Scheme," *African Affairs*, v. 51 (October 1952), p. 306.

were "still far from being peasant farmers." [9] Admittedly, the requirements of strict disease control and of a rigid watering schedule do not permit very much independence in operation, but experience has shown that some earlier devolution should probably have been achieved. In the early 1940s Sir Douglas Newbold, then Civil Secretary in the Sudan government, wrote that "unless the Sudanese can soon have more intelligent participation in the Scheme than that of a labourer, we are bound to have trouble." [10] In an effort to improve this situation a program of devolution was worked out and a Devolution Officer appointed. His responsibilities are to encourage the farmers to take more interest in the agricultural aspects of the scheme by the delegation of some duties to local areas, and to organize democratically elected village councils to form the basis for further devolution.

The companies and the government have also been criticized for failure to give adequate attention to the social growth of the community. C. W. Beer, former Social Development Officer, writes that in the first 25 years "virtually nothing was done . . . to cope with the emerging social needs of nearly half a million people . . . who were undergoing a complete change in their way of life," [11] and that "it has only recently been realized that the operation of any development project creates new social needs, the solution of which must be found well in advance of their occurrence, and that this solution is as important as plans for overcoming the physical and engineering difficulties if a stable and contented population is to be maintained." [12] One can hardly quarrel with this argument, yet it must be questioned

[9] "The Gezira Scheme in the Anglo-Egyptian Sudan," World Crops, v. 4 (February 1952), p. 51.
[10] K. D. D. Henderson, The Making of the Modern Sudan, the Life and Letters of Sir Douglas Newbold (London: Faber and Faber, 1953), p. 516.
[11] "Some Further Comments on the Gezira," The Geographical Review, v. 44 (October 1954), pp. 595-596.
[12] Same. See also C. W. Beer, "Social Development in the Gezira Scheme," African Affairs, v. 54 (January 1955), pp. 42-51; "The Social and Administrative Effects of Large-scale Planned Agricultural Development," Journal of African Administration, v. 5 (July 1953), pp. 112-118.

whether heavy expenditure for social welfare would have
been justified or even possible in the difficult depression
years. The whole problem of proper allocation of limited
funds in the course of economic development is a thorny
one. It has been argued that emphasis upon expenditure to
achieve a sound economic base permits a greater expenditure on social welfare in the long run. It is also apparent
that any underdeveloped area has such great need for educational, health, and social services that it is all too easy to
build up recurrent expenses to such a point that investment
in economic betterment is dangerously diminished. One of
the dilemmas of Africa is that everything needs doing at
once.

In any case, a very considerable effort has been made in
recent years to give attention to social development in the
Gezira. One-tenth of the Gezira Board's share of the profits,
or 2 per cent of the entire profits, with a maximum of
£250,000 and a minimum of £60,000 a year, is allocated to
the Social Development Fund. In the fiscal year 1953–1954,
almost a million dollars was spent by the Social Development Committee, in addition to the considerable expenditures made by the government on medicine and education.
About 18 per cent of the Social Development Fund was devoted to education, including grants for buildings, provision
of recreation facilities, subsidization of a social and agricultural paper, *El Gezira*, provision of a mobile cinema, assistance to cooperative societies, and educational visits of tenants to other parts of the Sudan and abroad. Forty-four per
cent of the allocation provided aid to public health, including two-thirds of the costs of anti-malarial spraying of every
building and house in the Gezira twice a year, and improvement of domestic water supply by deep wells and surface
installations. Lesser amounts went to support two training
farms for tenants' sons, and the planting of eucalyptus timber plots for building-poles and rafters. An effort is being
made to convert into fuel briquettes the cotton-bush stalks
now being burned in the field to prevent infestation of subsequent crops. A long-term village farming experiment has

been started with the major aim of developing a mixed agriculture less dependent on cotton. Incidentally, this helps to meet two criticisms of the scheme: that there is overemphasis upon one cash crop and that the large animal population is not integrated into the farming system. Another appropriation covers the investigation of low-cost housing techniques, using chemical earth-stabilizers and water proofers to decrease cracking of sun-baked clay bricks. All of these programs, it is hoped, will make for a contented population, able to withstand the blandishments of socially disruptive ideologies.

In analyzing the position of the tenants in the Gezira Scheme, the first thing to note is that a low-productive, largely self-sufficient area has become a major producer of high-value cotton. The standard of living of 29,000 tenant families has been raised from one of poverty and uncertainty to a level that compares very favorably with that of other peasants in Africa and the Middle East. Thousands of others have benefited through direct employment by the Board or by the tenants as laborers. There is security of tenure. The Tenants Reserve Fund and the allowance of ample space for subsistence and fodder crops insure that any unusual reduction in cash returns will not unduly reduce standards of health and nutrition. Tenants have benefited by application of the best available scientific knowledge to their farming operations, and now benefit by increased expenditures on social welfare. There is reward for self-improvement in the methods of payment for cotton and in the tax-free allotment of land for other crops. The farmers have, on the other hand, become part of an agricultural factory where there is restricted opportunity for individual initiative and where all must shoulder, in some measure, the misfortunes and inadequacies of their fellow peasants.

Whatever one's final assessment of the Gezira may be, its successes have been great enough to justify careful study and to stimulate emulation in other African areas. One measure of its success is seen in the vigor with which the Managil extension is being pushed by the independent Sudan government.

THE GEZIRA EXPERIENCE APPLIED TO OTHER PROJECTS

One of the best tests of the Gezira approach would be its successful application to other schemes and to areas with different physical milieux. A number of projects in Africa have borrowed, directly or indirectly, in part or more fully, from the Gezira experience, but investigation reveals that firm conclusions cannot as yet be made regarding most of them. In some cases measurable progress has been made while others have failed. For most, information is inadequate or they have started too recently to justify conclusions regarding their success or failure.

The Niger Project, French West Africa

The Niger Project, the largest single development project in French territories south of the Sahara, is comparable in many ways to the Gezira. What is now the Upper Niger River once flooded over large stretches of fertile land on the southern margins of the Sahara, giving support to a much greater population than now inhabits the region. The Lower Niger, moving headward, diverted the river to the east, causing deterioration of the area and forcing migration to other regions. The aim of the Niger Project is to rejuvenate the dead inland delta by controlling and directing the flow of the river.

The major engineering features of the project are the half-mile long Sansanding Dam, in use since 1941 but not completed until 1947, a navigation canal, and a feeder-canal leading to the Sahel and Macina canals. In some sections the former distributaries of the river have been used as natural canals, while lesser canals lead the waters across the fossil delta to fields that have been mechanically leveled and prepared. About 100,000 acres have thus far been brought into the scheme; it is claimed that over two million acres may eventually be put under control.[13] Some 27,000 Africans are now settled on the project.

It was originally planned that cotton should be the economic mainstay of the project, which was frequently referred to as "the French Nile." But the relatively thin alluvial soils, the poor standards of the peasants, and the high cost of transport to Dakar, caused this goal to be at least temporarily abandoned, and cotton now occupies only about 15 per cent of the irrigated lands. Rice has become the major concern, occupying about 60 per cent of the controlled area. Peanuts are grown as a subsistence crop on the sandy soils in the north and small quantities of fruits and vegetables are also produced.

The Niger Office, a non-profit, semi-autonomous, government agency manages the community and is, therefore, comparable with the Sudan Gezira Board. It is responsible for extending the engineering features of the scheme, for the mechanized plowing of some of the fields, for furnishing seed and technical advice based upon its Research Service, and for general planning of the yearly work. It is repaid in part by a yearly tax of one quarter of the commercial crop. The Board of Directors of the Niger Office includes experts employed by the Office, delegates of the administrative authorities, and representatives of the farmers.

The farmers, grouped by ethnic affinities, are responsible for labor for most of the agricultural operations. They are provided with huts, gardens, animals, and simple tools. Land is at first assigned to the farmer on a temporary basis. After ten years, providing it has been developed according to directions, the tenant obtains full possession of all the buildings on his lot and the rights to the full proceeds of his labor. He may then transmit his concession to his heirs, but he may not sell it, an arrangement which is calculated to promote social stability in the area. The French have fostered the development of native agricultural cooperative

[13] Service de Presse et d'Information, Ambassade de France, *African Affairs*, no. 11 (New York, June 1954), "A Modern Agricultural Community in French West Africa: The Niger Office," 6 p.

associations to assist in training the new farmers, in developing their property, and in collecting and disposing of the crops.

The accounting system is fairly complex, but bears comparison with the division of costs and proceeds in the Gezira. The Niger scheme appears to be at least fairly successful, though it has not progressed as rapidly as had been hoped and its remoteness has proved to be a heavy charge. Some $80 million have so far been invested by the Niger Office, but far greater sums will be required if the proposed total acreage is to be irrigated. It is hoped that the annual net profit per African "family"—including an indefinite number of relatives—which was $680 in 1953, will soon reach $1,000.

Projects in the Sudan

In the Sudan itself, the Gash and Tokar Deltas, small producers of high-grade cotton, are managed under a system similar to that of the Gezira, while in the extreme south the relatively new Zande Scheme has leaned heavily upon the Gezira example. Successful operations have been carried on in the two deltas for many years, but the Zande Scheme, with much more difficult problems and hence more ambitious goals, cannot be fully assessed for perhaps a generation.

The area of the Zande project was deliberately selected because of its remoteness, and the scheme was conceived as an experiment in the social emergence of indigenous peoples in remote areas. This emergence was to be achieved by greatly improving the standards of local self-sufficiency, and by stimulating a limited amount of trade with the northern Sudan in factory-produced textiles to provide exchange for outside necessities.

The Zande district is in a savanna region with heavy seasonal precipitation and leached, acidic soils. Its largely untouched inhabitants, the Azande, were accustomed to practicing a shifting agriculture with a great variety of crops. Cattle could not be kept in the area because of the tsetse fly, so the desire for proteins was partially satisfied by eating termites, rodents, and occasional larger "game."

Because scattered and haphazard plots made supervision and introduction of new crops and rotation systems impracticable, a system of organized shifting agriculture was adopted. Over 60,000 Azande have been resettled into elongated village units. Individual holdings of from 25 to 40 acres run at right angles to the roads or cycle tracks on which the huts are situated. The holdings, about 150 feet wide and quite deep, are subdivided into plots running parallel with the road; the plots are separated from others on the same farm by "hedges" of distinctive trees, so each plot can be given a familiar name. In any year all the peasants in a village will be farming adjacent plots, while other strips will be in bush or grass fallow.

This regularized, rectangular layout is intended to permit the rapid introduction of new crops, the establishment of a uniform rotation system designed to preserve the fertility of the soil, and the simplification of the direction and supervision of the whole project. Eventually, it may permit more ready introduction of mechanical operations, since a machine could run the full length of the village strip scheduled for attention. Incidentally, the land pattern adopted bears close resemblance to the organized shifting agriculture adopted independently by the Belgians in the *paysannat indigène* system of the Congo.

The economic mainstay of the scheme is short-staple, rain-grown cotton. Acceptance of a tenancy requires the planting of at least one-half acre to this crop, plus one-tenth of an acre for each additional wife. Some dura, sesame, peanuts, sugar cane, and palm oil are also produced as cash crops, while corn, millet, cassava, and bananas are important subsistence crops. In 1956, experiments with coffee and chillies were reported. Because of the remote location, it was not expected that cotton could be exported from the area (though high prices made this possible in the early years). Rather, a cotton spinning and weaving plant was erected to produce cloth, part of which is sold in the northern provinces of the Sudan. This is expected to be by far the most important source of exchange to pay for products the area is incapable of producing itself. Productive capacity of the mill is now over two million yards a year. Other small plants, including a sugar mill and an oil and soap factory, produce largely for the regional market.

The Zande Scheme is most like the Gezira in the insistence upon continuous scientific research—which began years before the first appropriation was made to the scheme in 1946—in the high degree of direction involved, and in the partnership type of organization. The Equatoria Project Board is the counterpart of the Gezira Board and is a semi-independent administrative authority.

Early results of the Zande operation surpassed expectations, partially because of the enthusiastic support of the Azande, partially because of unusually high cotton prices. The scheme is now settling down for the longer pull. Whether the Sudan government will give it the same attention bestowed by the British, and whether the Azande will display continued enthusiasm in the face of lower profits, are important tests for the future.

The Damongo Scheme, Ghana

The Damongo, or Gonja, Scheme, situated 76 miles west of Tamale in the Northern Territories of Ghana, had two major objectives: to determine whether mechanized agriculture is practical under dry savanna conditions for the production of local food and of surplus food for the south, and to resettle farmers from congested areas. The Gonja Development Company, a government body, is the manager, and receives two-thirds of the production in return for developing, plowing, fertilizing, and planting the land. The tenant weeds and harvests, receiving one-third of the production except for the yam crop, for which the proportion is reversed. The original goal of 50,000 acres has been reduced to 32,000, but by 1955 only 3,438 acres were being cultivated.

Ploughed belts, each with a different crop, run along the

contours and are separated by wide uncultivated strips as a further measure to prevent soil erosion. The farms run up and down hill to permit each peasant to have his share of the several strips and crops. Each farmer is expected to look after about thirty acres, eighteen acres being mechanically tilled, ten being in fallow, and two being used for kitchen gardens. The farmer thus receives his income from three main sources: from his share of the cultivated crops, from his private vegetable plot, and from assisting with the mechanical cultivation.

Guinea corn and dwarf sorghum are the major crops; rice is grown in some of the valleys; peanuts, tobacco, and yams are also produced. The soils of the western Gonja area are quite infertile, so yields have not been good.

The success of the Damongo Scheme is questionable. The Gonja Development Company has invested £11½ million although only 250 settler families are expected to be involved. In 1954, some difficulty was reported because the local tribes were not accustomed to freehold tenure and were showing reluctance in taking up the land. R. J. Harrison Church suggests that a better soil area should have been selected for experimenting with mechanical cultivation and that the sums invested "might have been more profitably injected into existing farmed areas. . . ." [14]

The Mokwa Scheme, Nigeria

The Mokwa Scheme, located in the Emirates of Bida and Kantagora in a sparsely populated part of the savanna of Nigeria, was developed on the basis of a visit to the Gezira. Its first two managers had experience in that scheme. It had a tri-partite partnership arrangement. The government leased the land, provided villages, built roads, supplied the water, and undertook tsetse clearance. The Niger Agricultural Project Ltd. developed and administered the settlement area, provided minor roads, fertilizers, tractors, and other agricultural implements, supplied the technical and managerial staff, and was responsible for the financial de-

[14] *West Africa* (London: Longmans, Green, 1957), pp. 383-384.

tails of the scheme. The settler-cultivators provided labor and received security of tenure as long as good husbandry practices were followed. The proceeds were distributed one-third to the settlers and two-thirds to the government managing company.

This scheme, which was launched in 1950 with an appropriation of over one million dollars, has been abandoned. Available evidence does not permit adequate assessment of the causes for failure, but they apparently included the excessive cost of resettlement, inadequate research prior to launching the scheme, the ravages of particularly industrious ants, and, possibly, too great emphasis on the sociological aspects of a socio-economic scheme.

Agricultural Schemes in British East Africa

The Tanganyika Agricultural Corporation, a governmental body, was successor to the Overseas Food Corporation after the abortive Tanganyika Groundnuts Scheme was largely abandoned. One of its present schemes, for African small-settlers who produce both food and cash crops, is somewhat similar to the Gezira in organization. The corporation generally manages the scheme, prepares the land by tractor, and sells the cash crops. The costs of the corporation's operations are deducted from the proceeds, and the remaining profits are divided between the corporation and the tenants.

The Makueni Settlement Scheme in Kenya is also like the Gezira, particularly in the degree of direction employed. Registered holders of new lands in this scheme receive security of tenure as long as directions set down by the authorities covering all aspects of agricultural and animal husbandry are followed. Additional time is required before an analysis of these two schemes, the first one essentially experimental, can be meaningful.

CONCLUSION

The Gezira Scheme and the several schemes that have been patterned in part upon it are examples of one among many possible approaches to agricultural advancement in Africa. But there probably is no short cut to full productivity of the land. Simple persuasion and advice, the use of monetary incentive or rewards, communal projects and self-help schemes, organized and directed programs, the *paysannat indigène* system of the Belgians, cooperative societies, and the French *Sociétés mutuelles de production rurale*, may all have their place, depending upon the physical, human, and economic circumstances that exist in different regions. A comparative study of approaches to agricultural development would be helpful, however, in evaluating the great variety of techniques that have already been tested and might contain lessons of considerable value to those concerned with advancing African agriculture.

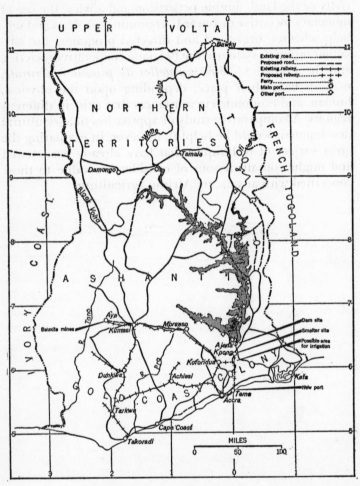

Map 2. The Volta River Project

Chapter 3

THE PROPOSED VOLTA RIVER PROJECT, A STUDY IN INDUSTRIAL DEVELOPMENT

THE proposed Volta River Project in newly independent Ghana is a multi-faceted scheme involving mining of bauxite, its reduction to aluminum using the power from a hydroelectric development on the Volta River, the irrigation of a part of the Accra Plains, improvement of transport, provision of power for urban and industrial uses, and minor additional features. The backbone of the project is the aluminum smelter, since it is the only apparent consumer large enough to justify a scheme of the dimensions involved.

At least three parties would be partners in the development: the United Kingdom, which would lend a substantial part of the capital required, the companies producing aluminum, and the Ghana government, which would be responsible for most of the transport and supplementary features. It is possible that the International Bank might become a fourth partner.

The possibility of harnessing the Volta River has long been recognized, and as long ago as 1924 the Gold Coast government considered its development. In the 1930s Duncan Rose, a South African, drew up a general plan closely comparable to that being considered today, but the second World War interrupted a preliminary commercial investigation. In 1945 private interests formed West Africa Aluminium Ltd. to carry forward the scheme, and two years later Aluminium Ltd. displayed its interest by acquiring an extensive bauxite concession. In 1949 the latter firm secured an interest in West Africa Aluminium Ltd., and in the same year the Gold Coast appointed Sir William Halcrow and Partners to investigate the potential value of the Volta River to the Gold Coast economy. The United Kingdom assisted in the examination through a joint mission with Aluminium Ltd. and the British Aluminium Company. Reports from Halcrow and from the joint mission, submitted in 1951, were favorable.

It became apparent that the size of the venture would require governmental participation, and in 1951 and 1952 exploratory conferences were held among representatives of the United Kingdom and Gold Coast governments, Aluminium Ltd., and the British Aluminium Company. Pursuant to their recommendation that much more investigatory work was required, a Preparatory Commission [1] was set up in 1953 under the chairmanship of Commander R. G. A. Jackson, an Australian who had played an important part in UNRRA and who later had experience with hydroelectric installations in Australia.

The United Kingdom and Gold Coast governments agreed to share the costs of the Commission, which would be charged to the project should it be adopted. The Commission was instructed to study all aspects of the scheme: the bauxite resources, engineering features, manpower availability, financial arrangements, and the impact of the project on the Gold Coast economy. The aluminum companies appointed a resident representative in the Gold Coast to maintain close liaison with the Preparatory Commission and the Commission's consulting engineers worked in close collaboration with the staff of Aluminium Laboratories, a subsidiary of Aluminium Ltd. with wide knowledge and experience in the development of hydroelectric schemes.

The Gold Coast appointed a National Committee for the Volta River Project, consisting of two ministers and three members nominated by the Legislative Assembly, to lend assistance to the Commission and to assure that all matters

---

[1] It had been suggested in the White Paper on the *Volta River Aluminium Scheme*, Cmd. 8702 (London: HMSO, November 1952). The paper is reproduced as Appendix 1 in v. 2 of *The Volta River Project* (London: HMSO, for the Governments of the United Kingdom and the Gold Coast, 1956), pp. 1-19.

of concern to the Gold Coast were thoroughly investigated. This committee, which included members of different political parties, was also intended to make the project a matter of national concern. Some of its members visited aluminum installations in Canada and the United Kingdom in 1953 and 1955. The Gold Coast government also asked Professor W. Arthur Lewis of Manchester University to advise independently on the position the Gold Coast should take toward the project, as the assessment of possible advantages and disadvantages was not the direct concern of the Preparatory Commission.

After almost three years' work, the report of the Preparatory Commission was published in 1956.[2] It soon became apparent that no commitment would be made until the Gold Coast became independent, to obviate any possible claim that the agreement had been concluded while the country was still not entirely self-governing. The country became independent on March 6, 1957, taking the new name of Ghana and accepting membership in the Commonwealth of Nations. Although it had been realized that some time would be required by all parties to digest and assess the report, the Commission set a tentative timetable involving commencement of construction operations in 1957. Enthusiasm for the project has not developed, however, at least on the part of the outside parties and no action has been taken. It must be stressed that no party had at any time committed itself to the scheme. It is impossible to say whether any action will be forthcoming in the near future, though it seems possible that Ghana may make a concerted effort in 1958 to stimulate its prospective partners, the International Bank and perhaps the United States government, to conclude a definitive agreement. The decline in the price and the demand for aluminum in 1957 naturally had a dampening effect on the whole industry.

[2] *The Volta River Project*, v. 1, *Report of the Preparatory Commission;* v. 2, *Appendices to the Report of the Preparatory Commission;* v. 3, *Engineering Report*, by Sir William Halcrow and Partners (London: HMSO, for the Governments of the United Kingdom and the Gold Coast, 1956).

THE SIGNIFICANCE OF THE VOLTA PROJECT

Despite the uncertainty regarding final outcome, the Volta Project has interest and implications of very considerable dimensions.

First, its size alone attracts attention. Under the scheme, Ghana would become one of the world's leading producers of bauxite (c. 1,200,000 tons a year) and aluminum (210,000 tons a year) in the free world. Tables 1 and 2 show the production of bauxite and primary aluminum for major free-world producers in selected years, to suggest the relative magnitude of the proposed Ghana production. The ultimate continuous generating capacity of the power station would be 617,000 kilowatts. The reservoir created by the dam would be one of the largest man-made lakes in the world.

More important, the Volta River Project (VRP) is a fascinating study in the problems of investment in underdeveloped areas. The facts that Ghana has so recently become independent and that its government is entirely African heighten the interest. The attitudes of Ghanaian administrators, politicians, and public are significant not only for this development but for a wide variety of projects elsewhere. Ghana's position will serve as an example of note to other nations, and, should the project be adopted, patterns may well be set that will affect foreign investment for years to come. As the Commission stated, "the failure or success of this scheme could have a profound influence on the possibility of raising finance for . . . other large-scale schemes in the less developed parts of the world." [3]

Third, the influence of the project on a developing economy would provide important lessons of wide application. Although Ghana exports a variety of mineral and vegetable products, its heavy dependence on cocoa is commonplace knowledge and the broadening effect of the VRP would be closely watched. The scope of the scheme would also make

[3] Same, v. 1, p. 2.

Table 1

BAUXITE PRODUCTION IN MAJOR PRODUCING COUNTRIES FOR SELECTED YEARS, 1938–1956

(Thousand metric tons)

	1938	1943	1949	1955	1956
World [a]	3,700	13,600	7,900	15,200	16,578
Surinam	377	1,694	2,162	3,123	3,483
British Guiana	455	1,973	1,827	2,474	2,521
Jamaica	—	—	—	2,238	3,192
United States	316	6,333	1,167	1,847	1,771
France	649	916	767	1,493	1,466
Greece	180	25	45	500	700
French West Africa	—	—	10	493	451
Italy	361	286	105	327	n.a.
Gold Coast [b]	—	107	147	118	140

[a] Excluding U.S.S.R. (1956 estimated production 1,100,000 tons).
[b] Exports.
n.a. Not available.

Sources: Statistical Yearbook 1956, UN Doc., 1956.XVII.5 (New York, 1956), p. 157; U.S. Bureau of Mines, Mineral Trade Notes, v. 45 (July 1957), p. 7.

Table 2

PRODUCTION OF PRIMARY ALUMINUM IN SELECTED COUNTRIES FOR SELECTED YEARS, 1938–1956

(Thousand metric tons)

	1938	1943	1949	1955	1956
World [a]	540	1,880	1,140	2,650	c.2,870
United States	130	835	548	1,420	1,523
Canada	65	450	335	530	558
Germany	166 [b]	250 [b]	29	137	147
France	45	47	54	129	149
Norway	29	24	35	73	95
United Kingdom	23	57	31	25	28

[a] Excluding U.S.S.R. and China mainland.
[b] Including Austria.

Sources: Statistical Yearbook 1956 (UN), cited, p. 269; Monthly Bulletin of Statistics (UN), v. 11 (November 1957), p. 61.

it worthy of note for what it showed about the interconnections of economic development and social factors.

Lastly, political problems of some dimensions are more or less closely involved in the scheme. These include the evolving attitudes toward national prerogatives, the possible conflict of regional interests, and the international problem of the Ewe peoples.

DESCRIPTION OF THE SCHEME

Description of the scheme's major components will permit a more meaningful analysis of the benefits and losses that might accrue to each of the parties and an understanding of some of the major problems.

The Aluminum Scheme

The production of aluminum in the VRP would be one of the most ideally integrated operations of this light metal industry in the world. The exploitation of the huge bauxite reserves within Ghana, the short haul of the bauxite to the alumina plant, the nearness of this plant to the reduction smelter where the alumina is processed into aluminum by use of cheap hydroelectricity, and the proximity of a good nearby port for export of the metal, mean that the cost of transport could be considerably less than for most aluminum operations in the United States, Canada, and the United Kingdom. These nations depend heavily on bauxite shipped long distances from such producers as Jamaica, Surinam, and British Guiana.

The largest deposits of bauxite in Ghana are in the Western Province and in Ashanti (Map 2). Working in the western deposits began in 1941, and the British Aluminium Company, mining at Awaso, 55 miles northwest of Dunkwa, is the only firm now in operation in Ghana. Its output of bauxite is shipped through Takoradi. The largest deposit is situated at Aya, 35 miles west of Kumasi, and it is this body that would be developed under the VRP. Some 140 million tons of bauxite have been proved in this area, where total reserves are usually estimated to be about 200 million tons. Most of the ore occurs as cappings 20-50 feet thick on the flat tops of hills, permitting low-cost surface operations and gravity loading. Another deposit occurs at Mt. Ejuanema with an estimated reserve of 4 million tons. The total Ghana reserves of bauxite are placed at 225-229 million tons of good quality ore, averaging about 50-56 per cent aluminum oxide.[4]

Production of bauxite at Aya would require the construction of a 40-mile branch line from Kumasi. Duncan Rose's original plan called for laying track northward to the upper branches of the Afram River, whence the ore would be floated by barge to the dam site at Ajena. After careful study, the Preparatory Commission found that direct rail shipment would be more favorable than any of the alternatives, including a part water route, highway transport, long-distance conveyor belt, or pumping as sludge through pipelines. Mining would be highly mechanized at Aya, and the only processing would involve crushing the ore before its shipment in special railway cars. It was originally thought that about one million tons of ore a year would be adequate for a production of 210,000 tons of aluminum; the aluminum companies suggest that the ratio should be nearer $5\frac{3}{4}$ to 1, so the proposed final stage would involve mining about 1,207,500 tons of bauxite a year.

Conversion of bauxite to aluminum requires two stages: the recovery of commercially pure aluminum oxide or alumina by "digesting" dried and ground ore in very strong caustic soda, and the electrolytic reduction of alumina to aluminum in specially designed cells with high electrode consumption. This processing would take place near Kpong, 12 miles from the dam at Ajena and 207 miles from the bauxite mines. This site is readily accessible from the road leading from the port of Tema to the new bridge across the Volta River at Adomi and could be reached by new rail

[4] See N. R. Junner, "The Mineral Resources of the British West African Colonies," *Proceedings of the Fourth Empire Mining and Metallurgical Congress*, Part I (London, 1949), pp. 110-123.

lines without difficulty. Initial capacity of the smelter would be 80,000 tons of metal a year; ultimate capacity would be 210,000 tons. The first ingots would be produced about eight years after inception of the scheme.

Since every pound of aluminum requires about ten kilowatt hours of electricity, the production of aluminum is strongly oriented to sources of cheap power. Aluminum ingots have, in fact, been aptly described as "packaged power." Interesting new processes involving lower power consumption are under scientific investigation in the United Kingdom and elsewhere but it will probably be a long time before commercial development is practical.

Power for the aluminum smelter would be obtained by harnessing the Volta River near Ajena, in the gorge of the Akwapim Hills 70 miles from the coast. The Volta is a large stream, even by African standards, with a catchment area of some 150,000 square miles and a main course length of about 1,000 miles. But most of the tributaries, with the exception of the Black Volta, are dry for about seven months of the year, while from May to October they are in flood. The present flow of the river at Ajena varies from below 1,000 cusecs (cubic feet per second) in the driest months to a peak which may be from 125,000 to 390,000 cusecs during the months of September and October. This high variability of flow requires the erection of a storage reservoir, while the need to create a suitable head of water dictates placing the dam and power station where the stream has a steep gradient as it cuts through the Akwapim Hills.

The projected dam, with a 4,100-foot crest 310 feet above the river bed at the deepest part, would create a reservoir lake covering an area of some 3,500 square miles stretching over 200 miles upstream from the dam. The dam would raise the water level to 276 feet above sea level, and discharge could be regulated to give a firm rate of 38,000 cusecs. The normal maximum fall in the level of the water during the year would be 24 feet; the drop to the turbines would be increased by cutting a channel 300 feet wide and 28 feet deep through the Senchi Rapids, eight miles downstream from the dam, and later by making an additional small cut in the crest of the Kpong Rapids, five miles below Senchi. The power plant, which would be located on the eastern flank of the dam, would thus have a continuous generating capacity of 617,000 kw., if the water drawn off for irrigation did not exceed 710,000 acre feet. If all the water were used for producing power, the plant's capacity could be raised to 633,000 kw. The first power would become available in the eighth year after work began.

As the cost of power is so vital to the success of the scheme, the Preparatory Commission made every effort to estimate it accurately. Table 3, which summarizes the results, shows the effect of several variables. Two different assumptions are made about evaporation losses, and three possible rates of interest on capital are shown. In the upper half of the table, prices in September 1955 are used, while in the lower half these estimates are increased by 45 per cent, which the Commission suggested as an appropriate allowance for inflation and increased prices. The Commission found that the cost per unit was so greatly reduced upon moving from the preliminary to the final stage, that it recommended that every effort be made to install the full project as rapidly as possible. This is because the bulk of the capital expense of the dam and power plant would be required before any power at all could be generated. At 0.199 pence per kwh., the Commission's best estimate, the cost of power was considered to "be fully competitive with that from any other schemes of similar magnitude which have recently been completed, or from those now under consideration for which estimates have been published." [5]

The aluminum smelter would be the chief consumer of power, requiring 83 to 90 per cent of the total generated. In fact, the whole scheme would be unjustified at the present time without this firm demand. When the Preparatory Commission report revealed that costs would be consider-

[5] The Volta River Project, cited, v. 1, p. 4.

Table 3

ESTIMATED COST OF POWER AT SUBSTATION AT FINAL STAGE
(Pence per kilowatt hour)

	September 1955 Prices		
Rate of	4%	5%	6%
Assuming 55″ evaporation	0.166d.	0.199d.	0.235d.
Assuming 65″ evaporation	0.177d.	0.211d.	0.249d.
	With 45% Added		
Assuming 55″ evaporation	0.241d.	0.289d.	0.341d.
Assuming 65″ evaporation	0.257d.	0.306d.	0.361d.

Source: The Volta River Project, cited, v. 1, pp. 81 and 83.

ably higher than those given in the preliminary White Paper, several suggestions were made for smaller-scale schemes which might "touch-off" an industrial revolution in Ghana.[6] However, smaller-scale projects would face not only the prospects of higher unit costs for electricity but also great uncertainties regarding the attraction of firm consumers.

It is contemplated that 75 per cent of the aluminum ingots produced at the smelter would be made available to United Kingdom purchasers. There is little likelihood of more than small-scale fabrication taking place in Ghana. Hence almost all the ingots would move by rail to Tema for export to overseas markets.

Transportation Improvements and Extensions

The southern part of Ghana is relatively well served by rail lines and roads, with a considerable mileage even of paved roads. The only modern, deepwater port has been Takoradi, with a capacity that has been increased to what is considered its maximum of 2.5 million tons. Actual traffic has been about 2.1 million tons a year. Accra has been the most important of the surf ports, but surf-loading operations are a slow, dangerous, and expensive anachro-

[6] "A Baby Volta?", West Africa (London), January 19, 1957, p. 51.

nism in the modern transport scene. In addition to new rail lines and roads tapping the bauxite reserves and leading to the dam and smelter sites, therefore, the original proposal called for erection of new, modern port facilities. The off-center location of Takoradi also suggested the need for better port facilities toward the east. An indication of the requirements for expanded port capacity is the increase in volume of imports from 1948 to 1955 of 267 per cent, with the total cargo handled by all Gold Coast ports in 1955 reaching about 3 million tons.

It was originally suggested that aluminum ingots be shipped down a canalized Volta River from Kpong to the river-mouth port of Ada, which would be improved. However, Ada is about 70 miles east of Accra and not so well placed to handle general Ghana traffic as the point selected, Tema, about 17 miles east of the capital. The need for additional port facilities was sufficiently great to cause the government to proceed with the construction of Tema before a decision was reached on the VRP itself.

Construction of an 18-mile rail connection from Achimota, just north of Accra, and of a main road to Tema was begun in 1952, and work began on the port in late 1954. The new port, which will be one of the most modern in Africa, will be capable of expansion to far greater capacity than the present port of Takoradi. The first stage of construction will provide four berths at a single finger-quay capable of handling 800,000 tons of cargo a year, but the largely artificial harbor can be expanded to handle up to 20 ships. One berth was originally planned to be in use in 1957, the remaining three in the first stage by 1959. The major engineering features of the harbor are a 7,700-foot weather breakwater and a 4,800-foot lee breakwater which enclose 500 acres of calm water with a depth of at least 26 feet without dredging. About 3.5 million tons of rock are being quarried from the Shai Hills, 17 miles to the north, and the rail line to the quarries would be part of the line extending to Kpong if the VRP is adopted. Other facilities at Tema will include: special oil berths inside the lee breakwater; a small dry dock; a fishery harbor; and a slipway, berths, and repair yard for harbor craft.

The building of this new port at an estimated cost of $42 million was described by Prime Minister Kwame Nkrumah in 1955 as "without doubt the largest and most ambitious project yet undertaken in the Gold Coast." [7] Its completion prior to the adoption of the VRP will permit the landing of material to be used in setting up the hydroelectric scheme and aluminum smelter without delays. The port also assures the ready export of aluminum ingots from the country. Lessons learned in the recruitment and training of labor and in the provision of housing and other amenities would be valuable for application to the larger project.

Some question has been raised respecting the need for this new port if the VRP is not adopted. But there is a good prospect that the capacity of the first four berths will rapidly be fully used. The traffic of Accra, amounting to about 600,000 tons in 1956, will be transferred at an early date. Some heavy lift cargo destined for the east and now landed at Takoradi will automatically move to Tema. In addition, it is expected that the port will handle 120,000 tons of cocoa and 30,000 tons of general cargo a year. If the VRP is adopted, it is thought that a second finger-quay with another four berths would soon be required. It is possible that two berths would be equipped and operated by the smelter companies. The estimated total expenditure on the port and township of Tema and on the necessary connecting roads and bridges is $110 million.

The need for new roads and rail lines has already been indicated. The total additional trackage required is not great: 39.8 miles from the mines to Kumasi, 28.7 miles from Koforidua to the smelter site, and 14.6 miles from the smelter to the railway to Tema at Shai Hills. The first-class Eastern Trunk Road is under construction from Tema and will eventually lead to Bawku in the extreme northeast. It crosses the Volta by a 1,115-foot bridge, with one

[7] West Africa, April 16, 1955, p. 339.

of the largest single-span arches in Africa. The road will be useful for transportation to and from Kpong and it should stimulate traffic for Tema from the trans-Volta area.

The formation of a lake over 200 miles in length obviously suggests the possibility of developing waterway traffic. The lake would not lie along any present transport route, and there would be no pre-existing traffic for the service to tap. Some traffic should develop from Kete Krachi, where road traffic would be completely changed; the lake might carry agricultural produce from the Gonja district; and the expanded lake fisheries should involve some build-up of tonnage on the inland waterway. But it would be unrealistic to expect any large use of the lake for some years.

Additional Features of the Project

A number of supplementary features associated with the VRP are worthy of note, including the transmission of power to urban and mining consumers, irrigation and water supply, and the development of fisheries.

About 100,000 kw. of the capacity of the power project would be available for general purposes in Ghana, and a preliminary study has been made regarding its possible use. It was originally proposed that a high-voltage, overhead grid run from Ajena to Tema, Accra, Takoradi, Tarkwa (for the gold and manganese mines), Kumasi, and the mining areas of Aya, Bibiani, and Awaso. Almost all of the major consuming centers would thus be supplied with electric power at a rate expected to be below that of the present diesel plants. As such a grid would not be justified without the power from Ajena, and because it could be constructed in four years, it was agreed that the grid would be reconsidered after a decision had been taken on the project.

An assessment of the potential power requirements of Accra, Tema, Sekondi-Takoradi, and Kumasi estimated that the maximum installed capacity needed would rise from 19,000 kw. in 1958 to 28,000 kw. in 1963 and 55,000 kw. in 1973.[8] Pending a decision on the VRP, a new thermal station with an installed capacity of 20,000 kw. is being constructed at Tema and additional plants are being installed at Accra and other centers.

Irrigation and water supply are other uses to which the waters of the Volta River would be put under the VRP. The Accra Plain, gently undulating open scrub country lying between the Akwapim Hills and the sea, would be the only major irrigated area. It has an unusually dry climate for the Guinea Coast, possibly because of the influence on air masses of cool waters welling up off the coast. Irrigation might, therefore, permit a very great intensification of agricultural production. At present, large parts of the plain are uncultivated and unoccupied, though nomadic herds of cattle graze over some portions. The proximity of large urban centers such as Accra, Tema, and potentially Kpong, provides incentive to increase production of foodstuffs. Comprehensive soil and topographical surveys have confirmed that thousands of acres of the plain can be developed by irrigation. A pilot scheme has been established on about 1,000 acres near Kpong to test the suitability of the area for intensified irrigation farming. A second phase will involve extension of pilot operations to an 18,000-acre area; eventually 200,000 to 300,000 acres might be irrigated.

Another possibility opened up by the VRP would be the promotion of a fishing industry of considerable magnitude on the lake. The inadequate supply of proteins in the diet and the difficulties of keeping cattle in the tsetse-ridden south make any increased fish catch highly desirable. Experiments with raising *tilapia* in artificial fish ponds suggest that large production per acre is possible. A survey of the fisheries in the Volta River revealed that the river and its branches are all well stocked with fish, and that set and cast netting result in good catches wherever they are used. Some 400 families engaged in fishing were estimated to be

[8] Gold Coast Government, *Economic Survey, 1954* (Accra: Government Printer, 1955), pp. 38-39.

catching at least 600 tons a year. Inhabitants of the upper river areas show little concern with fishing, and long stretches are practically untouched. It has been estimated conservatively that the lake might produce 18,000 tons of fish a year, equal to the present total catch off the coast of Ghana. Achieving this level would require a large number of additional fishermen, the introduction of new techniques, and building up a marketing organization.

Cost of the Project and Proposed Financial Arrangements

The original White Paper, issued in 1952, estimated that the total investment required to complete the final stage (when 210,000 tons of aluminum ingots would be produced) would be $403 million. The Preparatory Commission raised this estimate to almost $650 million at September 30, 1955, prices. Three factors are cited to explain the increase: the 1955 plan involves 10 per cent more power than originally contemplated; additional costs were revealed by the Commission's exhaustive investigations; and prices increased between 1952 and 1955. But in view of the experience with development projects in many parts of the world, the Commission recommended that allowance be made for a further increase of from 40 to 50 per cent in the cost of the project's major features. Increasing the estimated cost by 45 per cent would raise the total to $867 million, or over twice the original figure.

Table 4 summarizes the several cost estimates, and is confined to the final stage figures, because the evidence suggests clearly that the project should only be undertaken with the intention of moving to full-scale production as rapidly as possible. As the table shows, Ghana would assume responsibility for those aspects of the project that could be classified as public works, plus costs of railway construction and supplementary items. It was contemplated that the United Kingdom would finance most of the power development, while equity in the company producing bauxite and aluminum would be provided by Aluminium Ltd. of Canada and the British Aluminium

Table 4

SUMMARY AND DIVISION OF ESTIMATED COSTS OF THE VOLTA RIVER PROJECT AT 210,000 TON SMELTER CAPACITY

(Million $)

	1952 Estimate (Cmd. 8702)	*1955 Estimate* (Preparatory Commission)	*1955* Plus 45% for Specified Parts
Jointly Financed			
Power Project	151.2	189.3	271.6
Smelter and Mines	179.2	255.4	369.6
Ghana Gov't Financed			
Railways		50.7	73.5
Port, Town, Road Development		110.3	110.3[a]
Other		42.0	42.0[a]
Total	72.8	203.0	225.8
TOTAL	403.2	647.7	867.0

[a] No increase was calculated for these items, partly because they included non-constructional expenses, partly because much of the expenditure (i.e., for Tema) has already been incurred.

Source: The Volta River Project, cited, v. 1, pp. 4 and 83; v. 2, p. 15.

Company. In return for the United Kingdom investment there would be a commitment to offer probably 75 per cent of the aluminum produced to purchasers in the United Kingdom at world prices. The aluminum companies would have the major responsibility in developing the mines and erecting the smelter and township of Kpong.

To coordinate the project the government of Ghana would set up a statutory public authority to be known as the Volta River Authority (VRA). Responsible to the Ghana government, the VRA's board would have a majority of African members but the companies would also be represented. So long as any part of its loan was outstanding, the United Kingdom would be represented and would have the right to approve the selection of the chairman.

EVALUATION OF THE SCHEME

Against this background of the physical, engineering, and financial aspects of the scheme, we can now assess the benefits and losses that might be involved in the VRP. The standpoint of each of the parties involved provides the best basis for analyzing the attributes and limitations, the possible advantages and disadvantages, of the scheme.

The Position of the Aluminum Companies

The aluminum companies' primary interest must be to make a reasonable profit on their investments. Before participating in the VRP they must, therefore, be satisfied that there will be an increasing demand for aluminum, that the engineering and cost estimates of the operation are sound, and that their investments will be politically secure.

With regard to demand, the world consumption of aluminum has been increasing at a far greater rate than that of almost all other non-ferrous metals during the last few decades. Table 2 indicates that world production of aluminum, excluding the U.S.S.R. and China, was more than five times greater in 1956 than in 1938. The Alumi-

nium Industry Council in the United Kingdom has predicted an average rate of increase in consumption of 5 per
cent, and the Paley Commission estimated that world consumption of aluminum in 1975 would be four to five times
the 1950 level. In late 1956 supply finally caught up with
demand in Britain and the United States. Production was
cut back in 1957 but there is no evidence of a basic change
in the long-run trend.

From the standpoint of costs to the companies, the most
favorable comparative aspect of the VRP is the proximity
of the bauxite deposit to the source of power, permitting
a considerable potential reduction in costs of transportation. The 207 miles from Aya to Kpong compare with
5,000 from Jamaica to Kitimat. But the companies look
with some misgiving on the present Ghana freight rates
and on their stability. At 1956 rates, transport of bauxite
from Aya to Kpong would cost half as much as shipping
alumina 5,000 miles from Jamaica to Canada. The companies consider this unreasonably high.

Questions also arise regarding the total investment required and the unit cost of the power. On the basis of the
Preparatory Commission's figures, Aluminium Ltd. stated
in 1956 that "the prospective return on capital in the proposed aluminium producing company is now substantially
lower than estimated. . . ." in 1952.[9] Doubling the capital
costs would obviously influence power costs unfavorably.
The Economist noted that a cost of 0.289d. per kwh. would
compare with about 0.34d. paid by a new American smelter
and about 0.17d. by Norwegian firms.[10] The long period
required for completion of the project is a further disadvantage, increasing the difficulties of estimating changes in
local and world economic conditions that might influence
the investment required. Note has been taken, however, of
the remarkable stability of wage rates in the Gold Coast
from 1952 to 1955, apparently linked with the stable price

[9] "Official Comments on the Volta River Project," *West Africa*, August 4,
1956, p. 569.
[10] "Pause on the Volta River," *The Economist* (July 28, 1956), p. 323.

paid to farmers for cocoa. Also, the Commission felt that efforts to maximize the mechanization of construction would reduce the significance of any wage increases.

All parties agree that the human factors of the project would be the most important single element in its success or failure. As far as the companies are concerned, the utilization, training, and housing of the African employees is particularly important. Other outside observers have also placed major emphasis on these considerations. The White Paper estimated a peak requirement for manpower of 25,000 but the Preparatory Commission reduced this figure to 16,000 by assuming that every effort would be made to mechanize operations in order to reduce wage, housing, and health costs. A summary of manpower requirements in selected years of the constructional phase and at the final operating stage is given in Table 5.

Table 5

MANPOWER REQUIREMENTS OF THE VOLTA RIVER PROJECT

Construction Phase

	AFRICANS				OVER-SEAS STAFF
	Professional and skilled	Semi-skilled	Un-skilled	Total	
First year	1,020	535	2,720	4,275	210
Sixth (peak) year	4,650	2,340	8,305	15,295	785
Eighth (final) year	1,390	575	2,550	4,515	245

Full Operating Stage (All Staff)

	Supervisory	Skilled and semi-skilled	Unskilled	Total
Mines	40	560	220	820
Power Project	18	67	60	145
Smelter	400	7,670	1,430	9,500
Total	458	8,297	1,710	10,465

Source: The Volta River Project, cited, v. 1, p. 28.

Both training indigenous workers and bringing in a considerable expatriate staff are likely to be fairly costly, but there is complete agreement by the companies that the training of Africans at all levels, and in all professions and skills, should be a most important objective of the scheme. The danger is that political pressure might arise to Africanize the operation more rapidly than the companies considered desirable. This danger might be minimized by drawing management personnel from a number of countries so no dominant group could be accused of running the show; by selecting overseas applicants not only for technical skill but for skill in getting along with people; and by having each individual assume certain training responsibilities. But the low supply of technical skills in Ghana, the competition for managerial and technical talent, the propensity for Ghanaian students to prefer non-technical training, and the length of time required for experience as well as training, are negative factors that must be considered. In this regard the Commission warns that some of the most responsible posts throughout the scheme could probably not be filled by Africans for a considerable number of years.

Much discussion arose over the cost of Ajena township, estimated at almost $14 million, a figure which the companies feel to be excessive. An important explanation for this high cost is the proposal to house family units and not just single men. The Commission states that such a policy would greatly reduce undesirable social disturbance and actually pay dividends in the form of reduced labor turnover and hence lower training expenditures.

The companies also apparently have some reservations regarding the nature of the guarantees that would be given them. They feel that the major risks would be theirs, as they would be in the position of guaranteeing the financial success of the scheme. If the smelter closed down, the companies would still have to pay enough to amortize the debt of the power plant. Thus the United Kingdom and Ghana would be assured of getting back the money which they had invested in the hydroelectric project.

The position of the companies regarding the VRP depends in part on alternative investment possibilities. Known world reserves of bauxite are estimated at some 1,600 to 1,700 million tons, of which one-third is in colonial areas; total reserves are probably enormously greater than these estimates would suggest. The aluminum companies could, therefore, turn elsewhere for increased supplies, though there are few places where ore and power are so close to one another. There are also certain hydroelectric sites which might be harnessed at lower cost than the Volta River and which would not require the erection of a storage reservoir and head-creating dam. Certainly, competitive locations are sufficiently available so the companies need not commit themselves to the scheme unless terms are reasonably favorable. It should be apparent that Ghana needs capital more than the capital needs Ghana.

Nor have the aluminum companies been neglecting the opportunities for comparable development in other African areas. The first aluminum ingot produced in Africa came from the smelter at Edea in French Cameroun in 1957; this smelter is scheduled to produce 45,000 tons in 1959. Aluminium Ltd. is reported to be investing the equivalent of $100 million in a bauxite and alumina project in French Guinea through its French subsidiary, Bauxites du Midi, and to be examining a joint investment with Péchiney and the French government in harnessing the Konkouré for production of aluminum. Belgian concern with the huge Inga project with a total potential of 20 million kw. cannot fail to attract the interest of major aluminum producers.

The whole question of security of investment is the crux of the problem to the companies. If Aya and the Volta were located in New Jersey, even the differences in cost estimates presented by the Preparatory Commission would not be serious. But adding all the uncertainties of investing and operating in a newly independent, underdeveloped, African country to the known indefinite elements that occur anywhere raises the element of risk substantially.

Regarding the normal climate of opinion in the colonial world of West Africa, *The Economist* stated in 1954:

The dominant ideas reflect the typical education given to colonial students in England, and even in the United States. They tend to be dogmatically left-wing on all matters concerning the creation and ownership of wealth and the future relations with the metropolitan power. In practical terms, they are hostile to foreign enterprise and distrustful of foreign administrators. While the people at large expect programmes which only western standards of wealth and administration can secure, the educated minority from which the local government must be drawn, tend to distrust—because they are western—the only sources from which capital and administrators can be drawn in the short run.[11]

The attitude of the responsible Ghana officials has not reflected these general opinions. Members of the Ghana government have taken pains to state that the government was anxious to give foreign enterprise every encouragement to invest in their country. Prime Minister Nkrumah has repeatedly told the Assembly that the government had accepted the fact that it would be many years before Ghanaians would be in a position to combine capital with the experience required in the development and management of new enterprises, and that the country must, therefore, rely to a large extent on foreign investment.

In 1951 the Gold Coast set up an Industrial Development Corporation whose functions include the attempt to attract foreign capital. The government has announced its intention of assisting would-be investors in arranging for sites, for purchase of land, for provision of services, and for the housing of staff. The 1954 *Economic Survey* reiterated that "the government has no plans for nationalizing industry," [12] a statement that was made earlier in the year by the Prime Minister. Mr. Ako Adjei, Gold Coast Minis-

[11] "Growing Pains in West Africa," *The Economist* (March 20, 1954), p. 871.
[12] Gold Coast Government, *Economic Survey, 1954*, cited, p. 16.

ter of Trade and Labor, repeated the statement in London
in June 1955, adding that if it seemed to the outside world
that the government was playing an unduly large part in
industry, then that was to be explained by the lack of private capital to start certain industries.[13] The position of
the Prime Minister regarding capital investment has been
incorporated as Appendix 15 to the report of the Preparatory Commission and his undertaking was implemented by
a constitutional amendment stating that no nationalization
would take place without fair compensation.

Of course, final decisions regarding a long-term investment such as is contemplated in the Volta scheme cannot
be made solely on the basis of stated policies of the government that happens to be in power at the inception of the
scheme. Estimates must be made concerning the stability
of that government and of the durability of the attitudes
it professes, as well as of the degree of public acceptance of
its policies. It is impossible with second- and third-hand
sources to make such an estimate in New York. About all
that can be concluded is that the Ghana government has
thus far adopted an eminently reasonable position, and
that there is every likelihood that the extreme left will de-
nounce the position with vehemence.

Certain other political problems that might influence
the attitude of the aluminum companies are all-pervasive
and are discussed briefly later.

The Position of the United Kingdom Government

The White Paper (Cmd. 8702) presented to Parliament
in 1952 listed two main explanations for United Kingdom
interest in the Volta Project: to increase sterling area supplies of aluminum at competitive prices, and to further its
policy of encouraging the development of the resources of
the Commonwealth.

As has already been indicated, the consumption of
aluminum is expected to increase rapidly in the years
ahead. The Aluminium Industry Council, representing

13 *The Times* (London), June 24, 1955.

various sections of the United Kingdom aluminum industry, predicted a threefold increase in consumption from
1951 to 1975. The consumption in 1951 was 203,000 tons
of virgin metal and 113,000 tons of secondary metal. Even
by 1956 the fabricating industry had increased its capacity
to about 500,000 tons a year.

Power is too expensive in the United Kingdom to justify expansion of smelter capacity there, and the United
Kingdom would prefer to secure its aluminum ingots from
the Commonwealth for strategic and financial reasons. But
Canada is not the most practical source of virgin metal, because it is not a member of the sterling area and because
it is so closely tied strategically with the United States. At
present, about four-fifths of the United Kingdom's supply
of primary aluminum comes from dollar sources, and a
shift to colonial or soft-currency areas would benefit the
dollar position. The sterling area production of primary
aluminum was only 32,000 tons in 1955 and expected increases in India and Australia are modest in amount. The
Volta is considered as possibly the most promising site for
large-scale expansion in the sterling area. Cost of transportation from Ghana would not compare unfavorably with
transport costs from Canada, while bauxite sales from British Guiana could earn increased foreign exchange, particularly from Canada. Thus both the dollar-saving and dollar-
earning programs of the British would be benefited. These
basic desires remain as valid objectives in 1958, but it is
not certain that the United Kingdom is as well placed to
contemplate heavy new commitments as it was in 1952.

United Kingdom taxpayers, like the companies, would
also wish to be assured of the security of their investment.
The memories of Abadan and of the colossal failure of the
Tanganyika Groundnuts Scheme are still sufficiently fresh
in the public mind to counsel caution in large-scale programs in underdeveloped areas. Regarding the Volta
scheme, the White Paper states that "its magnitude is such
that it should not be embarked upon without every prac-

ticable assurance that it can be carried through to a successful conclusion." [14]

Certain partial safeguards for the United Kingdom would be included in the proposed arrangements: the investment would be in the form of a loan to the VRA repayable over 80 years; the companies would guarantee amortization of the loan; the United Kingdom would be represented on the Board and would appoint the chairman jointly with Ghana; not less than 75 per cent of the metal produced is to be offered to United Kingdom buyers. In its final decision, however, the United Kingdom must face the same uncertainties regarding security of investment as the companies. But if the whole scheme were brought off to the satisfaction and demonstrable benefit of all parties concerned, the United Kingdom might benefit greatly from its role as a model in the conclusion of other agreements throughout the underdeveloped parts of the Commonwealth.

Some concern has been expressed in Britain that graft and corruption might endanger the successful completion of the project and the investment of the outside parties. In 1954, the Gold Coast government was faced with the accusation that ministers had been guilty of malpractices, and the London *Times* wrote regarding the subsequent inquiry that "a clear lesson to be learnt from the findings is the hazard of withdrawing the British financial watchdog before Africans have fully found their bearings in a new world." [15] It concluded, however, that the inquiry report offered "no argument against the progress of self-rule." Barbara Ward, the wife of Commander Jackson, minimized the extent of corruption in the Gold Coast, writing that the "malicious pre-judging of the issue undoubtedly shook the confidence of many Africans in the sincerity of Western support for their efforts at self-government." [16] In 1956

[14] Cmd. 8702, cited, p. 1.
[15] *The Times* (London), April 27, 1954.
[16] Barbara Ward Jackson, "The Gold Coast, an Experiment in Partnership," *Foreign Affairs*, v. 32 (July 1954), p. 613.

the Cocoa Purchasing Company was accused of bribery, corruption, nepotism, and inefficiency, which the Jobowu Commission found to be fully justified, noting that the Convention Peoples Party, Dr. Nkrumah himself, and another minister were involved in the company. *The Times,* reporting that neither the allegations nor the conclusions had any influence on the electoral campaign, suggested that this indicated "a somewhat different standard of values from that obtaining in a more politically mature community." [17]

The Position of Ghana

The impact of the VRP on Ghana would be far more pervasive and complex than upon either of the other partners, and Ghana would also probably be the chief beneficiary.

Some of the benefits to Ghana have been brought out in describing the project: improved rail, road, and water transport; increased opportunities for fishery operations; and intensified agricultural production on the irrigated Accra Plain. Certain of these features, however, require further analysis. Ghanaian officials and the public have displayed great curiosity and perseverance in questioning every aspect of the proposed scheme, as it is entirely appropriate that they should. Every effort was made by the Preparatory Commission to see that objective answers were given to their queries.

The question of availability of power is a case in point. Although the scheme would be completely unjustified at present without a large-scale consumer of electric power, Ghana must ask itself whether it would be committing too large a share of its available power for too long a period. Some 100,000 kw. of capacity at the Ajena station would be available for allocation by Ghana. An additional 65,000 kw. could be developed at Bui on the Black Volta at an estimated cost of about $54 million based on September 1955 prices. The consulting engineers calculated that

[17] *The Times* (London), September 19, 1956.

power from Bui could be delivered 140 miles to Kumasi at an average cost of 0.57d. per kwh. No complete survey of the total potential water power of Ghana has been made, but there are undoubtedly lesser sites that could also be developed. The evidence suggests, therefore, that power for general purposes would probably be available in excess of demand for many years, and it is entirely possible that additional power might be offered to the aluminum companies should they agree to expand the smelter capacity. The Ghana government has asked the Technical Assistance Administration of the United Nations to send a mission to Ghana to review those aspects of the power position not covered by the Preparatory Commission, and to give particular attention to rural as well as urban needs and to the feasibility of producing fertilizers based on low-cost hydro-electricity.

Ghana has also asked whether the bauxite reserves are sufficient to justify production at the maximum rate proposed, and whether they should not be reserved until such time as Ghana would be in a position to fabricate aluminum products itself. In answer to the first question, it is apparent that the reserves are adequate to last at least 185 years at the rate of 210,000 tons of aluminum ingots a year, assuming that 5¾ tons of bauxite are required to produce one ton of aluminum. The answer to the second question is concerned with comparative opportunities, and it can be pointed out that exploitation of mineral deposits in underdeveloped areas is often the quickest way to increase revenue and thus to provide capital for additional development. The countries with attractive mineral reserves are likely to be considerably ahead of resource-poor countries in the progress of economic development. It is still not possible, unfortunately, to have one's cake and eat it. Ghana would have the advantage under the Volta Project of the location of important processing plants on its territory. Since only a part of the ingot output is preempted, it would have the possibility of building up the fabricating industries. It should be realized, however, that

these industries are largely market-oriented and that the
West African market is not a large one.

One of the losses to Ghana would result from the inundation of an area of 3,500 square miles, or about one-thir-
tieth of the country. The Commission attempted to examine the ramifications of this problem exhaustively, in-
vestigating everything from the existence of important local
fetishes and common rights of snail collecting to the acreage of cocoa trees and current building costs in villages
that would be affected. Fortunately, the greater part of
this area is sparsely populated, there is relatively little cultivation, and many of the soils are poor. The Commission
found that about 62,500 people inhabit the area which
would be submerged, and allocated about $11.2 million of
estimated expenditures to cover the cost of compensation
and resettlement. The problem of resettlement would be
reduced because most of the population has access to land
outside the area on which it could settle, and because
those engaged in fishing would gain advantages. No minerals of economic significance are known to exist in the
area to be flooded, with the possible exception of a small
limestone deposit. Some disturbance of roads and ferries
would occur, but little new road construction would be
required. The possible use of the lake as a new north-south
routeway has already been mentioned.

There would also be some disturbance in the area below
the dam, particularly to local water supplies and to the
fishing industry in the creeks behind the banks of the main
stream. Some 54,000 persons at present depend to some degree on the Lower Volta for their livelihood, but most of
the area is characterized by poor soils, isolation, and a stagnant economy. Investigation indicated that the water supply would be improved by the more even flow of the river
preventing salt penetration beyond the estuary, that production of salt and onions in Keta Lagoon could be improved, and that any adverse effect on salt production at
Songaw Lagoon could be more than offset by either cutting
a sluice gate in the bar or pumping sea water into the pans.

Nevertheless, $1.4 million was allocated to mitigate the effects below the dam and to cover any possible liability that might arise.

Careful attention was given by several scientific teams and by the regular government departments to health and disease problems that might arise. The conclusion was that "the creation of the new lake would bring with it many health problems." [18] Specifically, it might encourage the breeding of *Anopheles gambiae* and *A. funestus;* the lake would become infested with snails carrying bilharziasis, and a new routeway would be provided for bringing diseases from the north. Control programs would be necessary, involving some clearance of marginal and emergent vegetation, siting of new villages away from the lake where possible, provision of adequate water supplies to reduce the necessity of using the lake, and rigid control measures at lake ferry and port towns. Fear had been expressed that onchocerciasis or "river blindness," transmitted by the fly, *Simulium damnosum,* would become more prevalent after the creation of Lake Volta, but a medical report concluded that the lake should reduce or even eliminate the breeding of the fly. As a survey revealed present infection rates as high as 68 per cent, the lake should materially improve health conditions as far as "river blindness" is concerned. It is contemplated that a modern health program would be provided for the workers employed on the VRP, including provisions for a balanced diet, general medical services, and full hospital facilities.

Perhaps the most important incentive for Ghana to seek adoption of the Volta Project is the wish to broaden the base of its economy. It is estimated that of the nearly two-thirds of the adult population of Ghana who are engaged in food production, one-quarter have the cultivation of cocoa as their primary occupation, and that perhaps two-fifths of the population is directly concerned with the cultivation, harvesting, and marketing of cocoa. Cocoa has provided over two-thirds of total export value and one-

[18] *The Volta River Project,* cited, v. 1, p. 60.

third of government revenue. Four-fifths of the money for the 1951 to 1957 Development Plan came either from the export duty on cocoa or from loans made by the state-controlled Cocoa Marketing Board.[19]

Cocoa sales at high prices have permitted Ghana farmers to be classed among the elite of African peasants, with a per capita income in 1955 of about $143, more than double that of other West African countries. But the dangers of a "one-crop economy" have become increasingly clear. The actual damage and acceptance of the potentially disastrous effect of "swollen shoot" disease on the country's cocoa farms have been the most important factors in pointing up the dangers, but persistently low prices for cocoa since 1955 have driven them home. Furthermore, production levels have been below prewar figures, even in the better crop years of 1948–1949 and 1956–1957, and the results of an international survey were not optimistic regarding the possibilities of increasing output in the future.[20]

Ghana is also interested in broadening its base because its population is increasing rapidly. Although population statistics for Africa must be accepted with reservations, the population of what is now Ghana is estimated to have risen from 3,490,000 in 1937 to 4,763,000 in 1957. The need for supplementary avenues of employment and income is obvious. The estimates of direct manpower requirements of the VRP were given in Table 5. A peak of about 15,000 Ghanaians would be employed in construction and some 10,000 in operations. These figures compare with about 25,000 in gold mining, 3,000 in diamond mining, and 2,000 in manganese operations. Balogh makes the criticism that the level of employment expected minimizes the impact of the project on the country,[21] but the priming effect of this direct employment, plus the supplementary

[19] "Potential Prosperity of Ghana," The Times Review of Industry (London), March 1957, p. 79.
[20] OEEC, The Main Products of the Overseas Territories: Cocoa, Doc. C(56)60 (Paris, 1956), pp. 13-50.
[21] T. Balogh, "Time and the Volta—Once More," West Africa, October 6, 1956, p. 775.

improvements in agriculture and fishing, should spread the benefits much more widely. The township of Kpong, for example, with an expected population of 50,000, should stimulate production in the area very considerably. And for the Commission to have selected a more expensive method of construction in order to provide more employment would have been economic nonsense. Ghana demands a vigorous implementation on the part of foreign investors of a policy for training Africans. Nkrumah has stated that the degree of warmth with which any enterprise was welcomed would be conditioned by the arrangements proposed for the employment, training, and promotion of Africans.

Increased income for Ghana would come not only from the earnings of the workers in mining, the power plant, and the smelter, but through expanded government revenues. The government would collect export duty on an estimated additional $100 million at full production. It would profit from increased railway receipts, port dues, sale of excess power, improved local rate collections, and increased corporation tax revenue. It has been estimated that income from all sources—payrolls, taxes, port dues, etc.—would be on the order of $28 million a year.

Additional gain would redound to Ghana through a somewhat more balanced regional development. At present the most productive areas of the country are the cocoa district of Ashanti and the mining areas tapped by the western railway and its branches. The volume of commercial traffic is heavily weighted westward. The Volta scheme, concentrated in the east except for bauxite mining, should result in a more even development across the south, and should benefit the backward north through lower transport costs on Lake Volta.

Although the possible advantages of the scheme to Ghana make an impressive list, there are certain disadvantages and problems that must be noted. The expenditure of $650 to $870 million in Ghana in a relatively short period raises social and economic problems of no small weight.

Social problems are involved in the recruitment of labor, the forcible moving of people in the lake area, the conflict of permanent employment with the migratory habits of many tribes, the prevalence of enervating diseases, and the provision of food, adequate housing, and other amenities in the proposed mining, construction, industrial, and commercial communities.

Fears have been expressed that the country would not be able to supply the labor required, and that workers would be withdrawn from the present mines and commercial enterprises, some of which now have a chronic shortage of labor. A project such as the Volta scheme could be quite disruptive in this way unless care were taken to prevent it. Although realizing the need to be aware of potentially undesirable effects, the Commission did not express concern about any major problem except the lack of skilled and semi-skilled workers. There are also several favorable elements regarding the labor supply: the reduction of earlier estimated requirements; the prior construction of the port and some of the transport routes, which has probably reduced the peak needs; and the existence of substantial concealed rural unemployment, which might be tapped for a part of the labor supply. Finally, French Togolese and Nigerian migrant workers could be recruited if this proved necessary.

If the VRP is adopted, the problems that will face Ghana can be considered under several headings: the availability of adequate capital; possible inflationary effects of the scheme; risks of disrupting the long- and short-term development programs of the country; and possible loss of economic control through excessive foreign borrowing.

The question of availability of adequate capital now appears much more serious than it did when the White Paper was published, for not only have the capital requirements increased, but the revenues from sale of cocoa have declined considerably. An article in *West Africa* in August

1956 stated that the Gold Coast has " 'liquid' reserves which are much smaller than is commonly assumed. . . . no more than £50 m. of existing resources are available for future development." [22] *The Times Review of Industry* estimated that at the end of 1955 total overseas balances were $235 million for the Ghana government, $176 million for the Cocoa Marketing Board, and $34 million for other official institutions.[23] It should be noted that Ghana has already provided $92 million for public works that would be required by the project but which were considered desirable even if the project were not adopted. The Preparatory Commission, estimating that the government would have set aside about three-fourths of the total required by the time construction began, felt that Ghana should be able to find the required funds without excessive strain.

The Preparatory Commission gave careful attention to the possible reciprocal impact of the VRP and the regular development program, concluding that the VRP could only be achieved on schedule if future development plans of Ghana were not excessive and were most carefully coordinated with the requirements of the project to ensure that there was no undesirable competition for manpower and materials. On its part, the government has stated that it would defer or rephase other parts of its development program which seemed likely to conflict with the scheme.

Although there is obvious danger of inflation resulting from a large-scale investment in Ghana, the remarkably conservative economic approach of the present government suggests that strong efforts would be taken to prevent it. Inflationary tendencies would also be reduced by the prior construction of Tema, by the employment of mechanical equipment wherever possible, by continued control of cocoa prices, and by the fact that over two-thirds of capital investment in the eight-year construction period would be

[22] "Time, Money and the Volta," *West Africa*, August 4, 1956, p. 554. See also, "How Poor Is Ghana?", same, March 30, 1957, pp. 295-296.
[23] "Potential Prosperity of Ghana," cited, p. 80.

expended externally, representing imported plant, equipment, and materials.

Ghana, as might be expected, is extremely sensitive about retaining full control over its economic destiny. In a three-day debate in the Gold Coast Legislative Assembly in March 1953, one member stated that the eighty-year period for paying off the debt would place the country "in *economic* slavery under an economic governor"; [24] another said that it "mortgaged the Gold Coast for 80 years to England." [25] In response to this and similar remarks the Prime Minister said: "We are considering entering upon this gigantic scheme, not as beggars, not as dupes, but as free and equal partners, the owners of our land and the masters of our own House. We have nothing to fear if, in all our negotiations, we bear constantly and sincerely in mind the well-being of our country and people." [26]

An examination of the many comments made regarding this aspect of the VRP financing suggests that it is the large scale of the United Kingdom and company investment that attracts attention and that there are few criticisms regarding the organizational arrangements proposed. As the VRA would be responsible to the Ghana government and have a majority of Ghanaian members, and as the project would be situated in Ghana and soon be self-sustaining, it is difficult to justify local fears of economic domination. Participation of the International Bank would undoubtedly make the scale of foreign investment more palatable to Ghana.

The Ghana government is undoubtedly aware, on the positive side, of the prestige that would accrue to an independent, underdeveloped area that was successful in attracting so large an investment project as the VRP, and of the possibility of attracting additional capital on the basis of fair treatment of the Volta partners. The position of the

[24] *Gold Coast Weekly Review* (issued on behalf of the Gold Coast government), March 11, 1953, p. 4.
[25] *The Times* (London), March 18, 1953.
[26] *Gold Coast Weekly Review*, cited, p. 2.

United Kingdom and the companies in this regard is a most difficult one, for adoption by them of too critical or too suspicious a view would be quite likely to change the present reasonable position.

POLITICAL PROBLEMS OF POSSIBLE SIGNIFICANCE

Several political problems are, or may be, of considerable significance in deciding upon or implementing the Volta Project. Some have already been briefly discussed, including the attitude toward nationalization of foreign investment and the stability of the local government. Two others are less directly connected with the VRP but nonetheless worthy of brief note: the Ewe situation, and the federalist movement.

The Ewe Situation

The Ewe, described as being fiercely tribalistic, reside partly in that part of Togoland which has been under French trusteeship (about 175,000) and partly in Ghana (about 450,000). Before Ghana came into being, the Ewe were further divided between British Togoland and the Gold Coast, and if this division had been continued it might have proved impossible to carry out the VRP, for the Volta Basin would have been split politically. The plebiscite of May 1956 in British Togoland, however, showed a clear majority of voters (58 per cent) in favor of integration with the Gold Coast, and when Ghana came into being, Southern Togoland became part of the Trans-Volta/Togoland Region. The immediate threat to the VRP was thus largely removed.

But an international problem still exists. Some Ewe were dissatisfied with integration and disturbances on March 6, 1957, led to several deaths and numerous arrests. Undercurrents of discontent still exist. Leaders of the Togoland Congress Party, which opposed integration, now accept the accomplished fact, but would like a separate Southern Togoland Region able to negotiate with the adjoining

French Togoland. The Congress holds that all of Southern Togoland and the adjoining French territory are dominated by the Ewe tribe which should be united in a single country. The leader of the Congress has been reported as promising that unrest would continue despite any action the Ghana government might take to reduce the nationalistic determination of the Ewe.

The Federalist Movement

A greater potential threat to the VRP exists in the federalist movement in Ghana. In 1954 a group of influential Ashanti leaders formed an organization called the National Liberation Movement (NLM) whose purpose was to substitute a federal for a unitary form of government. Three major explanations may be cited for this movement: the desire to prevent domination of Ashanti by the minority of European-educated coastal intellectuals who largely run the government in Accra; desire to secure a greater share of the funds received for the sale of cocoa for the many Ashanti cocoa farmers; and the desire to retain a degree of power in hereditary tribal groups.[27]

The NLM acquired considerable force in the ensuing years, to the point that some fears were expressed in 1956 that civil war might break out over the widening breach between Nkrumah's party and the NLM. And only a month before independence the chairman of the NLM was quoted as threatening to secede by force. The Nkrumah government has taken the attitude that it would be economic and political folly to split a country as small as Ghana, but the strength of the federalists forced concessions in the form of checks on the executive power and provision for regional assemblies. Although the Asantehene's group has been the most powerful one agitating for decentralization, it received support from certain leaders in the Northern Territories and in Togoland.

The whole problem is complicated by the so-called Brong question. The Brongs are a widespread tribal group-

27 "Revolt in Ashanti," *The Economist* (February 19, 1955), p. 618.

ing inhabiting a part of the Ashanti Region. The Convention People's Party (Nkrumah's party) promised support to the Brongs in their drive for establishing a Brong Region separate from the Ashanti Region. The NLM bitterly oppose this movement which would reduce the Asantehene's region and possibly produce an additional regional assembly favorable to Nkrumah.

It is obvious that these separatist tendencies are potentially unfavorable to the VRP, making it more difficult to channel funds into a national project, threatening to reduce the amounts available for development, and creating uncertainty regarding governmental stability.

CONCLUSION

A study of the Volta River Project, which might be the greatest single project that had ever been undertaken in tropical Africa, reveals the ramifications and complications that are involved in almost any African development. The interconnection of physical, economic, social, and political features is striking.

The outcome of the VRP remains unknown. But it is obvious that the attitudes toward it on the part of the two outside parties are less cordial in 1958 than in 1952. Neither the United Kingdom nor the aluminum companies appear anxious to invest the far greater sums now called for; the desire of the companies is reduced by the demand situation and by the requirements of other developments. In the meantime, Ghana's resources are more restricted, though the reduced cocoa revenues creating the difficulties argue at the same time the increased necessity for other developments. Possibly the greatest hope is in attracting capital from outside, in acquiring a fourth partner such as the International Bank. Not only would this relieve the financial pressure but it would increase the feeling of security of each of the partners.

Time has been an important factor regarding the VRP. There is no question that the deliberate, searching, investigation-studded approach that has characterized consideration of the project was adopted in part to permit time for the development of a more definitely assessable climate of opinion. The outside partners have had to be satisfied that all parties were being apprised of the details of the arrangements and were being given an opportunity to consider and criticize them. The Ghana government shares the same position to a degree, for it would be easy for the opposition to make political capital of a hasty or steamrollered adoption of the scheme. But it now appears as though the continued delays have placed Ghana in a somewhat more difficult bargaining position. Whereas there was a feeling earlier that it was the United Kingdom and the companies who were the chief proponents, it now appears that it will have to be Ghana that takes the initiative. It will be regrettable if time shows only that it had been more difficult to effect an investment in an independent area while other aluminum projects were developed in non-self-governing territories.

Taking the long view, however, there is no reason to be pessimistic. The bauxite reserves and the Volta River are enduring, and the major incentives of all three parties for their development are likely to strengthen—the United Kingdom need for sterling aluminum, the companies' needs for new productive sites, and the need for Ghana to broaden its economy.

Chapter 4

TRANSPORT IN TROPICAL AFRICA

ALTHOUGH one may not agree with Lord Lugard's statement that "the material development of Africa may be summed up in one word—transport," [1] there can be no serious doubt that in sociological, political, and economic terms transport problems are among the most important Africa faces. Improved transport and communications are fundamental to all other types of development.

African ports, roads, and railways have been grossly overburdened in postwar years, as is clearly demonstrated by the great groundnut mounds at Kano, the periodic inability to move copper and chrome from interior central Africa, and the congestion and slow turn-around time characteristic of many African ports. Development plans have had to be scaled downward in many areas because of inadequate transport facilities.

It is no wonder that congestion has been common in the tropical African area, for there was a two- or threefold increase from 1938 to 1956 in net ton-miles of railway traffic, better than a twofold increase in goods loaded in overseas trade, and almost a threefold increase in goods unloaded in overseas trade.[2] There have been even more striking increases in the use of highways, in the number of motor vehicles, which more than quadrupled from 1938 to 1957, and in both passenger and freight traffic by air. This chapter surveys the present state of transport in middle Africa, and then outlines the major difficulties that

[1] Sir F. D. Lugard, *The Dual Mandate in Tropical Africa* (Edinburgh: Blackwood, 1922), p. 5.
[2] *Statistical Yearbook 1956*, UN Doc., 1956.XVII.5 (New York, 1956), pp. 328-329, 342-344; *Monthly Bulletin of Statistics* (UN), v. 11 (November 1957), pp. 75-79, 81-85.

help to explain the present inadequacies and that will affect future expansion in transportation.

THE PRESENT TRANSPORT PATTERN IN TROPICAL AFRICA

Americans and Western Europeans are inclined to take transport for granted. They have available well-developed road, rail, air, and waterway systems which offer a choice of routes and of modes of transport. Service is usually regular and is interrupted only by major storms and floods. In these circumstances one forgets the tremendous significance of transport, not only in economic life but in making possible social and political intercourse. One must approach African transportation with an entirely different outlook. Its shortcomings and problems intrude constantly in the study of other matters. There are still vast areas without any regular service, while it would be difficult to claim that any region is adequately served. A few illustrations will show the great power of improved transport to quicken the economic pulse of a region.

Before construction of the Dahomey rail line, carriage of goods from Cotonou to Niamey required 70 days by human porterage. When the line reached Parakou in 1934, the time was reduced to three days, and an air service now covers the route in three to four hours. The transport of 4,200 tons of cereals in the Ivory Coast during the first World War required 2,500,000 man days and 125,000 porters. It is estimated that an average African train can perform the work of 15,000-20,000 human porters for one-fifth to one-tenth the cost, and that one 5-ton truck can replace 500 head bearers. Before the rail line was built in northern Nigeria, two- or four-wheeled carts were used between Zungeru and Kano, requiring 25 days to cover 250 miles at a cost of £42 per ton, and even this service was confined to the dry season. After the line was completed the 25 days were reduced to less than that number of hours.[3] The most

[3] Most of these examples come from R. J. Harrison Church, *Modern Colonization* (London: Hutchinson, 1951), pp. 84, 101, and also "The Transport Pattern of British West Africa," in *Geographical Essays on British Tropical Lands* (London: Philip, 1956), pp. 70-71.

spectacular result of this line was a quite unexpected and rapid increase in the exports of groundnuts, now one of the two leading exports of the country. A more recent example of the high cost of primitive transport is from Kenya. Before a new road was completed in the coastal belt of northern Kenya in 1953, it cost $1.00-1.75 per ton-mile to bring market crops by porter or by donkey to coastal villages. Trucks now handle this produce at a charge of 50 to 75 cents per ton-mile. The earlier charges effectively confined the production of marketable crops to a belt only six to eight miles inland from the coast, which resulted in premature exhaustion of the area. That the cost of transport is still a heavy charge upon remote areas is indicated by the fact that a ton of cement costs four and a half times as much at Niamey as at Dakar.

Almost nowhere in tropical Africa is there a fully integrated transport complex permitting a rational selection of either road, rail, or air transport. Transport has to a considerable degree developed without proper planning. Political factors have often outweighed economic considerations to the detriment of some of the transport agencies, individual territories, and particularly regions which are forced to use longer, higher-cost routes than might have been necessary. The goal should be integrated development. This will require an over-all transport plan, not only for each territory, but for the large continental regions where transit and other international movements are important. There are now signs, rather conspicuously absent in the past, that the international cooperation and coordination required to achieve the goal are beginning to be realized.

Ports

Africa has the shortest coastline in relation to its area of any of the continents. The tropical area is notoriously poor in good natural harbors. The Guinea Gulf countries, Tanganyika, British Somaliland, and Somaliland under Italian administration, have been particularly handicapped by the absence of desirable sites for ports. River mouths and estuaries have all too frequently been plagued by shifting sand bars or by the presence of offshore bars. Lighterage ports and surf ports are still important. Some are situated in protected waters, but many have completely open roadsteads, and their piers have more than once been partially or entirely destroyed by storms. In any case, surf loading is slow, expensive, inefficient, and dangerous. Waves frequently preclude working the two end hatches by surf boats, further slowing the operation and requiring special arrangements in loading cargo.

Great progress has been made, however, in improving the port situation of tropical Africa. There are now first-class ports along most coastal stretches, extensions of existing ports are under way, and new ports are being constructed and planned in several territories. It is no longer sound to make general statements that African development is hampered by the absence of ports, though certain territories are still handicapped in this regard, and many areas continue to suffer from more or less chronic congestion in the ports which handle their traffic.

As an example of this congestion, vessels of the West African Conference Lines were delayed a total of 741 days in five West African ports from January-June of 1956, which was still a marked improvement over the previous year.[4] The greatest delays occurred at Lagos, where there were 88 days lost by vessels awaiting working berths in June alone. Shipping companies have applied surcharges of as much as 60 per cent to shipments in and out of the most congested African ports during their worst periods. The increased costs resulting from port delays are numerous. There is first the cost of chartering additional vessels to offset time lost, which averaged £550 per day in 1955 and was £1,000 per day in January 1956 for West African Conference Lines.[5] Other increased costs result from pay-

[4] "Port Capacity and Shipping Turnround in West Africa," United Africa Company Limited, *Statistical and Economic Review*, no. 19 (March 1957), p. 15.
[5] Same, pp. 15-17.

ment of overtime wages, greater spoilage, breakage, and pilferage, penalties in use of transit sheds, and larger interest payments on goods tied up in shipment. Sometimes there are losses resulting from failure to deliver goods to market at the most propitious time. The United Africa Company estimated that an annual saving in capital costs alone of £400,000 could be realized by companies serving West Africa if the amount of time spent in port on a round trip voyage could be reduced by five days.[6] The calculated saving of eight ships was based upon the estimate that 160 vessels were providing regular service from Europe and that the present average round trip time was 100 days.

Port delays do not, of course, reflect only inadequate port capacity. Frequently the feeding rail lines are more responsible for congestion than the ports themselves. An important feature of postwar traffic should also be noted— the much greater increase in goods landed than in goods embarked from African ports. The tremendous variety of import packages makes them much more difficult to handle than most export cargoes, which typically contain a large proportion of homogeneous produce such as sisal, cocoa, cotton, or palm oil.

Turning to a rapid survey of the individual ports and starting on the west, *Dakar* is the first good port encountered south of Morocco. Protected on the north and west by the basalt peninsula of Cape Verde, it is largely an artificial port enclosed by two long moles, of which the southerly one may eventually be connected with Ile Gorée for even greater protection. Started only a century ago, Dakar now has a population close to 300,000 and ranks third among all French ports—metropolitan and overseas—in tonnage handled. It is equipped with three miles of quays which can accommodate 33 vessels. With excellent petroleum facilities, well-planned, modern piers, and adequate handling gear, it is one of the few examples of an African port which is probably overdeveloped in relation

6 Same, p. 9.

to its hinterland. Its significance in naval terms helps to account for the surplus capacity, and its importance in bunkering is a second major explanation. Of the total port traffic of 3.99 million tons in 1956, 2.87 million tons were petroleum products. The position of Dakar at the narrowest point of the Atlantic and the furthest west point in Africa, and approximately at the mid-point of many important sea routes, accounts in large part for the high tonnage of bunker fuels. Although more ships call at Dakar than at any other tropical African port, the high proportion of bunker traffic means that it is not as important to Africa as certain other ports. A distinct disadvantage in the long run is the fact that the tributary area is largely semiarid country not capable of intensified output except in relatively small, favored sections. A considerable tonnage of peanuts from Senegal is exported from Kaolack, on the Saloum River, Ziguinchor on the Casamance, and Bathurst in Gambia, further reducing the traffic of Dakar. St. Louis, north of Dakar, fell into decay as a port with construction of the rail line to Dakar in 1885. Shifting sand bars prevented it from benefiting from its position at the mouth of the Senegal River.

Bathurst is situated on the navigable Gambia River, but its development has been severely limited by the small hinterland it serves, largely confined to the tiny territory of Gambia. Before its deepwater berth was completed in 1952 its wharves could accommodate only vessels under 2,000 tons. Even now, the 290-foot berth is long enough to permit discharge from only four of the usual five hatches, but the port is considered to have an adequate capacity for its present volume of about 100,000 tons a year.

Portuguese Guinea is served only by lighterage ports, of which *Bissau* is by far the most important. The navigability for about 100 miles of its three main rivers has reduced the necessity for connecting rail lines and has facilitated assemblage and delivery of goods.

Conakry in French Guinea, situated at the end of one of the few peninsulas in West Africa, has been greatly im-

proved in postwar years, especially for the mechanical loading of iron ore and bananas, but further extensions are
required to give full protection to the port. Three vessels
can be berthed alongside for general cargo movements in
addition to those utilizing the special gear. Port traffic in
1956 totaled 1.59 million tons of which over a million
were iron ore and bauxite.

Freetown in Sierra Leone has one of the largest harbors
in the world and probably the best natural harbor in West
Africa, situated in a deepwater estuary, which is kept free
of mud and sand by rapid tidal currents. Loading and unloading was handled by a fleet of lighters until 1954 when
the 1,250-foot Queen Elizabeth II Quay was opened, capable of berthing two ocean vessels and one coastal steamer.
In 1956, Freetown opened big new fuel oil bunkering facilities, hoping to draw some of this trade from Las Palmas in
the Canaries, Dakar, and St. Vincent in the Cape Verde
Islands. Freetown, with a 1.84 million ton traffic in 1956,
is still congested, and there is no spare capacity at the deepwater quay, but the shortage of railway rolling stock is
the major cause of present difficulties. In 1957 a program
of further extending the deepwater quays was announced.
Pepel, across the bay from Freetown, handles a high percentage of the country's export tonnage, approximately
1.5 million tons of iron ore, but is relatively insignificant
in import and general cargo shipments. Its completely
mechanized loading gear, capable of handling 1,500 to
2,000 tons of ore per hour, or more than can be loaded in
most West African ports in a day, is a good example of the
relative ease of moving homogeneous, bulk cargoes.

The port situation in Liberia has been enormously improved by the erection of an artificial port at *Monrovia,*
constructed in 1945–1948 as an American lend-lease project
at a cost of $20-22 million. Two breakwaters of 7,702- and
7,250-foot lengths protect the harbor area, and there is a
2,000-foot pier capable of berthing three or four vessels.
Though this was originally thought by many to be excessive in relation to the economy of the country, the develop-

ment of the Bomi Hills iron ore, increased shipments of rubber, and expanded imports occasioned by many new developments, have already raised the question of need for expansion. The improvement in handling rubber shipments from the Firestone plantations illustrates the benefits derived from adequate port facilities. Under the previous surf-loading operations it took seven to eight days to load a vessel. Now the rubber is brought to Monrovia by coaster and loading the same tonnage requires only one or two days.

Below Monrovia is a stretch of more than 500 miles without any harbors of significance until the magnificent new harbor of *Abidjan* is reached. The whole Ivory Coast, the most productive part of French West Africa, was formerly without a decent port. Port Bouet and Grand Bassam had wharves extending into the Gulf; the pier at Port Bouet was destroyed at an early date and Grand Bassam was considered an unusually unhealthy locality. The port of Abidjan was finally opened to ocean traffic by cutting the Vridi Canal through the coastal bar, thus giving access to the large and well-protected Ebrié Lagoon. The problem of silting by longshore currents, the curse of the whole Guinea coast, was met by extending the canal's western dike further than the eastern dike and by narrowing the seaward lip of the canal, thus creating a current to direct any sand deposited at the mouth to a deep offshore fosse known as the *trou sans fond*. Some concept of the nature of the problem may be gained from earlier experiences in cutting through the bar at Abidjan. The first attempt, made in 1904–1907, was badly sited and the canal silted up in a few months. In 1933, a yard-wide ditch was cut along the abandoned canal to release unusually high flood waters from the lagoon. In eight days the ditch had widened to 375 yards, but six months later the outlet had already been blocked by the action of the sea.[7] The port of Abidjan has been equipped with a 1,250-yard deepwater quay and a

[7] R. J. Harrison Church, *West Africa* (London: Longmans, Green, 1957), p. 12.

190-yard quay will be added for barge traffic. In 1956, its traffic totaled 1.1 million tons, and, if the recent rapid increases continue, plans will have to be made to augment the existing port facilities. The population of Abidjan, estimated at 125,153 in 1955, increased over fivefold in postwar years, revealing the benefits of the improved facilities.

The port of *Takoradi* in Ghana is an entirely artificial harbor built at great expense in the face of severe natural difficulties, especially control of silt moving from west to east and the difficulty of hardening cement in warm tropical waters. Its original cost (1921 to 1928) was $16,500,000; postwar extensions costing $8,500,000 have increased its capacity to about 2.5 million tons a year, considered the maximum possible with the present layout. Traffic reached 2.31 million tons in 1956. Takoradi has seven deepwater berths plus eight mooring posts served by lighters and special facilities for handling timber and bauxite.

Even with the recently completed improvements, however, Takoradi has been incapable of meeting the requirements of Ghana, so surf loading at Accra has continued to be important. Minor surf ports such as Sekondi, Cape Coast, Winneba, and Keta are still served regularly, and there is even some surf loading at Takoradi itself. Although *Accra* is classified as a surf port, it has improved oil-handling equipment in the form of a floating dock two miles off shore connected with a tank farm three miles inland by a submarine pipe. Port traffic at Accra totaled 600,000 tons in 1956. Completion of the new port of Tema, described in the previous chapter, will give Ghana two modern, well-equipped ports, whose combined capacities should be adequate for the country's needs for some years.

Togoland and Dahomey are served by the inadequate lighterage and surf ports of *Lomé* and *Cotonou*, which handled 102,000 tons and 256,000 tons respectively in 1956. In addition, some cargo was brought from Lagos via the connecting lagoons. A factor which complicates the situation at these ports is the high concentration of export traffic in four or five months, which results in greater pressure on port facilities than total traffic figures might suggest. A debate now rages among the various interested parties regarding the most suitable way of meeting the need for new facilities. There are three main proposals: to improve Cotonou with construction of a deepwater interior port, to improve both ports, and to consolidate traffic by opening either an interior or an exterior port at an intermediate point. Arguments in favor of concentrating upon Cotonou include the fact that it has the larger traffic, that it is already so severely congested that it has been necessary to impose a 15 per cent surcharge on the port, and that it serves not only Dahomey, but French Niger and, to some extent, the Upper Volta. Opponents of this solution claim that Cotonou is too far east to serve Togoland, and particularly to handle shipments of low-value phosphate which is being developed in that country, and that the need for continuous dredging after construction of a port at Cotonou would add greatly to the costs involved. The main reason for favoring improved facilities at Lomé is to permit export of about 500,000 tons of phosphate, though it is questionable whether this would require more than a pier with special mechanical gear. Proponents of Lomé also point out that unless new facilities are provided for Togoland, there is danger that a considerable portion of traffic will use the Ghana port of Tema. The advantages of consolidating the two ports at some halfway point are obvious; the disadvantages are that no good lagoon site exists, that it would be necessary to duplicate warehouses and other establishments now at Lomé and Cotonou, and that it is uncertain whether the phosphate could bear the cost of shipment to an intermediate location.[8]

[8] Pierre Dore, "Le problème crucial de l'évacuation des produits du Dahomey-Togo," *Marchés Coloniaux du Monde,* 11th year, no. 495 (May 7, 1955), pp. 1165-1166; "La question du port en eau profonde sur la côte du Dahomey," same, no. 509 (August 13, 1955); Jean-Pierre Atea, "Cotonou, centre de gravité du Dahomey," *France Outremer,* 32nd year, no. 307 (June 1955), pp. 35-37.

The prime port of Nigeria is *Lagos/Apapa*. A lagoon harbor, as the name suggests, it normally handles about 70 per cent of the import tonnage and 45 per cent of the export tonnage of the country. Lagos became an ocean port in 1913 when an opening was cut in the sand bar separating the lagoon from the sea. Customs Wharf along the Lagos front was the main part of the port for years and, despite entirely inadequate berthing facilities and great congestion, it continues to handle more imports than the new extension at Apapa. The Apapa wharves were first opened with four berths in 1926, and in 1956 five additional berths became available. This portion of the port now has specially designed lighterage berths, portal cranes, and other facilities of an entirely modern port establishment. In addition to the problem of continued congestion at Customs Wharf, Lagos has a problem of maintaining its protecting sand bar which will apparently require more or less continuous transferal of sand. Lagos/Apapa handled about 670,000 tons in 1938 and 2.56 million tons in 1956.

Port Harcourt, 41 miles up the Bonny River, is the second ranking Nigerian port and the best of a number of river ports. The terminus of the eastern rail line, it accounts for about one-fifth of total Nigerian overseas shipments. In 1956 it handled 869,000 tons of overseas traffic plus 201,000 tons of coastwise trade. Port Harcourt is handicapped by site features which require an angled wharf, reducing the usable length of berths and limiting the space for port facilities, thus impeding movement of goods to and from the transit sheds. In addition, there are no wharf cranes and the sheds were built without end doors, which restricts the use of trucks in port operations. As might be expected, Port Harcourt is badly overworked and is likely to remain congested until the three extra deepwater berths that are planned have been installed.

Eight other ports divide the remaining one-fifth to one-quarter of Nigerian shipments. Access to all the other river ports is more or less restricted by shifting bars. Vessels of comparatively shallow draft may be employed, larger vessels may go in and out only partially laden, or produce may be evacuated by coastal craft and transshipped at Lagos, often an expensive proposition. The minor ports include: Warri and Sapele, controlled by the Escravos Bar with minimum depths of 11 feet; Burutu, controlled by the Forcados Bar with a 12-foot minimum clearance; and Calabar, a lighterage port 48 miles up the Calabar River. Sapele ranks third in Nigerian tonnage exports thanks to the presence of the United Africa Company lumber and plywood factory. Burutu, with berths for three ocean-going vessels, is the base of that company's Niger River fleet, and transshipments account for its ranking third in tonnage coming into the country.[9] A project has recently been approved for dredging the Escravos Bar to provide access at all tidal stages for vessels drawing 20 feet and to arrest silting of the bar by littoral drift. This will increase the permissible cargo limit from 2,000 to 5,000 tons.

Douala, the main commercial city of French Cameroun,[10] is situated on the estuary of the Wouri River. Deepwater berths, quay extensions, and new mechanical gear have increased the capacity of Douala threefold in postwar years, and completion of a bridge across the Wouri in 1955 has permitted the linking of the two rail lines of the country, thus obviating transshipments from the western line across the estuary. Port traffic totaled 838,000 tons in 1956. Kribi, a lighterage port used in shipments of timber products and some cocoa, is the only other port of any significance in French Cameroun.

Libreville ranks first among French Equatorial African ports in tonnage embarked, but is relatively insignificant in imports. Libreville and *Port Gentil* are of particular importance only to the forestry industry, the latter being the site of a large plywood factory. Both have good protection for their lighterage operations and deepwater berths are

[9] "The Company's River Fleet and Port, Nigeria," The United Africa Company Limited, *Statistical and Economic Review,* no. 2 (September 1948), pp. 33-48.
[10] See "Douala et Yaoundé," *Encyclopédie Mensuelle d'Outremer,* v. 5, fasc. 57 (May 1955), pp. 221-225.

planned for both. Goods loaded totaled 292,000 tons at
Libreville and 192,000 tons at Port Gentil in 1956; goods
unloaded at the two ports were only 36,000 tons and 54,000
tons respectively.

Pointe Noire is the only fully equipped modern port of
French Equatorial Africa. It is an artificial port whose construction was facilitated by the existence of a submarine
spur. Although it is connected by rail to Brazzaville and
hence is the gateway for that part of French Africa served
by the Congo-Ubangi waterways, its traffic was only about
456,000 tons in 1956, far below its estimated capacity of
1 million tons. Developments in the Niari Valley, and opening of the huge manganese deposits at Franceville could
greatly increase the traffic of this port.

Matadi is the sole ocean terminal of importance in
Belgian Africa.[11] Boma, serving only the Mayumbe area,
handles about 6 per cent of shipments of Congo ports and
Banana is of even lesser importance. Matadi is situated in
the narrow land corridor connecting the vast interior of the
Belgian Congo with the sea. It is located at the only point
which is at the same time on the lower navigable Congo, in
Belgian territory, and capable of being connected by rail
with Léopoldville at the base of navigation on the inland
Congo without crossing international boundaries or having
to bridge the Congo itself. This site has numerous disadvantages: access to it is hindered by powerful currents at
the entrance to the estuary, by unstable sand banks choking
the middle section of the lower river, by sharp turnings near
the port, and by the whirlpools of the Devil's Cauldron just
below; operations at the site itself are handicapped by
extremely restricted flatland and, again, by rapid currents.
The lower Congo has been improved by constant dredging

[11] See William A. Hance and Irene S. van Dongen, "The Port of Matadi
(Belgian Congo) and Its Hinterland," *Annals of the Association of American Geographers*, v. 48 (March 1958). The author is particularly indebted
to Mrs. van Dongen, Associate in Research at Columbia University, for her
diligent research on Matadi and the remaining ports of middle Africa. Most
of the material on these ports and on the rail lines serving them is summarized from articles written jointly with Mrs. van Dongen for a Columbia
University contract with the Office of Naval Research, Geography Branch.

and by the installation of luminous buoys to permit night navigation under pilotage. But the constricted situation of Matadi and the absence of any immediate hinterland has made it primarily a transshipment point, strictly dependent upon its rail connection with Léopoldville and the main basin of the Congo River. This dependence, which is characteristic of other middle African ports, stands in contrast with the position of most major West African ports, which are frequently the leading cities and the political capitals of their respective territories.

Matadi now ranks as one of the leading African ports. Its total traffic increased from 531 thousand tons in 1938 to about 1.8 million tons in 1956. Outbound cargo is chiefly agricultural and forestry products, as most minerals are shipped via ports connected directly by rail with the producing regions. To offset this loss to the national port every effort is made to route as much of incoming cargo as possible via Matadi.

The main port now has two deepwater quays totaling 1,150 yards, a 130-yard cabotage quay, a section of partly improved shore used mainly for storage, and bulk palm oil handling facilities. A new 600-yard quay, started in 1949, has not been completed because of unforeseen construction difficulties. The port annex of Ango Ango, several miles downstream, is the petroleum port and receives small vessels incapable of passing the Devil's Cauldron. The capacity of the combined sections is about 2.6 million tons, but acute congestion has frequently existed at Matadi. Eventually it may be necessary, unless there is greater willingness to utilize extra-national ports, to bridge the Congo and construct a rail line through difficult terrain to Boma or Banana.

The two great Portuguese territories of Angola and Mozambique stand in sharp contrast with most African territories in having several excellent natural harbors spaced rather well along their coasts. Although some of these ports were slow to develop and to acquire large-scale traffic, evidence now clearly suggests that they will be far more important in the future. Up to the early thirties only a few primitive jetties existed along the Angolan coast;[12] today, there are three excellent, modern ports. *Luanda*, the capital city, handles a greater value of domestic shipments than the other ports, but it ranks below Lobito, which has the only railway connected with outside areas, in total tonnage and value of traffic. Luanda's model pier, constructed in 1945, has five berths, giving it a capacity far in excess of the present traffic of about 400,000 tons. The harbors of both Luanda and Lobito are protected by sandspits built up by the northward-flowing Benguela current.

Lobito was opened to traffic in 1928 and received its first deepwater quay in 1937. With a new quay opened in 1957, the port now has space for eight or nine vessels, plus a 160-yard coastal quay. Its trade was slow to develop, being only 210,000 tons in 1938,[13] but it reached 1,309,000 tons in 1956. Great pressure upon the other ports and railways serving interior central Africa has finally brought Lobito into its own. In recent years it has handled about one-fourth of copper mined by Union Minière, one-half of the zinc, and all of the cobalt and manganese. Manganese shipments have increased from about 13,000 tons in 1948 to 246,000 tons in 1954. Imports of coal to relieve the acute fuel shortages in the Katanga and Copperbelt mining industries have greatly increased tonnage of cargo landed at Lobito.

Moçâmedes, whose 400-yard deepwater quay was formally opened in 1957, is the third modern port of Angola but its traffic was only 31,700 tons in 1956. It has been improved as part of an integrated project in south Angola involving a large settlement scheme and irrigation and power developments. Close to the Southwest African border is Baia dos Tigres (Tiger Bay), now only a fishing hamlet in barren sands, but possessing excellent maritime features which

[12] William A. Hance and Irene S. van Dongen, "Port Development and Rail Lines in Portuguese West Africa," Eighteenth International Geographical Congress, Rio de Janeiro, August 1956.
[13] William A. Hance and Irene S. van Dongen, "The Port of Lobito and the Benguela Railway," *The Geographical Review*, v. 66 (October 1956), pp. 460-487.

might be developed if a new railway were constructed to the Rhodesias.

Turning to the Indian Ocean coast and continuing to move counterclockwise around the continent, *Lourenço Marques*, in the extreme south of Mozambique, has long been an important gateway for that area and one of the major ports serving the Transvaal in the Union of South Africa.[14] With a large, easily accessible, and well-protected anchorage area, it has been considered for centuries as the finest harbor of the entire eastern coast. It received one of the earliest deepwater wharves in tropical Africa in 1903, and the port area had almost assumed its present form by the first World War. The port can accommodate 15 ocean-going vessels at 2,640 yards of quay, and it has two large mechanized coal loaders and a large cold-storage plant. Four miles upstream at Matola are a pier for petroleum shipments and lumber wharves. With an actual traffic of close to 4.75 million tons in 1956 and a theoretical capacity of 7 million tons, Lourenço Marques was naturally attractive as a second outlet for the Rhodesias, which were linked with the port in 1955.

Beira has long been the prime gateway to the Rhodesias and Nyasaland [15] and handles some exports from the Katanga. Unlike Lourenço Marques, it has a mediocre physical site on a low, unstable flatland of marsh and silt. The harbor is generally shallow; its mouth is restricted by sandbanks; and it has problems of silting and excessively high tidal ranges. Installations at Beira include 900 yards of deepwater quays, a 490-yard lighterage wharf, and mechanical loading gear for chrome ore at a T-head pier also used for discharging tankers. Beira's traffic increased from 200,-000 tons in 1915 to 1 million tons in 1929, 3.05 million tons in 1955, and to about 3.22 million tons in 1957. Before the connection to Lourenço Marques was completed

14 William A. Hance and Irene S. van Dongen, "Lourenço Marques in Delagoa Bay," *Economic Geography*, v. 33 (July 1957), pp. 238-256.
15 William A. Hance and Irene S. van Dongen, "Beira, Mozambique Gateway to Central Africa," *Annals of the Association of American Geographers*, v. 47 (December 1957), pp. 307-335.

it handled 80 per cent of the total overseas trade of British Central Africa. Congestion on the Rhodesia Railways and on the line to Beira, plus difficulties in the port itself, combined to make Beira one of the most overworked ports in Africa in postwar years, but the new outlet to Lourenço Marques and an agreement releasing some traffic to move via Lobito have greatly relieved the port.

The little-known but promising port of *Nacala* is situated in Fernão Velosa Bay in northern Mozambique.[16] Deepwater wharves are nearing completion in this large, completely sheltered bay, which caters to the Niassa area of northern Mozambique, the most important region for production of cash crops by Africans. Nacala's traffic was 108,000 tons in 1955. The Portuguese also plan limited deepwater berthing at Porto Amelia, further north in another well-protected bay.

Tanganyika has three ports of significance: Mtwara, Dar es Salaam, and Tanga, though some of its overseas shipments move via Mombasa in Kenya. *Mtwara,* in the south, has been variously dubbed "the peanut port," the "Cinderella of Tanganyika," and "the ghost port." Built as a part of the Groundnuts Scheme to replace the inadequate port of Lindi, the main reason for its existence disappeared with the collapse of that scheme. It is hoped that the southern hinterland will be sufficiently stimulated to build up the traffic of the port, now inadequate to justify the 416-yard deepwater quay.

Dar es Salaam is Tanganyika's leading port, but it was a lighterage harbor until 1956 when the 600-yard Princess Margaret Quay was opened. Its harbor is only fair, being somewhat small and possessing a narrow entry. Its traffic has risen rapidly in postwar years to nearly one million tons in 1956.[17] The need for improved facilities is obvious when one considers that a port designed to handle 120,000

[16] Irene S. van Dongen, "Nacala, Newest Mozambique Gateway to Interior Africa," *Tijdschrift voor Economische en Sociale Geografie,* 48th year (March 1957), pp. 65-73.
[17] William A. Hance and Irene S. van Dongen, "Dar es Salaam, the Port and Its Tributary Area," forthcoming.

tons was moving over eight times that figure. *Tanga* is an improved lighterage port which handles a large tonnage of sisal exports from northern Tanganyika. Although it has been heavily used in postwar years (328,000 tons in 1956), it may lose some traffic to the improved port of Mombasa.

Mombasa handles about 98 per cent of the overseas trade of Kenya and Uganda plus a portion of the trade of Tanganyika. Its traffic totaled 3.2 million tons in 1956. It has been another of the more congested African ports, but construction of new quays at Kilindini has bettered its position. Mombasa now has about ten berth spaces fully equipped with modern cranes, handling equipment, and storage facilities. Its large harbor is capable of further expansion and additional deepwater quays are planned. Zanzibar City was at one time a great entrepôt port for the east African coast, but improvement of the coastal ports has largely eliminated this function. A fairly well-equipped lighterage and dhow port, it is the main outlet for Zanzibar and Pemba, which had a trade valued at $32 million in 1955 and $15 million in the first half of 1957.

The horn of Africa is one of the most disfavored stretches of the entire continent from the standpoint of good harbors. *Chisimaio (Kismayu)* is the only natural harbor in Somaliland under Italian administration. The poverty of its hinterland does not justify large expenditure, and Ethiopia is not yet interested in improving its outlets to the south through this territory. *Mogadiscio*, the main city of Italian Somaliland, is its main importing point despite inferior conditions. A lighterage and dhow port, it has no protection at any time for larger vessels and lacks shelter even for small craft during the southwest monsoon.

Berbera, in British Somaliland, is a dhow port protected from the sea by a sandspit. Its trade with Ethiopia was eliminated by the improvement of Djibouti and by recurrent tribal warfare in the interior, and now totals about 150,-000 tons a year. *Djibouti*, the major outlet for Ethiopia, is a modern port situated in the deeply indented Gulf of Tadjoura. The port and its rail line are the chief economic assets of French Somaliland and support about one-third of its population. The traffic of Djibouti increased from 195,000 tons in 1938 to 731,000 tons in 1956.

Massawa in Eritrea, the "world's hottest seaport," has good facilities and remains the leading gateway for that country, but it is far from the productive parts of the other member of the Federation, Ethiopia. Assab, in the south, may be developed as an outlet within the Federation for the main Ethiopian massif. Finally, *Port Sudan* is the major outlet for that country. A modern installation, it has replaced Suakin, which had restricted space and a difficult entry. Its construction was begun in 1905 in a large bay called Mersa Sheikh Barghut, connected with the Red Sea by a channel through fringing coral reefs.

Waterways

The plateau character of Africa and the high seasonality of precipitation away from the equatorial core have meant that navigable waterways have only limited importance in most African areas.

In West Africa, the Niger continues to be significant, especially for bulk shipments of forest products, palm oil, peanuts, and imported petroleum products. The lower Niger is navigable for 537 miles from Burutu to Jebba, but shallow draft barges are required seasonally for most of this distance. Its major eastern affluent, the Benue, is navigable for six months in the lower stretches and for several months to Garoua in French Cameroun. The varying regimes on the lower Niger and the Benue require an intricate timing of river operations:

The river fleets with power-craft and barges must concentrate their efforts on the short Benue season, then switch to the Niger between Lokoja and Jebba, and then retreat to the lower reaches from Lokoja southwards. This series of operations, which follows an annual rhythm, must be delicately handled by those in charge of river organizations. If they let the craft stay up the Benue a day too long, the vessels will be stuck on sandbanks for ten months! Yet if through caution or misinformation they withdraw the fleet too soon, much valuable merchandise is left behind and can only be evacuated by land at much greater cost.[18]

The French first planned to use the upper and middle Niger as the major axis for transport in the steppe areas of French West Africa, but this is no longer considered practicable. The Upper Niger is navigable from Kouroussa to Bamako for four months; the Middle Niger is usable from Koulikoro to Gao (c. 756 miles) and in a short stretch from Niamey to Gaya. Although these sections are chiefly significant in carriage of local trade, there are plans for improving the services on them and for running a special steamer for tourists on one of the more attractive stretches.

Small ships can operate all year on 177 miles of the Senegal River from St. Louis to Podor and in August and September on 603 miles, to Kayes. But the river suffers from great fluctuations in volume and is now much less important than the competing railway. The Gambia River might have been a major routeway in West Africa had it been included in French territory. Ocean-going vessels drawing no more than 13 feet can use the Gambia to Kuntaur, 150 miles from Bathurst; smaller vessels can travel 288 miles upriver. With 58 river stations, at 33 of which the government steamers call regularly, the Gambia is the major transport artery of that peanut-producing country.

Of considerable benefit to several territories in West Africa are the systems of coastal lagoons and tidal creeks. A canal in the Ivory Coast permits movement by lagoon across half the coast, permitting the assemblage and dispersal of goods by Abidjan at reduced costs. Porto Novo in Dahomey is tied by lagoons to Lagos, which is used for the importation of petroleum products and some goods too difficult to unload at Cotonou. Lagos is, in turn, tied with the Niger Delta ports, the connecting waterways being used for a sizable transshipment traffic. Lastly, mention must be made of the proposed use of Lake Volta in Ghana, which would

[18] F. J. Pedlar, Economic Geography of West Africa (London: Longmans, Green, 1955), p. 118.

permit low-cost water transport from the dam creating the lake into the Northern Territories.

The Congo system is the most important inland water-way of tropical Africa and the natural feeding system of the Matadi-Léopoldville axis. Generally speaking, water routes are used in the Belgian Congo wherever possible and rail lines have been constructed only as accessories to the rivers, either to go around rapids or to link the waterways with areas lacking navigable streams. There are about 9,000 miles of navigable rivers in the Congo, of which 1,650 are classi-fied as first-class routes. The most important stretches are on the main river from Léopoldville to Stanleyville, a distance of 1,082 miles, and from Léopoldville to Port Francqui, 378 miles up the Kasai River from its junction with the Congo. Each of these routes handles about 400,000 tons of traffic yearly. Léopoldville, with a total river traffic of 1.4 million tons in 1955, ranks as one of the leading ports of Africa, though it is hundreds of feet above sea level. Ef-forts have been intensified in recent years to rationalize river traffic on the Congo. Some of the most restricting shoals have been removed, the major ports have been modernized, luminous beacons and mirrors have been installed, vessels have been equipped with radar, and the river fleet is being dieselized. It has also been decided to adopt the American system of pushtows, whose contradictory appellation, it may be hoped, will disappear in translation. The Congo and its tributary the Ubangi are also important to French Equato-rial Africa, but traffic for Brazzaville is considerably below that going to its neighboring capital across Stanley Pool. In 1955, 101,000 tons of goods were landed and 86,000 tons were loaded at the river port of Brazzaville.

The East African Lakes are of some importance in inland navigation. Shipping on Lake Victoria, about as large as Ireland, permits low-cost movement of goods to and from the rail-heads of Kisumu in the north and Mwanza in the south. The 1956 traffic on Lake Victoria totaled 215,000 tons. The value of the long, narrow, rift-valley lakes can easily be exaggerated for they are, to a considerable degree, barriers to movement rather than aids. Lake Tanganyika, for example, is now the only break in a transcontinental rail route from Lobito to Dar es Salaam.

A few of the rivers flowing into the Indian Ocean, such as the Zambesi, the Rufiji, and the Tana, are navigable for short stretches, but none are important routeways. Lastly, the middle Nile is used in the Sudan. In 1955–1956, goods totaling 87,000 tons were carried on the southern steamers in that country, but the low level of development in the south and its extreme remoteness do not suggest that traffic will reach important levels for many years.

Railways

The railway map of tropical Africa is notable chiefly for its emptiness. In most areas, single-track routes stretch inland with few branch lines and even fewer connecting links with other lines. The only point on the west coast that is connected by rail to the east coast is Lobito; only Beira and Lourenço Marques are so connected on the east. However, railways are the most important means of transport in Africa; only in limited areas have trucks assumed real significance in the carriage of freight.

In French West Africa, Dakar is connected by an 800-mile line via Kayes on the Senegal River to Bamako and Koulikoro on the Niger, and by a branch line to St. Louis. French Guinea has a 410-mile line to Kankan, built through precipitous country in the face of appalling engineering difficulties and at a great cost in lives, material, and money.[19] Its maximum elevation of only 2,346 feet conceals the very frequent steep gradients and sharp curves. The Ivory Coast has a 710-mile line from Abidjan to Ouagadougou, the capital of Upper Volta. Plans call for linking this eventually with the Dakar-Niger line. In Togoland and Dahomey there are two rail lines of 272 miles and 291 miles in length stretching inland in the typical African pattern. In total, French West Africa has 2,490 miles of rail lines, or only one mile for every 715 square miles of area. Unlike most

[19] Church, *West Africa,* cited, p. 298.

African lines, the tonnage carried has not increased over prewar years, having been about 1.4 million tons in 1938 and 1956, but the average distance of shipment doubled between 1938 and 1955.

Sierra Leone and Liberia have short lines serving the Marampa and Bomi Hills iron ore workings; the former line is being extended 73 miles to another iron ore deposit. Sierra Leone also has an "Emett-like," devious, narrow-gauge line from Freetown to Pendembu, a distance of 227 miles which requires 18 hours by "express." There are no railways in Portuguese Guinea.

The southern part of Ghana and Nigeria are better served by rail than most African areas, each having main eastern and western lines which are interconnected. In Ghana the western line from Sekondi-Takoradi serves the important mineral and forest areas and has its terminus at Kumasi. The eastern line, from Accra to Kumasi, traverses the most important cocoa area. An extension has been completed to the new port of Tema and a new connection permits routing traffic between Takoradi and Accra without going as far inland as Kumasi. About two million tons a year are handled on the Ghanaian lines, more than the tonnage on all the lines of French West Africa but less than one per cent of the tonnage carried in the United Kingdom.

Nigeria has 1,904 route miles of railroad, running from Apapa (on the bay of Lagos) to Kano and from Port Harcourt to Kaduna and the tin mining region at Jos. In the north the line extends to Kaura Namoda on the west and Nguru on the east; plans are in hand for a new 400-mile line from Jos to Maiduguri. In 1956 the Nigerian lines carried 2.86 million tons of freight. The rail lines of the whole West African area total approximately 5,052 miles or about 2.1 miles of railway for every 1,000 square mile area. This density compares with about 45 miles per 1,000 square miles in the United States.

In French Cameroun there is a 190-mile line from the port of Douala to the capital, Yaoundé, and a 125-mile line to N'Kongsamba. The 1956 rail traffic totaled 561,000

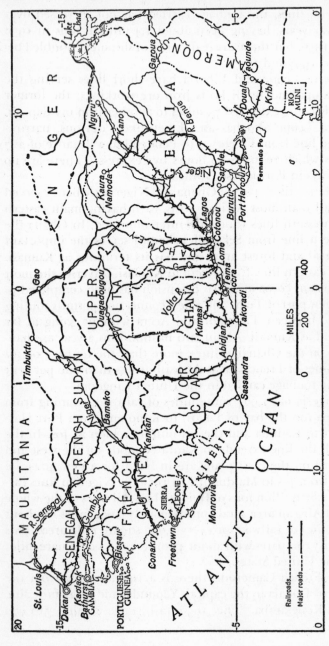

Map 3. Transportation in West Africa

tons. Traffic has increased from 38.7 million ton-kilometers in 1938 to 98.4 million in 1956. There is only one rail line in French Equatorial Africa, the 306-mile Congo-Ocean railway from Pointe Noire to Brazzaville, the difficult route to the capital city having been completed as late as 1930. This line had a traffic of 469,000 tons in 1956; still small, this represented more than a fourfold increase over the 1938 level. Taking the two French territories of Equatorial Africa and Cameroun as a unit, we have one of the poorest areas of Africa as far as railways are concerned. They have only one mile of track for every 1,829 square miles of area.

The Belgian Congo has six rail systems, only two of which are connected and three of which are very minor. The C.F.M.L. (Matadi-Léopoldville) has already been mentioned. It carries more freight per mile of open track than any of the other Congo systems, its total traffic having been 2.5 million tons in 1955, four times the prewar level. Its single track cuts laboriously through the Crystal Mountains in a route that has involved much cutting, filling, and bridging. It has been greatly improved from the initial 2-foot gauge railway completed in 1897. In 1932, it was converted to standard gauge (3 feet, 6 inches) and the route distance was shortened by 43 miles to the present 227 miles. Equipment has been augmented and modernized in postwar years and power equipment is now largely diesel-fueled. The line will doubtless be electrified if and when the huge Inga Falls project is completed. In the Congo's western corridor, the 2-foot gauge, 87-mile Mayumbe line extends from Boma to Tshela. Inadequate to serve the area, it will probably be replaced by a first-class highway.

In the north of the Congo is the Vicicongo system, built in the interwar period to tie the Uele region to the Congo waterways at Aketi. It is 425 miles long, has a 2-foot gauge and carried only 150,000 tons in 1955. In the eastern Congo the Compagnie des Chemins de Fer du Congo Supérieur aux Grands Lacs Africains (C.F.L.) operates a combined rail-water system with 673 miles of rail lines, 384 miles of river transport in two stretches of the Lualaba, and 412 miles of lake services. Its rail lines are in two sections, one circumventing the rapids above Stanleyville where the Lualaba becomes the Congo, the other running from Kindu to Albertville and connecting with the B.C.K. railway via the Kabalo-Kamina line, opened in 1956. This system presents a good example of the difficulties faced by surface transport in the Congo, particularly the necessity for repeated transshipments. Before 1956, the C.F.L. was not connected with any other line, and before 1939 an additional break existed along the short navigable stretch of the Lualaba between Kabalo and Kongolo. Even now, goods destined, say, for Bukavu in the extreme eastern Congo, must change carriers at Matadi, Léopoldville, Stanleyville, Ponthierville, Kindu, Albertville, and Usumbura if they are using the northern national route or at Matadi, Léopoldville, Port Francqui, Albertville, and Usumbura if they are using the other national routeway. The combined volume of the C.F.L. system was 1.18 million tons in 1955, of which 539,000 tons was carried on the rail sections. The new connection required standardizing the gauge on the greater part of the C.F.L. line, and a traffic increase of about 400 per cent over prewar years has necessitated a substantial re-equipment program. The third minor line of the Congo is the "Cefaki" or Kivu Railway running 58 miles from Uvira on Lake Tanganyika to Kamaniola. This line, which carried only 85,000 tons in 1955, may be abandoned when motor services are in a position to replace it.

Lastly, the Chemin de Fer du Bas-Congo au Katanga (B.C.K.), totaling 1,587 miles, serves the important mineral-producing areas of Upper Katanga. Its main line runs from the Rhodesian border, where it connects with the Rhodesia Railways, to Bukama at the head of navigation on the Lualaba. Extension of this line to Port Francqui in 1927 permitted reducing the distance from Matadi to the Katanga from 2,235 miles via the Congo-Lualaba to 1,720 miles via the Congo-Kasai. It also reduced the number of transshipments from seven to three. The B.C.K. was connected with the Benguela Railway in Angola in 1931 and, as noted above, with the C.F.L. in 1956. Measured by freight volume and ton-mileage the B.C.K. is the leading rail operator in Belgian Africa. In 1955, it carried 5.19 million tons of freight, half of which was mineral traffic. The capacity of the B.C.K. has been greatly raised by purchase of new power equipment and rolling stock and by re-laying with heavier track. It was the first railroad in central Africa to introduce partial electrification, on the Kolwezi-Elisabethville section. Despite the importance of the waterways of the Congo, then, it may be seen that rail traffic dominates in the southern and eastern portions of Belgian Africa, which include the most important mining areas. Proposals to extend the Congo railways include one to connect Kindu and Ponthierville which would link Stanleyville with Albertville and even, somewhat circuitously, with Cape Town. Although this would reduce the number of transshipments required on the major northern national route, it has not as yet aroused great interest. A second proposal to lay a railway from Stanleyville to Kivu has been superseded by construction of a first-class highway, now under way. The most important project involves linking the B.C.K. to the Matadi-Léopoldville route, which would obviate the necessity of using the Kasai waterway in shipments between Matadi and the Katanga. There is little doubt that this connection will eventually be made, but it is doubtful whether the high capital costs involved are justified at this time.

In Angola there are four railways, only one of which is of more than local importance. Porto Amboím has a short, narrow-gauge line and Luanda a 264-mile, meter-gauge railroad serving the most important Portuguese interior settlement area. This line may eventually be connected with the B.C.K. in the Belgian Congo. Moçâmedes's line was converted to standard gauge in 1953 and is now being extended to Vila Serpa Pinto, 450 miles from the port. It is not unlikely that this line will be pushed the remaining distance required to link it to the Rhodesia Railways near Livingstone.

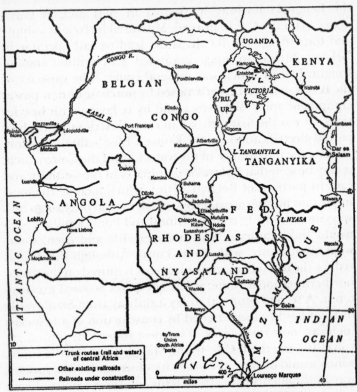

Map 4. Transportation in Central Africa

The most important line in Angola is that of the Benguela Railway running from Lobito to the Congo border where it connects with the B.C.K. Begun in 1903 with the aim of serving the Katanga, it did not reach the Congo border until 1928 and was not connected with the Belgian line until 1931. The depression and the Belgian policy favoring the national routes of the Congo kept the Benguela line's international traffic with the Katanga at a low level until recent years. Traffic with the Rhodesias was restricted as the result of agreements by which the Copperbelt producers used the Rhodesia Railways; these agreements were partially relaxed in 1957. Postwar congestion on the competing lines finally forced greater use of the Benguela Railway, which has the best geographic position for serving both the Katanga and the Copperbelt. Total freight hauled increased to 2.6 million tons in 1956 and transit flow represented four-fifths of the total ton-mile traffic in the same year.

In Mozambique, the southern railway system, based on Lourenço Marques, has a length of 325 miles, plus the new 400-mile Limpopo connection with the Rhodesia Railways. Before completion of this link, about 80 per cent of the rail traffic was transit traffic for the Union. The Mozambique Convention, first signed in 1909, guarantees to Lourenço Marques a minimum of 47.5 per cent of overseas traffic of a defined "competitive area" in the Transvaal, in return for the right of the Union of South Africa to recruit about 100,-000 Africans in Mozambique. Minerals and citrus fruit are the chief commodities moving to the port; petroleum and timber are forwarded to the Union. Traffic on the Limpopo Railway has increased rapidly and totaled 951,000 tons in the year ended July 31, 1957. This link makes possible savings of as much as ten days in shipments from Northern Rhodesia and is well placed for export of asbestos, chrome, and petalite from Southern Rhodesia.

The Beira Railway, first built in 1893–1896 and tied with Salisbury in 1899, soon became the major outlet for the Rhodesias, while the line to Nyasaland made Beira almost the sole ocean gateway for that country. Nyasaland traffic has never been large, the total carriage on the Nyasaland Railway being 658,000 tons in 1956. But the tremendous growth of the Rhodesias has flooded the Beira Railway, causing acute congestion in many postwar years. It still suffers from the poor alignment and inadequate roadbed associated with lack of planning and excessive speed of construction. But equipment has gradually been improved in quantity and quality, and the opening of Lourenço Marques to Rhodesian traffic has given the Beira Railway a slight breathing spell in which to effect additional improvements. Traffic on the Beira line totaled 2.79 million tons in 1955 and was reported at record levels in 1957. A branch line extends from the central rail system in Mozambique to Tete in the Zambesi Valley to serve the Moatize coal fields. But there is a relatively small carriage of domestic freight on all these lines, partly because they pass through sparsely settled areas, partly because the Portuguese made little effort to develop the hinterland until 1948–1949.

In the north of Mozambique, from Moçambique and Nacala, a rail line extends about 334 miles to Nova Freixo, and is scheduled to be continued to Porto Arroio on Lake Nyasa. This line carried 149,000 tons in 1955. A short rail line, built in 1922 from Quelimane to Mocuba, taps the fertile Zambesia area.

The present pattern of the Rhodesia Railways was largely achieved by the first World War. Although its capacity has been doubled in the years after the second World War, it still is inadequate, the magnitude of coal movements being a chief factor in congestion. The total tonnage hauled has increased from 5.1 million tons in 1949 to 9.4 million tons in 1956. Strenuous, if sometimes belated, efforts have been made to modernize equipment and to bolster the supply of engines. The Rhodesia Railways now has 23 diesel-electric locomotives and 12 more on order, while 45 Garratt steam engines were slated for delivery in 1957. A plan to install centralized traffic control at a cost of $11.2 million was announced in 1957.

In Tanganyika, the Southern Line extends 132 miles inland to Nachingwea but, like the port it serves, Mtwara, is not being used to capacity, the 1956 tonnage hauled having been 87,000 long tons. The main rail line is the Central Tanganyika railway from Dar es Salaam to Kigoma on Lake Tanganyika with branch lines to Mwanza on Lake Victoria and to the lead workings at Mpanda. It is a meter-gauge system with a total length of 1,283 miles, built largely by the Germans before the first World War and still not completely modernized. Its total traffic increased from 138,-000 long tons in 1938 to 872,000 tons in 1956, creating severe congestion not only on the line but at Dar es Salaam. In the north, a line extends from Tanga to Arusha and is tied with the Kenya-Uganda line by the Voi-Kahe connection. This line, which serves both the sisal estates along its route and the important African and European coffee-producing areas around Mounts Meru and Kilimanjaro, hauled 407,000 long tons of freight in 1956.

When the Tanganyika Railways were amalgamated with the Kenya and Uganda Railways in 1948 they were poorly equipped and under-maintained. "In fact little had been done to improve the capital equipment since the system was taken over from the Germans." [20] Although strenuous efforts have been and are being made to improve this position, the general shortage of capital has precluded a satisfactory modernization of the East African lines. Plans to build new lines have had to be curtailed.

The Kenya-Uganda Railway is the major transport line of these two territories. The Uganda line has recently been extended to Kasese near the Congo border to serve the Kilembe copper mine and the tea- and coffee-producing Toro region. In addition to the main line from Mombasa to Nairobi, Kampala, and beyond, there are branch lines to the soda deposits at Magadi, to the European farming areas of the Kenya Highlands, and to Kisumu, the major port of Lake Victoria. These lines have often been severely congested in postwar years and there is every reason to believe that the lines will continue to be under excessive pressure. In 1956 they carried 4,207,000 long tons of traffic as compared with 1,796,000 in 1938. British East Africa still has only about 3,300 miles of railway, or one mile for each 195 square miles of area.

In the northeast of Africa are two short lines in Italian Somaliland, the line from Massawa to Agordat in Eritrea, and the spectacular 490-mile railway from Djibouti to Addis Ababa built between 1896 and 1917. Traffic on this line, which is run at a heavy deficit, was only 232,000 tons in 1956.

The Sudan Railways run from Port Sudan to the Blue Nile at Sennar and to Khartoum via Atbara. A line from

[20] *East Africa Royal Commission 1953–1955 Report,* Cmd. 9475 (London: HMSO, 1955), p. 120.

Atbara also runs north to Merowe and to Wadi Halfa near the Egyptian border. The western branch to El Obeid is now being extended as far as El Qubba. In 1956 the Sudan Railways carried 1.67 million tons of paying freight, which resulted in the most successful year of its operation.

Roads

It is impractical to do more than summarize the road "system" of tropical Africa. There are no good road maps or touring services that may be relied upon for accurate and up-to-date information on the passability of roads. Bold red lines representing main roads on African maps often turn out to be more like tracks and are frequently impassable in the rainy season. On other maps the lines turn out to be future networks, not the present one, there being no roads at all where some are indicated. One questions the aptness of the term "road" for some routeways: those in Ethiopia have been described as the only roads where pedestrians overtake automobiles, and Gunther calls Liberia's best roads the worst in Africa.

Although roads in the rainforest areas are more likely to be built for year-round service because the constant rainfall requires it, they may still be periodically or even chronically non-negotiable or so rough that only powerful vehicles are capable of using them. Laterite is often a satisfactory surface when traffic is light, but it tends to corrugate or break down with increased use. In areas that are alternately wet and dry only the roads of greatest importance are likely to be open in the rainy season, and in the dry season it is sometimes more practical and more comfortable to drive alongside the road rather than in the rutted route. In the eastern Congo it is generally accepted that a car using cross-country roads—which are a lot better in this area than they are in the continent as a whole—has a life of about 20,000 miles. It may go further, but the repair time and expense mount rapidly beyond approximately this level. Dust and dirty gasoline are a menace to vehicles throughout the continent.

Much consideration has been given in postwar years to the comparative costs and values of roads and railroads. The view of many experts was well summarized in an economic report on a proposed north-south rail link between the Rhodesias and British East Africa:

In the past before the advent of the internal combustion engine and the heavy duty road vehicle, development, particularly of the remote areas of Africa, stood or fell on the construction of a rail line. . . . The railways of the early days of African development were competing with the ox-wagon. . . . It may well be that today the correct approach to the problem is to allow road transport to carry the burden hitherto borne by the low cost line and to postpone rail construction until traffic has begun to build up to such a point that higher standards of rail construction are warranted, and their sound economics assured. A special advantage of road transport, particularly during the early phases of development, lies in its greater flexibility and in the fact that the roads themselves can be constructed and vehicles obtained more quickly.[21]

Yet road construction has also proved more expensive than was thought likely in the immediate postwar years. The Firestone Company estimated that a first-class road to its Harbel Plantation in Liberia would cost $100,000 per mile; the cost of a minimum road in that country is set at $18,000 a mile. Both the French and the British failed to realize the high cost of constructing macadamized roads. In the seven years to 1955, for example, Tanganyika built 520 miles of paved and high-standard gravel roads at an average cost of $36,400 per mile. This was considered so high that it is not planned to build additional roads of this standard because the cost has prevented the proper improvement of other roads that serve productive or potentially productive areas.

Only a careful study of each area can reveal the appropriate choice among different modes of transport. Water transport is still normally the cheapest means; railways pro-

21 Quoted in Territory of Tanganyika, *Development Plan 1955–1960* (Dar es Salaam: Government Printer, 1955), p. 12.

vide the best transport for bulk and long-distance movements; roads are most suitable for shorter-distance hauls
and in newly developing regions or areas with a low-productive potential. The average charge of transport in pence
per ton-mile in certain West African services is revealing:
ocean steamer, 0.33d.; the Niger River Fleet, 2.34d.; the
Nigerian Railway 2.73d.; the Ghana Railway, 3.65d.; and
the Nigerian Railway road feeder services, 7.25d.[22] The last
figure undoubtedly exaggerates the average cost of road
transport, because it is confined to a regular service often
operating in areas of low-traffic density. Trucks have been
very successful in carrying goods in the south of Ghana and
Nigeria in competition with the railways.

A recent engineering study has estimated that Africa has
a total of 673,000 miles of roads and streets, of which 594,000
are unsurfaced, 37,000 stone and gravel, 1,000 concrete, and
41,000 asphalted.[23] This gives the continent only 2.9 per
cent of the free world's paved highways and streets and 8.5
per cent of its total road mileage.

TRANSPORT PROBLEMS IN TROPICAL AFRICA

The descriptions of the ports, waterways, and railways of
tropical Africa just given reveal many of the shortcomings
in African transport. What have been the explanations for
these inadequacies? What are the continuing handicaps to
transport development? There are many answers to these
questions. Furthermore, the physical, economic, social, and
political factors are often so closely interwoven that it is
difficult to tell which is cause and which effect. Nevertheless, analysis of each factor by itself is important in understanding the synthesis of problems and explanations.

Physical Problems

Africa is the "plateau continent," and the word "plateau"
immediately suggests some of the major problems besetting

[22] "Port Capacity and Shipping Turnround in West Africa," cited, p. 10.
[23] *The Lamp* (Standard Oil Company of New Jersey), Fall 1956, back cover.

transport by road, rail, and inland waterway. Almost everywhere the coastal plain, which averages for the continent only 20 miles in width, is backed by more or less formidable scarps, or, more accurately, by scarp zones. This fact is perhaps the single most important physical explanation for the isolation that characterized Africa until so late a period in its history, for the difficulty of surmounting the scarps is often very considerable. It was a high-cost proposition to build roads and rail lines up these steep slopes; it is difficult to maintain the lines, and expensive to operate on them. On the Benguela Railway, for example, the powerful Beyer-Garatt locomotives have their maximum load capacity reduced from the 1,720 metric tons prevailing on the coastal stretch from Lobito to Benguela to 520 metric tons on the scarp route.

The profile of many African railroads shows the difficulties involved. The Djibouti-Addis Ababa line requires 475 miles to cover a distance of 360 miles. In the first 60 miles it rises 2,320 feet, and in the final 180 miles, 4,625 feet. There are 1,426 bridges, numerous tunnels, and many viaducts on the line, which has maximum gradients that usually do not exceed 18 feet per thousand but that occasionally reach 28 per thousand. (Minimum radii on curves are generally greater than 300 meters but go as low as 150 meters.) It is said to cost as much to ship an automobile from Djibouti to Addis Ababa as it does to ship it from Detroit to Djibouti. So steep were the gradients on the Benguela line that it was built originally with a 5-mile rack-and-pinion section which was not converted to normal track until 1948. Even so, the minimum curve radii on the new line are 100 meters and gradients go up to 25 per thousand.

West African roads and rail lines do not face quite such difficult terrain problems. The plateau is lower than in east and central Africa, though the French Guinea and Sierra Leone Railways both have extremely difficult trajectories. In French Cameroun the great Adamoua Massif stands as a barrier of considerable dimensions to north-south routeways, while the remaining lines and the few roads penetrating from the west coast do so with very great difficulty.

In East Africa there is not only a coastal scarp but a series of scarps with antithetic slopes, so that much of the altitude gained on each difficult scarp is lost on the gentler plateau slopes. This area also has, in the rift zones, some of the most awesome landforms in the world. The term "rift valley," which is often applied to these zones, is misleadingly simple, as there are usually mountain masses on each side of the rifts, while scattered volcanic peaks complicate the pattern. The fact that the most productive parts of this region are frequently in the topographically more difficult areas does not ease the transportation problems.

Additional topographic difficulties in constructing land transport lines in Africa are occasioned by the fact that major routes of access and egress frequently run against the grain of the country. For example, a road or rail line across the Belgian Congo from west to east must cross innumerable valleys which follow a general north-south or northwest direction. This greatly handicaps that portion of the area south of the Congo which is not accessible to river transport, and has thus far precluded the building of roads and rail lines. Somewhat similarly in East Africa, the grain of the rift zones and of the many scarps runs north-south, in opposition to the major east-west routeways.

A problem of some dimensions in scattered areas is the absence of material suitable for ballast. This lack is particularly characteristic of the areas which require it the most because of climatic conditions. Cuttings and embankments in unstable soil have been troublesome and costly in certain areas.

The plateau character of the continent also has unfortunate effects on the stream pattern. Many of the major rivers of Africa, including the Volta, the Sanaga, the Ogooué, and the Congo, typically have a series of rapids in their lower courses as they cut through the escarpment rims. Even the short lower courses are usually difficult to navigate because of shifting bars, while offshore bars make access to river mouths troublesome if not impracticable. It is not entirely chance that explains the discovery of the middle Congo from the east, for the area between Matadi and Stanley Pool was a frightful barrier to penetration. The nature of the valleys also discourages their use as routes for roads and railways, quite in contrast to the situation in Europe or America.

The topographic factor is also important in explaining the shortage of good harbors on the African coast. The paucity of indentations, the closing of river mouths, and the problem of moving sands, have all been illustrated in the account of existing port development given earlier.

There is no question, then, that topographic difficulties help to explain the transport problems. They have made for high-cost construction, which is behind some of the financial problems which still beset the railways. Many of the lines were built on a shoestring, so there are now problems of realignment, reduction of gradients, and widening of curves to bring the capacity of the lines somewhat nearer modern requirements. In some cases these readjustments cost as much or more than putting in the original line. For example, realignment of the Sekondi-Kumasi line in the Gold Coast in 1922 cost £2 million in comparison with the original cost of £1.75 million. The necessity for realignments has been noted for the Congo-Ocean, Matadi-Léopoldville, Benguela, Beira, and Rhodesia Railways.

Climate is of tremendous direct and indirect importance in creating problems for African transport. Altogether, climate is more significant as a limiting factor than landforms. High temperatures make for a high consumption of water, and lines in steppe areas often have great problems in securing an adequate supply. This is true of the Benguela Railway on the Angolan plateau and of the Tanganyika Central Railway. In Kenya a 65-mile pipeline is under construction to carry water from the slopes of Kilimanjaro to points on the Mombasa-Nairobi line. Some railways have acquired special locomotives with condensors to reduce the consumption of water. High temperatures combined with high humidity create problems of oxidation and deterioration that are not easily solved. These help to account for the high maintenance costs characteristic of most African lines.

Precipitation—another climatic element—is even more important. In the rainforest belt, heavy year-round precipitation makes construction of roads and railways very costly. One mile of road with a high-tonnage capacity in Equatorial Africa costs up to $184,000.[24] I have seen new road-beds seriously eroded before it was possible to surface them. Laterite roads in rainforest areas fortunately tend to harden on exposure, but they cannot stand up to heavy truck traffic under the climatic conditions that prevail. The saving in cost of motor transport in West Africa resulting from bituminizing roads is said to be of the order of 18 per cent, or as much as 25 per cent when an unmade track is made into an earth road capable of carrying 15-ton trucks.[25]

In savanna and steppe areas, the marked seasonal distribution of precipitation together with its character—often torrential downpours—has meant that only the most important routeways are kept open on a year-round basis. For large parts of the rainy season most routes are utterly impassable. Wadis which are bone dry in winter become raging torrents, but building bridges across them is often not justified at the present level of economic development. Washouts are a regular occurrence, even on the permanent roads and railways.

The third element of climate, wind, is troublesome only in steppe and desert areas, where sand drift becomes a problem. It combines with temperature to make crossing the Sahara a hazardous experience, especially in the summer months.

Weather and climate are, of course, also important in

[24] Service de Presse et d'Information, Ambassade de France, *African Affairs*, no. 13 (New York, April 1955), "The Franco-African Transportation System: Key to Economic Development and Human Progress in Africa," 12 p.
[25] Pedlar, cited, p. 116.

ocean transport. Monsoons have for centuries permitted contact between east Africa and Arabia by ocean-going dhows. Less beneficial are the cyclones which affect portions of that coast, and the frequently wind-tossed seas, which interfere with lighterage and surfboat operations. Among the reasons for delays to Palm Line vessels in certain West African ports, weather, and particularly rain, accounted for one-third of the total days lost in 1954–1955, a figure appreciably higher than it would have been in nontropical regions.[26]

Climate also plays a major role in influencing the pattern of vegetation and the nature of the soils and hence, indirectly, the economic life, the surplus or deficit position, and often the density of population of individual areas. Because such a large part of tropical Africa is low-productive steppe, climate is of first-rank importance in explaining the economic problems and, consequently, the transportation problems of the continent.

The vegetation and animal life of Africa also influence transportation. From the standpoint of transport the most difficult vegetation zones in Africa have been the rain-forest areas. Original lines were often cut through the forest areas without adequate mapping, these regions being in any case very difficult to chart. The Ivory Coast line was placed where it is because the forest belt, the densest in West Africa, was narrowest at that point. The great tangle of vegetation along river valleys also helps to account for the selection of routes up the steeper scarp instead of along rivers descending from the high plateaus.

River transport on the Upper Nile is handicapped by floating vegetation known as "sudd," and although the main course is now kept open, vessels must be careful in tying up not to become enclosed in an impenetrable mass of growth. Recent reports tell of a new menace on the Congo, the water hyacinth, which was introduced as an attractive flowering plant, but which is now multiplying with such speed that it threatens to become a major im-

[26] "Port Capacity and Shipping Turnround in West Africa," cited, p. 20.

pediment to river traffic. Low-hanging vegetation is a hazard to navigation on minor Congo waterways.

Sometimes large game interfere with transport. The voracity of the man-eating lions of Tsavo was responsible for delays in construction of the Kenya rail line. Giraffe were constantly cutting telegraph lines on the Southern Tanganyika line. Hippopotami forced abandonment of a Sierra Leone waterway. But insects are today more important causes of transport difficulties. For example, the Southern Railway in Tanganyika, undertaken in haste to serve the postwar Groundnuts Scheme, was forced to use wooden sleepers because steel was not then available. These sleepers were soon so weakened by termites that it was necessary to re-lay the track with steel ties at considerable expense.[27] Termites have also been responsible for closing some of the minor airfields in northern Nigeria by creating mounds that impede runways.

One of the serious physical problems for African railways and inland waterways has been the general lack of suitable local fuels. Of the tropical African countries, only the Rhodesias, Mozambique, and Nigeria have produced significant quantities of coal for use by the railways. But the Wankie collieries in Southern Rhodesia have been incapable of providing adequate coal for the railways, power stations, and mineral smelting operations. The Nigerian coal is low grade and, although it has been important in reducing the import requirements of both Nigeria and the Gold Coast, its poor quality has led to higher maintenance costs of steam locomotives so that it is now planned gradually to dieselize these services. Some low-grade coal from Luena in the Congo has been used on the Belgian Congo rail lines; coal fields that may be exploited for future supply of fuel include those in southern Tanganyika, Northern Rhodesia, and Bechuanaland.

Many railways and water carriers have consumed large quantities of wood for fuel and continue to do so. This is

[27] "Tanganyika's New Port and Railway," *African World* (London, September 1954), p. 11.

an expensive business, however, and in places the forests have been denuded to such a degree that adequate supplies within reasonable distances of routeways are no longer available. In some countries, rapidly maturing eucalypts have been planted to replenish the supply. The use of wood is also a time-consuming affair. For example, refueling on the Vicicongo Railway requires a stop of 30 minutes every 36 miles and the procuring of some 81,000 cubic meters of wood yearly from a region that is not well wooded. Wood also occupies far more space than coal or oil, space that could be devoted to paying traffic. Incidentally, one of the advantages of the Vridi Canal in the Ivory Coast was that it permitted the line from Abidjan to discontinue using wood, its consumption having been 143,000 tons in 1949.

The possibilities of using domestically produced petroleum for manufacture of diesel fuels in tropical Africa remain largely a matter for conjecture. Only the field near Luanda in Angola shows promise of supplying fuel-oil in the near future. Hydroelectric facilities hold greater promise, but initial and conversion costs of railroad electrification have been prohibitively high. Nor can electrification be expected to solve the problem in arid and semi-arid areas.

The cost of fuel, then, whether it be domestically produced or imported, remains one of the factors accounting for the high operating expenses of many African lines and transport services and discourages the adoption of more efficient modes of transport.

Size and distance must not be forgotten in an analysis of the physical difficulties facing African transport. The continent is $3\frac{3}{4}$ times the size of the United States; tropical Africa alone is about $2\frac{3}{4}$ times as large. To provide an integrated transport system for so vast a region is obviously a staggering task. Many of the productive areas are far from the coast; to meet their needs long lines traversing low-productive regions with poor traffic potential must be constructed. For example, on the western Nigerian line there is practically no freight traffic between Oshogbo, 180 miles from Lagos, and Zaria, at 618 miles. On the eastern line little traffic develops between Enugu, 151 miles from Port Harcourt, and the Kafanchan Junction at 459 miles.[28] A large part of the navigable portions of the lower Niger and the Benue traverse a relatively sparsely populated and low-productive middle savanna belt. It would be much more advantageous to Nigeria if the river tapped the cotton and groundnut belts to the north. The Central Tanganyika line traverses great stretches of wasteland in crossing the country from Dar es Salaam to Lake Tanganyika, while the Kenya line produces little freight before Nairobi.

Distance also means time. Therefore, perishable crops cannot be grown for export in some favored areas. Sometimes air transport can meet this problem. Considerable quantities of meat are shipped from steppe areas to the protein-deficit cities of the rainforest such as Douala, Brazzaville, and Léopoldville. But air freight, although it has grown tremendously in postwar years, cannot be more than a limited solution. One interesting recent development is a coordinated service using ships from Belgium to Matadi and air carriers to inland Congo points. More than half of the cargo so far moved on this service has been tools and machine parts. Perhaps the greatest significance of airways is in the annihilation of time for moving people.

Equipment and Personnel Problems

In early postwar years most tropical African rail lines had too few engines and rolling stock. Marshaling yards, storage facilities, stations, and repair shops were grossly overburdened. Much of the available equipment was old and needed replacement of parts or complete overhaul. The ports lacked adequate berthing space. Pier and storage sheds had insufficient capacity, and cranage and mechanical handling gear, such as fork lift trucks and tractors, were woefully inadequate.

The slowness with which these deficiencies have been

[28] Church, *West Africa*, cited, p. 155.

overcome is partly explained by historical factors. Many of the lines were built at minimal cost at a time when funds were not available for a first-class construction job. In the depression years, expenditures were held to a minimum as the bottom dropped out of the world market for minerals and for the tropical staples and specialties that provided such a large percentage of the earnings of individual territories. The period between the depression and the second World War was too short to permit more than minor adjustments, while the war years saw a virtual stoppage of supplies of tracks, equipment, and port facilities. After the war the rail lines and ports were quite understandably incapable of coping with the vastly increased traffic that built up in response to increased world demand and the greatly enlarged expenditures on development in Africa.

Expansion and replacement of outworn equipment was slow. European ports and railways had suffered heavily from war damage. There was an unprecedented demand for new locomotives, cars, cranes, and other gear all over the world. The dollar shortage of the metropolitan powers precluded turning to American producers for more than a limited portion of the requirements. Consequently it took years to fill even small orders and in the interim the transport organs limped along as best they could.

Other factors also limited improvement. Often, for example, it was not possible to use more powerful locomotives, with greater speed, that could pull longer trains, because the track weights were too light and the bridge capacities too low. The situation was like the rolling snowball: the greater the congestion on rail lines and at ports, the slower the turn-around time, so more trains and ships were needed to handle the trade and even greater congestion resulted.

The cost of maintaining African road, rail, and harbor equipment has often been excessive. It becomes disproportionately high on short rail lines, especially where there is a variety of locomotives in use. As late as 1950 no less than 40 per cent of all Nigerian locomotives were under repair

at any time, while in 1952 the figure was still 33⅓ per
cent. This condition can be improved by modernization of
repair facilities, training of employees, and linking rail
routes. For example, connecting the 99-mile line from
Bonaberi to N'kongsamba and the 191-mile line from
Douala to Yaoundé in French Cameroun by constructing
a bridge across the Wouri permits not only a more efficient maintenance program, but also a more rational assignment of available equipment and personnel. Linking
the Belgian Congo routes from Kamina to Kabalo provides
comparable advances.

Maintenance difficulties largely explain recent decisions
to turn to diesel engines on several African lines. Diesels
require less frequent servicing than other locomotives, but
they will not solve the maintenance problems entirely, because the periodic complete overhauls that are necessary
are more difficult than are those of steam locomotives.
Dieselization was adopted earliest in French areas, and the
railways of French West Africa have now been almost completely converted. It was not adopted in British West Africa
until 1954.

Personnel problems go a long way toward explaining
the inability of African transport systems to cope with the
greatly increased traffic in postwar years. Managerial staffs
on railways and in ports have not always been composed of
people of high caliber. Management has sometimes been
unimaginative, short-sighted, and lacking in aggressiveness.
The top levels have failed to develop adequate plans for a
continuing growth of traffic. Shortcomings are also present
at the middle and lower levels, where inadequate training
and lack of interest are often apparent. The situation varies greatly from country to country, with a smoothly operating line or port usually reflecting a capable management.
Nor should the shortcomings in individual cases be permitted to obscure the very real achievements made elsewhere under the most difficult conditions.

Social and economic factors sometimes help to explain
the inadequacies of management and staff. In South Africa,

and to a lesser degree in the Rhodesias, many jobs on the railways are restricted to whites, but all too often it is the less well-qualified whites who are employed. To a degree, the rail lines have been the depository for whites who could not readily find employment elsewhere. It is highly unfortunate that the transport organizations, which are so basic to other forms of development, should be utilized as instruments for maintaining status.

In Nigeria, in contrast, Africanization proceeded more rapidly on the railways than in any other part of the government. Sometimes individuals were put in positions for which they were inadequately trained, which resulted in increased problems of operation, a higher accident rate, and greater maintenance requirements. These difficulties will be reduced in time, but it is a serious question whether there will be adequate technical and engineering talent on Nigerian, Ghanaian, or Sudanese railways for many years to come.

Financial and Economic Factors

Many of the rail lines of tropical Africa were built "as acts of faith in the hope that traffic would later justify the cost." [29] This is true of the non-mineral lines in West Africa. The Central Line in Tanganyika was primarily built for strategic reasons, and the Kenya-Uganda Railway was constructed partially to suppress the slave trade. When sufficient traffic developed it was not difficult to pay interest charges on capital borrowed for construction, but in some cases the rail lines ran at a loss for decades, and some are still a financial drain on their territories. As a consequence, they were sometimes not properly maintained, and the allocation of funds to cover operating costs precluded allotments to other development projects. The possible ramifications are well illustrated in Kenya, where the early government decision to attract white settlers was partly motivated by a desire to provide traffic for the railway, which was constructed at great expense and which had no

[29] Pedlar, cited, p. 113.

bulky or large-tonnage traffic to produce revenue. It is not stretching the point too far to suggest some correlation between building the Kenya line with inadequate economic justification and the recent Mau Mau difficulties.

Most of the railways of tropical Africa are government owned, since private capital does not usually come forward unless there are obvious possibilities for sustained heavy shipments. There has been, therefore, a more or less chronic shortage of capital for investment in railways and ports. The position has sometimes been worse for roads than for railways, because roads do not result in directly increased revenues to the government, while railways begin to secure income even before their completion.

The precarious position of some of the railways, plus the importance of others as sources of governmental income, help to explain some of the transport policies adopted by many African territories. The preoccupation with railways often resulted in a failure to develop an adequate road network and, more often, in failure to develop an over-all plan in which each means of transport would be used where it was most practical.

In a number of cases the policy was so weighted in favor of railways that road-building was deliberately obstructed or made to follow devious routes that minimized possible competition with railways. Elsewhere, laws were passed to keep trucks from taking traffic away from the railroads. In Sierra Leone, for example, the government restricted competition by imposing tolls on certain roads. In the Gold Coast the government prohibited, after 1936, the carriage by truck of cocoa, beer, and all imported goods over sixteen sections of road.[30] In Kenya no private trucking was allowed to operate between Nairobi and Mombasa, even when the rail system could not handle the traffic. Examples of unnecessarily devious routing of roads are seen in Nigeria, where it is still necessary to make great detours in proceeding by road from Zaria to Kano, the rail route being 87 miles and the road 112 miles in length. In Ghana

30 Church, "The Transport Pattern of British West Africa," cited, p. 66.

the road distance between Dunkwa and Kumasi is almost twice the 68-mile rail route. In the Sudan there is still no good road between the two major cities of Khartoum and Wad Medani, which are connected by rail.

There are examples of better linking of road and rail transport, including the use of feeder truck services, in northern Nigeria, the eastern Congo, Mozambique, and British East Africa. The competition between trucks and railroads in southwestern Nigeria in the carriage of high-value cocoa to port is another example of a desirable development. It is difficult to justify the railway's desire to restrict this competition in view of its recurrent inability to carry the produce offered to it.

In some areas long-standing agreements have bound important users to specific transport routes. In the Rhodesias, for example, the Copperbelt producers agreed to use the Beira route exclusively until 1956 in return for special rates on coal supplied from Wankie and copper shipped to Beira. It augurs well that this agreement was partially relaxed on January 1, 1957, permitting use of the shorter and less congested B.C.K.—Benguela route to Lobito.

Rate stability is important to transportation, particularly in encouraging other investments and hence in the long-run development of traffic. In Africa the situation varies greatly from territory to territory. For example, the Central African Federation has been notably favored by stability, but in the Congo the policy of having flexible rates has introduced such an element of uncertainty in estimating costs that several potential American investors have given this explanation for their failure to follow through with proposed projects. The Belgians insist that their rates are often kept excessively low in order to support the weaker elements of the economy, but this in turn is likely to mean that the successful producer will be subject to rates based on what the traffic can bear. The fact that strong monopolies exist in Congo transport has also inhibited foreign investors. In several territories freight rates are a carefully guarded secret and assignment of tariffs for particular cases appears to be a matter for negotiation. As a consequence of these and other factors, occasional distortions of almost absurd proportions arise. It cannot be safely concluded that the shortest route to and from an area will be the cheapest route. The Benguela Railway has perhaps suffered more than any other from these distortions. Rates on much longer routes to interior central Africa and on routes where costs of shipment are greater are often set lower than the Benguela rates. It may be questioned whether the economy, charged with subsidizing these rates, is really benefited in the long run, and whether it would not be more practical to select the more natural routeways when they are available.

The Influence of Nationalism

Closely interwoven with the social, economic, and financial factors influencing transport in middle Africa are strong forces operating to favor the ports, roads, and railways in the territories of the several national powers and to route traffic via ocean carriers belonging to these powers. The nationalistic policies that have often plagued European transport unfortunately are often transferred to the colonies in an even more virulent form.

The techniques employed are highly diverse and often very difficult to uncover. Contracts for construction may include clauses requiring shipment by vessels of a specific flag; contracts for purchase of African minerals may prescribe the routes of shipment to be followed. In other cases, as in the eastern Congo, rates are highly distorted to encourage use of the *Voie Nationale*. There are understandable reasons for the desire to focus upon national routes— support of the territorial economy, assistance to sometimes shakily financed transport companies, and desire to save on expenditure of foreign exchange. But the result has been that some areas have probably had to pay excessively for their transport services, so their development has, therefore, been inhibited.

There are numerous interesting examples of these forces.

For example, in the tiny territory of Gambia Britain holds the best outlet for a large part of French West Africa. The Gambia River, which has no bar at its mouth, is one of the finest waterways in West Africa. Its value, however, has been greatly restricted by artificial boundaries, customs barriers, and the construction of the Dakar-Niger Railway which runs almost parallel to the river and in parts only some 30 miles from it.

A second example is found in French Guinea where the Conakry-Niger Railway was built in 1900–1914 to prevent the British from reaching the lands of the Upper Niger through Sierra Leone. Until recently, the French attempted to route traffic from that part of Guinea lying behind Sierra Leone and Liberia via Kankan and Conakry, despite the much greater distances involved. Today there is greater willingness to use the routes linking this region with Monrovia and Freetown.

In the Belgian Congo, extreme efforts have been made to concentrate traffic on national routes—the motto has been *tout pour le voie nationale.* Even when the Matadi-Léopoldville axis was highly congested, only a trickle of goods was permitted to use the Brazzaville-Pointe Noire Congo-Ocean Railway, which had excess capacity. Only in the past half-decade has there been a more rational use of the Benguela Railway to Lobito, which has a far superior natural site for port installations than Matadi. And policy continues to favor the national route even in the east and Ruanda-Urundi, which are 2,000 miles from the Atlantic and only half that distance from the Indian Ocean.

Other examples of this preoccupation with national routes include: efforts to keep traffic for Dahomey from using the port of Lagos in Nigeria and the linking lagoon system to Porto Novo; the deliberate selection of different gauges on the Sierra Leone and French Guinea lines to prevent their being joined; the unwillingness of the Rhodesian Railways to permit traffic to flow westward on a non-national line; and the plans of Ethiopia to improve the port of Assab, partially to offset Djibouti.

CONCLUSION

In conclusion, it may be reiterated that the shortcomings in African transport are numerous and weighty. The density of routes is typically low, the quality is often inferior, there are shortages of equipment, the personnel problems are frequently serious, and there is inadequate planning and coordination within and among the individual territories. The difficulties of ameliorating and eliminating these shortcomings are formidable. They include the inhibiting influences of physical environment, inadequate capital, the legacy of unfortunate economic and political policies, and the problems of building up a technically qualified staff with managerial talent at the top capable of the broad vision and imagination demanded by the dimensions of the problem.

Despite the difficulties, very considerable progress has been achieved in postwar years. Consider the new ports of Monrovia, Abidjan, Tema, Moçâmedes, Nacala, and Mtwara, the new rail links and extensions in the Upper Volta, Ghana, Angola, Congo, Rhodesia, Mozambique, Tanganyika, Uganda, and the Sudan, and the new roads in every territory. Very large expenditures have been made on transport. For example, in French territories south of the Sahara 50 per cent of the expenditures of the first Modernization and Equipment Plan (1946–1953) and 22 per cent of the second plan (1954–1957) were allocated to transportation.

But a glance at any modern map of transport routes in Africa reveals the continuing need (Maps 3 and 4). Centering on Chad, it is possible to draw a circle with a 675-mile radius that will not include within its area a single rail line. Six or seven transshipments are typical in forwarding freight from Europe to Ruanda-Urundi. Congestion is still common in many ports and on many railways. Heavy expenditures must obviously continue to be made in the transportation field, on which all basic development must in the last resort depend.

Chapter 5

ECONOMIC DEVELOPMENT AND POTENTIALITIES OF THE CENTRAL AFRICAN FEDERATION

THE Federation of Rhodesia and Nyasaland, which came into being on September 3, 1953, has the most rapidly expanding economy in tropical Africa. So tremendous has been the pace of growth that the Federation was recently likened to a "train careering along the rails at ever-increasing speed, with additional wagons being added every mile and new lengths of track being laid just in time for the train to pass over them." [1]

Every month brings announcements of new enterprises, new developments, new expansions. Already the second free-world producer of copper and cobalt, the Federation has developed new mines which will permit further increases in production when market conditions justify. Other minerals, such as manganese, lithium ores, nickel, and magnesite, are becoming more important, and surveys are constantly revealing greater potentialities in the mineral realm. Record production and receipts for the chief export crop, tobacco, have also been achieved, while new large-scale development of tea, sugar, and citrus estates has recently been announced. In the industrial sphere, the Federation takes first place among tropical African countries, with at least a beginning representation in each of the major divisions of manufacturing. For several years through 1956 the national product grew at the extraordinarily high rate of about 10 per cent annually. In 1957 the world demand for copper fell and its price dropped sharply (from a peak of £436 a ton in March 1956 to £185

[1] *African World* (May 1956), p. 21.

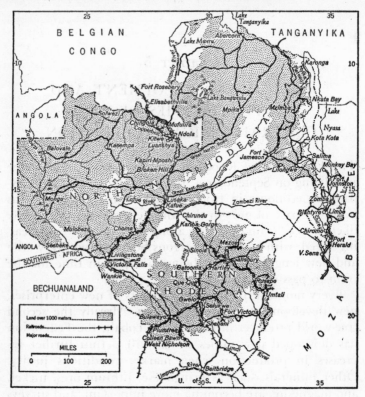

Map 5. Central African Federation

in late 1957). The result for the Federation was a considerable reduction in the value of exports and a deterioration in the balance of payments. In January 1958 the new Bancroft mine on the Copperbelt, which supported a community of 21,000 people, was forced to close down, and prospects for the copper industry appeared so unfavorable in the short run that an important segment of the Federation development plan was indefinitely postponed.

Although the virility of the Central African economy reflected a healthy state, at least until very recently, it is obvious that this state was not unaccompanied by problems, some present, some incipient, others only potential.

Some of these problems are characteristic of any under-developed economy, some have an African and a colonial aspect, some merely reflect the problems of coordinating and directing an economy bursting forward with as great rapidity as has probably ever been witnessed. It is important to distinguish between the "growing pains" and the more serious problems that might lead to deformities in the future economic body.

Without doubt the most difficult problem is that of developing successfully a multi-racial society in which there is equality for all. The Federation was based on the concept of racial partnership in both the political and economic spheres. Much has been done that is consonant with this goal. There is African representation in the Federal legislature; there are greatly expanded programs of betterment for the African reserves; some African ownership of land is now possible in Southern Rhodesian cities; the door is ajar for advancement of Africans on the Copperbelt. But much more remains to be accomplished. European trade unions offer intense opposition to weakening the industrial color bar; African trade unions are not recognized for collective bargaining in Southern Rhodesia; the four African representatives in the Federal legislature from Nyasaland and Northern Rhodesia are elected by African voters, but the two from Southern Rhodesia are elected primarily by whites; there are many written and unwritten economic and social impediments to African advancement. Africans did not generally support the Federation before its birth; they continue to express misgivings with respect to its political implications. A recent American report puts it as follows: "The sincerity and idealism of the Government's racial philosophy are not to be doubted, but the numerous anachronisms on the contemporary African scene testify to the obstacles attending full implementation of such philosophies." [2]

Another broad problem area is that of achieving a well-

[2] U. S. Department of Commerce, *Investment in Federation of Rhodesia and Nyasaland* (Washington: GPO, 1956), p. 102.

rounded, well-integrated economy. At the present time "the economy is overwhelmingly dependent on a few export commodities the yield from which is not at all closely connected with the general level of African productivity." [3] Approximately 70 per cent of foreign exchange receipts and more than half the public revenue of the Federation are derived directly from the mining industry alone. Broadening the economic base involves: developing an adequate infrastructure; diminishing the harmful influences of a migratory labor system on the agricultural base; evolving a system of agriculture which will improve dietal standards, contribute more fully to the Federation's economy, and preserve the land from depletion or outright destruction; establishing industry that is realistically based and not dependent upon direct or indirect subsidization for its life; and developing the untouched or almost untouched areas and resources of the country. The securing of an adequate supply of capital for this multitude of tasks is a problem in its own right.

The dynamic nature of many of the forces affecting the Federation economy must be noted. Depletion of ores, discovery of new mineral bodies, development of hydroelectric schemes, improved transport, organization of irrigation, control of insect pests, increased absorption of educational benefits, and many other forces require a constant reassessment of the Federation's economic future. Of great importance, also, is the now rapidly rising population. It may be expected that the African population will at least double in the next 25 years. This chapter describes the more important features of the Federation's present economy, and indicates the broad economic potentialities of the area in so far as the available information permits.

[3] H. W. Woodruff and C. W. Thompson, *Economic Development in Rhodesia and Nyasaland* (London: Dennis Hobson, 1955), p. 27.

Unity and Federation

Federation did not "unify" the three countries involved; it brought them together in a somewhat loose federation in which some of the most important powers of government are reserved for the individual territories. Southern Rhodesia was and continues to be an internally "self-governing colony"; Northern Rhodesia and Nyasaland are protectorates. Under the Federal constitution, the subjects of possible legislation are divided into three fields. There are "exclusive" subjects on which only the Federal legislature may make laws. "Concurrent" subjects are those with which both the Federal and Territorial legislatures may be concerned; the Federal law prevails in case of inconsistency. Subjects not listed under either of these two heads remain the responsibility of the individual territories. In particular, the Territories continue to be responsible for most matters affecting the daily life of the African and European inhabitants. This has "undoubtedly hampered the development of the idea of partnership at the Federal level,"[4] and may add to the anachronisms in racial relations that already exist. Achieving the professed goal of partnership among Africans and Europeans, which is basic to realization of the Federation's full potential, will certainly call for a high order of statesmanship on the part of African and European alike.

The constitution is scheduled to be reviewed in 1960, and lines have already been drawn for what may well be a bitter and protracted struggle. Europeans will wish the Federation to move very far toward or actually to achieve dominion status. Africans, particularly those in Nyasaland and Northern Rhodesia, are determined to retain the protection of the Colonial Office, while many Nyasalanders apparently will not be satisfied unless their country becomes another Ghana.

[4] Philip Mason, "Masters or Partners? Race Relations in the African Federation," *Foreign Affairs*, v. 35 (April 1957), p. 501.

The Physical Setting

The total area of the Federation is 486,973 square miles, nearly one-sixth the size of the United States. Northern Rhodesia accounts for almost three-fifths of the total area, Southern Rhodesia for about three-tenths, and Nyasaland for about one-tenth (Table 6). The land of the Rhodesias is mostly on the plateau of central Africa. Average elevations in Northern Rhodesia range between 3,000 and 5,000 feet above sea level. In many localities the level of the plateau is broken by hills, sometimes occurring as chains which develop into areas of broken country. The Muchinga Mountains, west of the Luangwa trough, form part of the great escarpment and have individual peaks rising to about 8,000 feet. The Luangwa trough itself is believed to be an ancient depression and is covered with sedimentary formations, in contrast to the bulk of the plateau area (Map 5).

In Southern Rhodesia a belt of generally level land above 4,000 feet runs nearly across the country from northeast to southwest. This area, about one-fifth of the country, contains most of the European population and the densest African settlement as well. It is the physical and economic backbone of the country. From this region of high veld the land drops off through a broad, more heavily eroded, middle veld to the low veld of the Zambesi Valley in the northwest and of the Limpopo and Sabi basins in the southeast. The margins of these troughs are everywhere marked by higher, rugged terrain, while the relief is gentle on the soft rocks of the troughs themselves. The Zambesi trough is deep and rather narrow, with very steep sides.[5] Largely because of aridity and insect pests it is just beginning to be developed. The southeastern low veld is considerably broader and also largely underdeveloped. The new rail link to Lourenço Marques passes through the area and promises to bring large-scale investment.

Nyasaland, a strip of land 520 miles long and 50 to 110 miles wide, is composed mainly of plateaus and highlands

[5] Derwent Whittlesey, "Southern Rhodesia: An African Compage," *Annals of the Association of American Geographers*, v. 46 (March 1956), pp. 9-10.

ranging from 3,300 to 10,000 feet, plus a portion of the Great Rift Valley occupied by Lake Nyasa in the north and by the Shire River in the south. Lake Nyasa stands at an elevation of about 1,500 feet, while the lower Shire Valley is only 200 to 300 feet above sea level.

From the standpoint of size alone, the Federation would appear to have ample room for the present population, as the over-all density is only 14.9 per square mile. The presence of much high land moderates the climate, making it attractive for white settlement and permitting a broad range of crops. Lowland tropical crops may be grown in the troughs, while other tropical, subtropical, and middle-latitude crops give potentially great diversity to the high veld, especially in Southern Rhodesia. The landform features do not present the difficulties of overland movement characteristic of East Africa, as is revealed in the low profile of the Rhodesia Railways' main line or in the new Limpopo or Pafuri Link to Lourenço Marques.

Population

The total population of the Federation is estimated to be 7,260,900, 96.1 per cent of whom are Africans (Table 6). The population is roughly equally divided among the three countries, which means that Nyasaland has by far the greatest density. Subtracting its water surface, that country has a density of about 70.2 per square mile, Southern Rhodesia has about 16.5 per square mile, and Northern Rhodesia has only 7.6 per square mile. None of these densities is high, but there is congestion in a number of areas, such as the southern shore of Lake Nyasa and some of the Lake Bangweulu islands in Northern Rhodesia, where densities of 300 per square mile are found. In much wider areas there is overpopulation, given the present agricultural systems.

Population growth is difficult to measure because of the inadequacy of statistics, but the African totals are believed to have increased from 2.5 million in 1911 and 4.0 million in 1931 to 6.2 million in 1951 and 6.98 million in 1956. It

Table 6

AREA AND POPULATION OF THE FEDERATION

Territory	Area (sq. mi.)	1956 POPULATION[a]			
		African	European	Other	Total
Northern Rhodesia	287,640	2,110,000	66,000	7,100	2,183,100
Southern Rhodesia	150,333	2,290,000	178,000	13,200	2,481,200
Nyasaland	49,000[b]	2,580,000	6,800	9,800	2,596,600
Federation	486,973	6,980,000	250,800	30,100	7,260,900

[a] Provisional figures.
[b] Including 12,000 sq. mi. of water surface.

Source: Central African Statistical Office, Federation of Rhodesia and Nyasaland, Monthly Digest of Statistics, v. 4 (July 1957), p. 12.

is generally estimated that the population will double in the next 25 years, but progressively improving health and sanitary conditions may well result in a sharper increase in the rate of growth.

Of the nearly 7 million Africans in the Federation, about 15 per cent are estimated to be wage earners, 601,000 in Southern Rhodesia, 258,300 in Northern Rhodesia, and 163,000 in Nyasaland. The important employment opportunities are concentrated in the mining communities of Northern and Southern Rhodesia, in the cities, and on the high-veld farms. This means that large numbers of Africans must migrate from the reserves, over a third of the able-bodied males normally being outside their tribal areas. About 142,000 of the 430,000 able-bodied African men in Nyasaland were estimated to be working outside the protectorate in 1956.

The European population has increased much more rapidly than the African, but still represents only 3.5 per cent of the total. It was about 26,000 in 1911, 65,600 in 1931, 179,040 in 1951, and 250,800 in 1956. Europeans are very unevenly distributed among and within the three territories: Nyasaland has only 2.7 per cent of the total, Northern Rhodesia has 26.3 per cent, and Southern Rhodesia 71 per cent.

Immigration has always been more important than natural growth in expanding the European populace. Strong preference is extended in immigration quotas and in assisted immigration to European citizens of the Commonwealth, and especially to citizens of the United Kingdom. In the period 1938–1952 approximately 96 per cent of non-African immigrants were of British nationality, about half from the British Isles and about 40 per cent from the Union of South Africa. As of May 8, 1956, Europeans born in the Federation comprised 30.2 per cent of the total European population; those born in South Africa totaled 31.8 per cent, and those in the British Isles 27.5 per cent. An additional 3.3 per cent came from other Commonwealth countries, making a total of 92.8 per cent born within the

Commonwealth. The number of Afrikaner immigrants is considered to be a critical factor,[6] since the core of the Southern Rhodesian political party that stands for segregation of the races is drawn from the approximately 16,000 Afrikaner residents. There has been some talk of relaxing the quotas sufficiently to attract southern Europeans, especially for development in some of the lower-lying areas.

Immigration continues heavy, having been 25,636 in 1956. In a number of postwar years there have been temporary cut-backs because of the lack of housing and other facilities. Not all of the immigrants are satisfied to remain in the area, and there has been a fairly strong emigration in some years. For the future, a white population of 700,-000 is mentioned as the goal for 1975. This will require, in particular, a continued expansion of industry and services, as farming is not attracting large numbers, and mining cannot be expected to absorb so large an increase. The absorptive capacity of the Federation will depend in part upon how far the color bar is relaxed. Many Rhodesians appear to feel that there is a restricted number of jobs, and that those which are not held for Europeans will be manned by Africans. But this neglects the tremendous need for skilled labor and managerial ability that the development and the potentialities of the country justify and require.

There was an average of 100,412 Europeans working in the Federation during 1956, 68.6 per cent in Southern Rhodesia, 27.7 per cent in Northern Rhodesia, and 3.7 per cent in Nyasaland. Over a quarter of the Europeans actively engaged in Northern Rhodesia in 1956 were employed by the Copperbelt mining companies, while 31,048 of the total of 66,000 in that territory reside in the mining and adjacent towns. In Southern Rhodesia the European population is highly urbanized, with over 92,000 of the 166,000 total in 1955 residing in the cities of Salisbury and Bulawayo and their suburbs. Many of the governmental employees of Northern Rhodesia and Nyasaland cannot be

6 Same, p. 94.

considered permanent residents, as they often retire at an early age and leave the area.

The 30,100 "other" non-African residents of the Federation are primarily Indians and Colored people (persons of mixed race). They are not an important element of the population, but their economic contribution is considerably greater than the 0.4 per cent of the total they represent.

TRANSPORTATION AND POWER

Because of the pervasive influence of transportation and power, it is desirable to survey these factors before turning to agriculture, mining, and industry. Almost any development in the Federation is dependent upon the availability of transport and most development results in a greater consumption of energy. These and other portions of the infrastructure, such as water supplies, sewerage systems, communication facilities, and construction, are basic to the whole economic advance of the region.

Transport

The existing rail lines and roads have been seriously inadequate to the demands made upon them in postwar years. This has resulted in temporary shut-downs of Copperbelt mining, in the accumulation of sizable chrome ore and asbestos stockpiles, in the rationing of power, and in great shortages of building materials. The fact that the area is landlocked complicates the picture, requiring improved facilities in adjoining territories as well.

One of the major explanations for the inadequacy of Rhodesian transport was the very high dependence until August 1955 on one seaport, Beira in central Mozambique. In a normal postwar year this gateway handled 65 per cent of the total external trade by value of British Central Africa, and 80 per cent of the total overseas trade. So severe was the congestion of Beira that ships sometimes lay at anchor 120 days waiting berth space. In 1950–1951, a 60 per cent surcharge was temporarily imposed by the East

African Shipping Conference Lines on all sea freight destined for the port, and an import quota system was applied, administered by the Beira Imports Advisory Committee, still in operation.[7] The Union ports handled the bulk of the remaining overseas traffic, but their distance from Rhodesian centers is a strong deterrent to their use (Map 4).

Nyasaland is served by one rail line running from Salima near Lake Nyasa to Beira. In 1956 the Nyasaland Railways carried 341,074 passengers and 724,236 short tons of freight. A 20-mile branch line is planned to run to Monkey Bay, at the tip of the peninsula which separates the two southern arms of Lake Nyasa, which would become the major lake port and headquarters of an improved lake shipping service.[8] Lake Nyasa is the most important inland waterway of the Federation, but tonnage carried on the ships operated by the Nyasaland Railways is still very low. Lake transport has been hindered by shifts in the level of the lake of as much as 20 feet and by dangerous storms, but improvement should result from a bund being erected at Liwonde on the Upper Shire to stabilize the lake. There are about 5,000 miles of motor roads in Nyasaland, only a very limited mileage being paved. The north-south trunk road, in process of improvement, is the main route, and will become part of the projected Capetown to Nairobi route to be built to international heavy-duty standards.

The backbone of the whole transport system of the two Rhodesias is the Rhodesia Railways running from Umtali to Salisbury, Bulawayo, Livingstone, Lusaka, and the Copperbelt. Linked for some years with the Beira Railway, the B.C.K. system in the Congo, and the South African Railways via Bechuanaland, a fourth international connection was completed in August 1955 to the southern Mozambique port of Lourenço Marques. This Pafuri Link or

[7] William A. Hance and Irene S. van Dongen, "Beira, Mozambique Gateway to Central Africa," *Annals of the Association of American Geographers*, v. 47 (December 1957), pp. 307-335.

[8] "Nyasaland Five-Year Plan," *The Times Review of Industry* (London), September 1956, p. 90.

Limpopo Line has given considerable relief to Beira and to the Rhodesia Railways as well as opening up a hitherto undeveloped part of the country. The line to South Africa is light and distances are excessive, but it is and will continue important in traffic between the Rhodesias and the Union.

The connection to the B.C.K. and then to Lobito via the Benguela Railway has never handled the Rhodesian traffic that it might have, or probably should have in view of the considerable distances saved on land and sea routes from Northern Rhodesia. In recent years, due to the inability either of Wankie to mine adequate coal or of the Rhodesia Railways to move enough of it to the Copperbelt, considerable tonnages of coal have been imported via the Benguela-B.C.K. Railways from South Africa and even from the United States. But copper was first exported by this route only in February 1957, after the Bulawayo Conference had agreed partially to release the Copperbelt from long-standing commitments to use the Rhodesia Railways to the east. This agreement has at least partly removed one of the outstanding anachronisms of the African transport scene.

Other rail improvements have been proposed. It will doubtless sooner or later be necessary to double-track portions of the main line. A saving of 150 miles on shipments from Northern Rhodesia and southwestern Southern Rhodesia could be effected by connecting the existing Gwelo-Umvuma branch in Southern Rhodesia to the main line at Odzi near Umtali, which would permit bypassing Salisbury. A link from Sinoia in Southern Rhodesia to Kafue in Northern Rhodesia would be even more desirable, for it would reduce the distance from Lusaka and the Copperbelt to Salisbury and Beira by 500 miles. Eventually, it may prove possible to join the rail system of Northern Rhodesia to that of Tanganyika, but this should not be attempted until the traffic potential of the area traversed is more apparent. Some interests in the Rhodesias would also like to see a new line to the Atlantic, perhaps to Baio dos Tigres or Moçâmedes in Angola or tying to the Benguela Railway without passing through Congo territory. If suggestions to export coal or pig iron in large quantities to Britain were pursued, a new link to the west coast would be much more necessary. Finally, it will probably be desirable to link the South African and Southern Rhodesian railways between West Nicholson and Beit Bridge. In no other part of Africa do such large rail extensions appear to be required, either now or in the not-too-distant future.

In addition to the need for new lines, there have been and continue to be heavy requirements for improvements on the existing line and to the locomotive park and rolling stock. The Railway Administration, which was not notably far-seeing in the early postwar years, now plans an expenditure of $134 million in the next four years on such a program. A large number of diesel locomotives, more powerful steam engines, and several thousand wagons have been ordered, and a plan for centralized control has been adopted. Total freight traffic on the Rhodesia Railways reached a record level of 10.8 million tons in the year ended March 31, 1957. Carriage of coal and coke, almost all from Wankie, represented 34.2 per cent of the total tonnage; other minerals made up 24.1 per cent of the total.

The trunk roads of the Rhodesias parallel the rail line, with numerous feeders acting to some extent as branch lines. The Great North Road from Kapiri Mposhi through the relatively neglected eastern lobe of Northern Rhodesia to Tanganyika has recently been partly improved, and is the chief transport artery in that region. Contact with this part of Northern Rhodesia is somewhat handicapped by the extension into the country of the Katanga pedicle of the Congo, while contact between Nyasaland and Southern Rhodesia is similarly affected by the extension of Mozambique territory up the Zambesi Valley. Motor services operate on some of the 29,000 miles of road in Southern Rhodesia and 18,000 miles in Northern Rhodesia, but most road haulers operate in confined areas around the main centers. Only a few hundred miles of road are two-laned, paved highways. There is a considerable mileage of strip roads, which have become more of a hazard than a help in some heavily traveled sections. The bulk of the mileage is in roads whose passage becomes highly precarious in the rainy season. There are heavy needs not only for improvement of present roads but for road extensions in some of the less developed areas.

Waterways are of little significance in the Rhodesias. There is a certain amount of traffic on the Zambesi above Victoria Falls to Mongu in Barotseland; the waters of Lake Bangweulu are used for local traffic; and some trade of the Abercorn area in the extreme north moves via Lake Tanganyika to the Central Tanganyika line.

The Central African Airways and the Hunting Line provide air coverage within the territory and to adjacent countries. Measured by miles flown in civil aviation, the airways of the Federation rank second to the Union on the African continent. Livingstone and Salisbury have first-class international airfields.

Power

The shortage of adequate fuel and power has been a severe problem in the Rhodesias in postwar years. Although during one period the difficulty was that the Wankie Collieries were unable to produce the required amounts of coal, in recent years the trouble has been that the railways were unable to deliver the coal produced. In January 1956, the capacity of Wankie was estimated to be 4.5 million tons a year, but during that year the railways moved only about 3.7 million tons. The combined capacity of the four collieries at Wankie is now about 5 million tons. As a consequence of coal shortages it has been necessary for the copper mining companies to burn large quantities of wood, which is estimated to cost three times as much as coal, and, as has already been noted, to import coal from South Africa and America. In 1953, for example, the Copperbelt needed 80,000 tons of coal a month but received only 54,000 tons from Wankie. The situation has improved since then, but in the first half of 1956 the Benguela Railway was again called upon to deliver 70,000 tons of coal. The shortage of fuel has made it necessary to ration electricity and has undoubtedly acted as something of a deterrent to industrial expansion. For example, a ferrochrome plant at Gwelo erected in the early fifties has been operating on a restricted scale pending additional supplies of power.

The shortage of fuel and power is not occasioned by a shortage of reserves. All three countries have substantial reserves of coal; there are excellent possibilities for developing hydroelectric resources, and, for the future, there may be sizable deposits of uranium ores. Knowledge regarding the extent of coal deposits and of hydroelectric resources is still somewhat sketchy, but enough is known to indicate that the power and fuel position is quite adequate to support a greatly expanded economy, and that the Federation compares very favorably with most African countries in this regard.

The major source of energy in the Federation has thus far been the Wankie Collieries, 200 miles northwest of Bulawayo and 68 miles southeast of Victoria Falls. Reserves there are estimated at 5,200 million tons of bituminous coal, a considerable portion of which is of coking quality. Much of the Wankie coal lies close to the surface; the main seam varies in thickness from 11 to 34 feet and is worked from inclined shafts at depths varying from 80 to 200 feet. The Wankie coal field has been called "in many respects . . . the most remarkable in Africa." [9] Output of coal has increased slowly to the level of 3,695,000 tons in the year ended August 31, 1956; the production of coke in this same period was 243,000 tons. The recent achievements at Wankie, bringing the capacity to 5 million tons, contrast with earlier repeated failures to meet commitments. Housing and other amenities have been greatly

[9] J. H. Wellington, *Southern Africa* (Cambridge: University Press, 1955), v. 2, p. 152.

improved, and the pits have been modernized. In the past, people had been reluctant to work at Wankie; the labor turnover was almost 100 per cent a year, and unmarried employees worked an average of only four months at a stretch.[10]

Coal is estimated to underlie some 400 square miles of low and middle veld in Southern Rhodesia, some in the southeast, but mostly in the northwestern part of the country. There has been discussion of opening production at Lubimbi, 50 miles east of Wankie and 30 miles north of the rail line, or at some point as close to Que Que as possible, to reduce the haul of coal to the iron and steel plant at nearby Riscom. Opening of the Pafuri Link has created interest in the West Sabi area, estimated to have a 4.25 billion ton reserve of non-coking coal occurring in beds whose average thickness is nearly 50 feet. However, an ash content of 35 per cent is likely to reduce interest in this field.

Coal has also been found in Northern Rhodesia north of the Zambesi and there are several known fields in Nyasaland, both in the north in the Vipya Mountains and in the extreme south. A find has recently been reported in the north which is only 5 miles from Lake Nyasa. In total, the coal reserves of the Federation are probably immense, certainly much greater than the 7.25 billion tons officially listed as "probable reserves." Although it is unlikely that more than a small percentage will prove to be of coking quality, these reserves appear to give British Central Africa greater possibilities than other tropical African countries for developing an integrated industrial economy.

The hydroelectric potential of the area is also very great. The area is handicapped by the markedly seasonal regime of even the larger rivers, but the very considerable potential heads of water and some excellent sites for storage are compensating factors. Relatively little electricity now comes from hydroelectric plants. Livingstone obtains its power from a small plant a short distance below Victoria

[10] *Investment in Federation of Rhodesia and Nyasaland*, cited, p. 70.

Falls. The Broken Hill lead-zinc operations secure power from the Mulungushi and Lunsemfwa Rivers and have decided to erect a new dam at Mita Hills, partly to provide a steady head and thus increase production at the existing plant.

The situation will be greatly changed, however, upon completion of the Kariba Gorge Project on the Zambesi, which will more than double the Federation's capacity for producing electricity. This project, which was adopted in 1955 as the most practical way of meeting the power shortage, represents one of the greatest investments in African development. It involves construction of a 400-foot high, 1,800-foot long dam which will create the largest man-made lake in the world to supply two underground power stations, one on each bank, each of which will have six 100,000 kilowatt units. The estimated cost of the project, which is expected to produce electricity at one farthing a unit, is $225 million.

It may be questioned why the natural site of Victoria Falls was not first developed before turning to a project requiring the construction of an expensive storage and head-creating dam. There were three objections to developing power at Victoria Falls: (1) the fear of destroying the beauty of a site with very considerable value to the tourist industry, (2) the great fluctuation in flow over the Falls, the mean maximum flow being about ten times the mean minimum flow, and (3) the considerably greater distance of the Falls from major consuming centers. Both the high veld of Southern Rhodesia and the Copperbelt lie within a radius of 250 miles of the Kariba site, though the transmission line to the Copperbelt will be nearer 300 miles in length.

There are numerous other sites that may later be developed for production of hydroelectricity, notably on the Kafue, on the Murchison Cataracts of the Shire in Nyasaland, and on the Chambezi headstream of the Congo. The Kafue gorge is almost the same length as the Kariba but there is a larger drop, so a net head of 1,680 feet would be

obtainable by damming the upper end and piping the
water to the lower end, perhaps in two stages. The smaller
volume of the Kafue, however, means that only about 38
per cent as much power could be developed there as at
Kariba. This is the main reason for the decision to develop
Kariba first, for there would have been little if any excess
power available after completion of the Kafue project, the
full output being immediately absorbed by Southern Rhodesian industry and the Copperbelt. If a site can be found
above Victoria Falls suitable for storage it would also be
possible to develop very considerable power at the Falls
without affecting their beauty, and indeed probably contributing to it.

There is, then, no physical reason for the Federation to
be short of fuel and power for many years. And despite
shortages that have existed in recent years the country
compares very favorably with its African neighbors in
production and consumption of energy. The estimated
consumption of energy per capita in 1955 was twice the
average for Africa and far ahead of all countries except the
Union. The Federation ranked first among tropical African
countries in installed capacity and production of electricity (Table 7).

In addition to the Kariba Gorge Project, which is scheduled to begin producing electricity in the early 1960s,
several other steps have been taken to improve the immediate power situation. The Wankie carboelectric plant
is being expanded to 24,500 kw. capacity, which will be
more than one-sixth of the total capacity of the generating
stations of the Electricity Supply Commission of Southern
Rhodesia. Increasing the capacity of this plant will not
increase the burden upon the railways. A third station is
scheduled for completion at Salisbury in 1957; the Lusaka
plant will have its capacity raised by 150 per cent in 1958;
and a new 20,000 kw. generator has been installed at
Umniati with another to follow. From 1957 until Kariba
power becomes available, electricity is being transmitted to
the Copperbelt from Le Marinel station on the Lualaba.

Table 7

THE ENERGY POSITION OF THE FEDERATION, 1955–1956

	Northern Rhodesia	Southern Rhodesia	Nyasa-land	Feder-ation
Production of coal, mil. m. tons, 1955		3.32		3.32
Electric energy Installed capacity, 'ooo kw., 1956	266.5	391.4	5.6	663.5
Of which, hydro-electric	37.0	.5	.6	38.1
Production, mil. kwh., 1955	1,268	1,179	9.45	2,456.45
Of which, hydro-electric	218	2	1.95	221.95
Consumption of energy, coal equivalents, 1955				
Total, 'ooo metric tons				3,910
Per capita, metric tons				0.55

Source: *Statistical Yearbook 1956*, UN Doc., 1956.XVII.5 (New York, 1956), pp. 138, 281, 288, 308; Central Africa Statistical Office, Federation of Rhodesia and Nyasaland, *Monthly Digest of Statistics*, v. 4 (July 1957), p. 12.

The agreement with Union Minière du Haut Katanga calls for supplying up to 500 million kwh. per annum. Le Marinel has an installed capacity of 248,000 kw. and is transmitting the electricity to Northern Rhodesia over a distance of 300 miles. Power production in Nyasaland is very small, but the Blantyre-Limbe carboelectric station now generates 12 times the amount consumed in 1949.

There are no known deposits of petroleum in the Federation nor are the geological formations encouraging. The success of the Union's oil-from-coal plant at Sasolburg near Vereeniging is being watched with interest with the thought of possible duplication on one of Southern Rhodesia's coal fields. The investigation of such a plant at the Lubimbi field is in the preliminary stages.

Uranium ores have been reported from a number of

localities and, should the deposits prove substantial, they may provide bargaining power for future acquisition of nuclear-electric plants. Prospecting for uranium should be greatly encouraged by a recent offer of the United Kingdom Atomic Energy Authority to buy chemical concentrates and ores for specific periods. An extensive search is planned in the Mpudzi River area near Umtali, while deposits have also been reported along the southeastern shores of Lake Nyasa, around Tambani Mountain in the Mwanza area of Nyasaland, and in the Copperbelt.

Although it is still true that the whole economy of the Federation rests upon the Wankie Collieries and a single track rail line, it is obvious that exciting and fundamental changes will take place within the next decade in the transportation and energy fields. The interior position of the territories will always make transport something of a problem, but the energy resources are sufficiently great to be considered a stimulant to economic growth.

AGRICULTURE IN THE FEDERATION

It takes but a brief examination to reveal the relative poorness of the Federation for intensive agricultural pursuits.[11] The basic physical handicaps are the climatic and soil characteristics. The highly seasonal pattern of precipitation, with rainfall almost entirely confined to the summer, means that cropping is also confined to this season unless irrigation can be applied. Secondly, the relatively small total precipitation over the bulk of the region suggests that arable areas are restricted, and that the larger portion is suitable only for less intensive grazing. A third major climatic handicap is the high degree of unreliability in rainfall; the rains are unreliable in their onset, their duration, their distribution within the season, and in their total amount. This is reflected in a wide variation in crop yields and in the carrying capacity of pastureland. Yields

[11] A portion of this section is taken from William A. Hance, "Economic Potentialities of the Central African Federation," *Political Science Quarterly*, v. 69 (March 1954), pp. 29-44.

of the staple food crop, corn, fluctuate widely, and imports and intra-territorial movements consequently vary sharply from year to year. Low yields are not only a result of low precipitation, but may be occasioned by excessively wet seasons.

Precipitation varies considerably with altitude, aspect, and latitudinal position. These differences will lead in the future to more clearly defined agricultural regions than now exist. The atypical areas, such as the lower lands of the Zambesi, Shire, and Sabi Rivers, or the higher lands of Nyasaland, will be looked to for specialized production to bring greater variety to the agricultural pattern.

Temperature characteristics are, in contrast to precipitation, unusually favorable. High temperatures usually associated with the tropics are considerably modified on the plateaus, and the light ground frosts which are likely during the winter at higher altitudes impose few limitations on the range of crops which may be grown. On the other hand, the prevailing high temperatures below 2,000 feet permit the production of such tropical lowland crops as sugar.

Although soil surveys are as yet entirely inadequate to permit any sound quantitative judgments, it is generally accepted that by far the larger part of the area has mediocre soils. There is a widespread deficiency of available phosphates, the nitrogen reserves are quickly depleted, and the structure of most soils tends to deteriorate rapidly when they are subjected to cultivation. Loss of structure is in turn followed by a sharp decline in productivity and by increased susceptibility to erosion. In general, the soils derived from the ancient rocks of the plateau are shallow and infertile, while it is mainly the younger soils of the lowlands and valleys that are really productive.

The primary result of the combination of soils and climates is that only a very small part of the area is favorable for intensive arable-mixed farming, while the bulk of the area, perhaps two-thirds, is suitable only for grazing. It is safe to say that the most important physical problem

facing the Federation is proper utilization of its land surface. But a speedy solution cannot be expected and, in the
meantime, existing land practices, as well as certain economic forces, are not conducive to the maintenance of
even the present level of quality.

Even the farming practices of the European population
leave much to be desired. There has been little attempt to
develop soil-conserving practices and farming systems. The
application of fertilizer is typically low. Emphasis on corn
or tobacco on many farms is carried to the point of mono-
culture. Only very recently have Europeans cooperated in
a program to halt soil erosion, although the need was
apparent as early as 1925.

The division of land between Africans and Europeans
is a subject that is likely to cause friction in the future.
The situation varies greatly from territory to territory,
with Southern Rhodesia having the largest percentage of
alienated land (Table 8). The amount of land listed as
alienated is somewhat misleading because part of it has
not been assigned and part of what has been assigned is
either not occupied or remains undeveloped. For example,
of the 48.6 million acres of alienated land in Southern
Rhodesia, only 33 million acres have been assigned, of
which 28.5 million are actually in farm holdings.

A more meaningful conception of the status of European
farming may be derived from the number of farmers and
farm holdings and from the area under cultivation. In
1956 only about 9,000 Europeans were employed on Federation farms, cultivating about 80,000 acres in Nyasaland,
207,500 acres in Northern Rhodesia, and 820,000 acres in
Southern Rhodesia. In Southern Rhodesia most of the
land taken up is in large ranches. It must also be remem-
bered that large numbers of Africans are resident or
employed upon European-owned land, there being about
26,000 natives in the European farming areas of Southern
Rhodesia.

The more important European farming areas are on the
high veld of Southern Rhodesia, particularly around

Table 8

LAND ALLOCATION IN THE FEDERATION

	Northern Rhodesia		Southern Rhodesia		Nyasaland[a]		Federation	
	Million Acres	%	Million Acres	%	Million Acres	%	Million Acres	%
Total area	184.4	100	96.2	100	23.7	100	304.3	100
Assigned to Africans	173.7	94.2	32.4	33.7	19.7	83.1	225.8	74.2
Alienated	4.6	2.5	48.6	50.5	1.2[b]	5.1	54.4	17.9
Other	6.1	3.3	15.2	15.8	2.8	11.8	24.1	7.9

[a] Land area.
[b] In 1954 the freehold area occupied by native squatters was nationalized, reducing this figure.

Sources: Colonial Office, Great Britain, An Economic Survey of the Colonial Territories (London: HMSO, 1952), v. 1, The Central African and High Commission Territories, Col. 281 (1), pp. 7, 35; Derwent Whittlesey, "Southern Africa—An African Compage," Annals of the Association of American Geographers, v. 46 (March 1956), p. 72.

Salisbury, and along the railway belt of Northern Rhodesia. Lesser areas are in the southern highlands of Nyasaland, in adjacent areas of Northern Rhodesia centered on Fort Jameson, and in the extreme north around Abercorn. Although a broad range of crops can be grown in these areas, there has been a high degree of concentration on a limited number.

Corn occupies the largest acreage on European farms. Some of it is used as cattle feed, but most of it is sold to help supply the staple African food. Because of the distance to the sea and to eventual markets, export crops are restricted to those having high value per unit weight. The chief export crop of all three countries is tobacco, produced by Europeans in the Rhodesias and by both Europeans and Africans in Nyasaland. It accounted for 16.1 per cent of total Federation exports by value in 1956, when tobacco exports weighed 165 million pounds. The very large increase in production in postwar years, one of the most spectacular in agricultural crops in Africa, was stimulated by assured sales in the British market, where the dollar shortage required sharp reductions of American tobacco imports. Tobacco makes heavy demands on the soil and there has not been adequate compensating fertilization. There is land available for expanding production, but the future will require proper rotational and fertilization practices. A subsidiary disadvantage of the concentration on tobacco has been at least a partial neglect in the production of a satisfactory food supply.

Other cash crops grown on European farms and estates include citrus fruit on three irrigated holdings in northeastern Southern Rhodesia, especially in the Mazoe Valley, and tea and tung in Nyasaland. Tung oil has not become as important as was hoped, partly because of the depressing effects of lowered world prices, but Nyasaland has become the leading African producer of tea. A number of new developments suggest that specialized crops will be of increasing importance in the future. Sugar is coming into production near Chirundu in the Zambesi Valley and a dam will be erected at Mtilikwe to irrigate a 16,000-acre sugar estate about 35 miles from the new line to Lourenço Marques. The proposed Kyle Dam near Fort Victoria will irrigate both sugar estates and the large Hippo Valley citrus estate, expected to achieve an annual gross turnover of $56 million and to be the greatest single agricultural project in the country and the biggest concentrated citrus estate in the world. Inyanga in Southern Rhodesia will be the site of a 10,000-acre tea estate to produce 12 million pounds a year, or almost three-fourths as much as the total tea exports of the Federation in 1955. Finally, the Rhodesian Selection Trust group of Copperbelt companies (RST) has decided to finance the establishment of farms to produce winter vegetables in Northern Rhodesia.

Many European farms, especially toward the drier southwest in Southern Rhodesia, are more concerned with raising cattle than crops. There are about 1,100,000 cattle on European farms in Southern Rhodesia and 120,000 head on Northern Rhodesian farms. The opening of 100,000 square miles of northeastern Northern Rhodesia for European ranches was reported in June 1956, but the presence of tsetse in about five-eighths of that country is a deterring factor. Southern Rhodesia is fortunate to be nine-tenths tsetse free.

African farming almost everywhere follows traditional practices. Some native systems display a keen sense of the relations between the character of the soil and the natural vegetation that grows on it. For example, a "soil selection" system is practiced in Barotseland in which there are at least six distinct and specialized garden types on which the crops grown, the soil treatment, and the periods of cultivation and fallow vary according to the fertility and regenerative capacity of the soil.[12]

A second example is *chitemene* cultivation, practiced in considerable areas of the Rhodesias. There are many varieties of *chitemene*, but the essential feature is the practice

12 C. G. Trapnell and J. N. Clothier, *The Soils, Vegetation and Agricultural Systems of North-western Rhodesia* (Lusaka: Government Printer, 1937), pp. 41-45.

of lopping branches or felling trees over a wide area surrounding the actual garden and then burning them on the garden.[13] Depending chiefly upon the quality of the soil, between 200 and 500 acres are required for the continued subsistence of a family of four. Burning destroys weeds, makes clay soils more friable, and provides a fertilizing ash. Given static conditions, these and other systems can be considered as somewhat ingenious adaptations to the environment.

Modern practices, however, have often led to the degeneration of the traditional native systems. Partly because of the absence in rural areas of from 40 to 70 per cent of the males, who migrate to the mines, industries, and European farms, annual garden extensions have often been abandoned, even when there is more than ample land. Secondary crops are often neglected, to the detriment of nutritional standards. In some areas, degeneration has resulted from the expansion of population and the consequent shortening of the bush or grass fallow, which should probably be close to 20 years on the old rock soils. These phenomena are by no means confined to British Central Africa; to an extent they represent a largely inevitable effect of the introduction of a modern economy. But the degradation of large areas must be recognized as a problem of major importance, and appropriate steps must be planned to offset its deleterious effects. An increased disharmony between rural and urban areas may otherwise prove to be a serious barrier to continued development in any sphere.

There is little commercial production for export on African farms except in Nyasaland, where natives produce all the cotton and part of the tobacco. There is sale of corn and vegetables from farms that are situated close to urban and mining communities or that are on the rail lines. The rather minor place of crop production, however, is suggested by the low percentage of total area in crops, estimated to be about 0.05 per cent in Northern Rhodesia and little more

[13] C. G. Trapnell, *The Soils, Vegetation and Agriculture of North-eastern Rhodesia* (Lusaka: Government Printer, 1953), p. 36.

than 2 per cent in Southern Rhodesia.[14] Crop production by Africans has shown a considerable increase, but it is doubtful whether the total production of foodstuffs in the country is keeping up with the growth of population.

Southern Rhodesia has recently adopted a program designed to revolutionize native farming, to double the average family's cash income in five years. This includes the substitution of individual holdings for communal tenure, the introduction of approved rotational systems, improved seed selection, and control of soil erosion.[15]

Natives have the larger share of the more than 3 million head of livestock in the Federation. Practices are uniformly bad. Little attention is paid to the animals, the value of the herd being measured in numbers and in length of horn. There is overgrazing, firing of grass, inadequate control of stock watering, etc. It is noteworthy, however, that sales of native cattle continue to rise, a record of 129,000 head having been sold in 1954.

The agricultural and land-use problems of the Federation call eloquently for increased attention if this portion of the economy is not to limit over-all development. Future emphases in areas suitable for cropping should probably be on mixed farming, because, with poor soils, any transformation to permanent cultivation will require composting with cattle manure. Furthermore, the general quality of the area suggests that livestock farming must eventually assume a very important part in the area's economy, primarily because of the climatic limitations on tillage agriculture. It is reasonable to predict that progress in combating trypanosomiasis and its carrier, the tsetse fly, will open up vast areas where grazing is now precluded.

Phosphatic fertilizers may also be made available in the future from large deposits of apatite at Dorowa in Southern Rhodesia, while nitrogenous fertilizers might be produced by fixation, using power from one of the proposed

14 Wellington, cited, v. 2, p. 3.
15 P. B. Fletcher, "A Revolution in African Agriculture," *Optima*, v. 6 (June 1956), pp. 55-59.

hydroelectric developments. A superphosphate plant is
scheduled for completion at Salisbury by 1958 and the production of nitrogenous fertilizers as a by-product of coke-
oven operations at Que Que is contemplated.

Meteorological, soil, and ecological surveys will disclose
the capabilities of lands at present but little used. In particular, lowland areas with sedimentary or alluvial floors,
such as the Luangwa trough in Northern Rhodesia, need
studying. Even the soils of the upland old-rock areas vary
considerably, while the soils of Nyasaland have greater variety than those of the Rhodesias. The better areas in all three
countries need careful delineation.

The general shortage of water, particularly during the
winter months, makes obvious the desirability of studying
irrigation potentialities, which are not inconsiderable. A
major project has been proposed for the Shire Valley in
southern Nyasaland which, in addition to stabilizing the
level of Lake Nyasa to the advantage of transport and fisheries and to the production of electric power, would make
possible the irrigation and reclamation of about 400,000
acres in Nyasaland plus additional acreage in Mozambique.
In Southern Rhodesia, between 300,000 and 400,000 acres
of the Sabi-Lundi area in the southeast might eventually
be brought under irrigation by the erection of a dam at
Condo on the Sabi River. The Kariba Dam will permit the
irrigation of sizable areas of the Zambesi Valley. Other projects include eight high-veld schemes that have been investigated in Southern Rhodesia, the Kyle Dam, and irrigation
in the Mazoe Valley. In Northern Rhodesia there are interesting possibilities for irrigating extensive lands for sugar,
rice, and other crops in the Luangwa Valley.

On the plateau surface, increasing attention will be given
to the potentialities of the swampy and seasonally flooded
areas, both the very large ones and the smaller *dambos* and
vleis, areas of impeded drainage. The seven largest swamps
and adjacent plains in Northern Rhodesia total 13,754
square miles, or no less than 6 per cent of the country. Just
what the appropriate combination of uses should be in these

areas will not be known until they have been much more thoroughly studied, but it is reasonable to believe that, with their apparently superior soils and with an excess of water, the effects of proper control will be highly rewarding. The pilot farm financed by the RST group, mentioned earlier, is one of the first projects devoted to research and development of such areas. It is situated in the better known eastern part of the Kafue flats, where there is a total of 1,300,000 acres subject to annual inundation. The preliminary study envisages the creation of large polders which will be cut into units of 160 acres for European farmers and smaller farms for an African settlement scheme.

A rather special interest in the production of food attaches to fishing. It is carried on to some extent in all the larger lakes and swamps, but would appear to be capable of very great extension, which would be highly beneficial to a population with a diet generally deficient in proteins and calcium. Fish farming could gradually become of real importance, with yields of 300-500 pounds per acre per year to be expected. It is hoped that a substantial fishing industry will be developed in the huge lake to be created by the Kariba Dam.

THE MINERAL INDUSTRY

The two Rhodesias produce a wide range of important minerals. Their production of copper, cobalt, petalite, chrome, and asbestos is of world significance. Other minerals are of less importance in international trade, but are of considerable actual and very great potential value to the area. The mineral industry occupies an outstanding position in the economy of Northern Rhodesia, accounting for over 95 per cent of the total value of exports, providing the principal source of employment for both Africans and Europeans, and yielding well over half of the total revenue of government. In Southern Rhodesia, the mineral industry is relatively less significant. It is marked by greater diversity in minerals produced and in the size of operation. Nyasaland has practically no mineral industry, though a number of bodies are known to exist. In the Federation as a whole, minerals accounted for 76 per cent of exports in 1956, exclusive of gold bullion and concentrates.

In Central Africa, "mining is much more than digging holes in the ground." [16] Provisions must be made for disease control, for health programs, for housing, and for recreational facilities and other amenities. The stimulus of mining to other aspects of the economy, such as transportation, agriculture, and industry, is difficult to measure but is tremendous. It was estimated in 1954 that mining used 28 per cent of the available coal and coke, consumed 66 per cent of the electricity produced, and provided 58 per cent of the tonnage hauled by the Rhodesian Railways.[17] And known mineral reserves suggest that mining will become of even greater importance in the future. The Rhodesias are extremely fortunate to have a large part of what is probably the world's greatest single metallogenetic zone, running discontinuously from the Katanga to the Bushveld Complex of the Union.

But there are, of course, accompanying problems. The evils of excessive migration and declining native farming are two. The high dependence upon products whose world prices have fluctuated notoriously is a third. Finally, it can never be forgotten that however great reserves may be, one is dealing with a wasting resource. Just as the Union looks upon reducing its relative dependence upon gold as a major goal of its economic policies, so the Federation will have to give similar attention to broadening its economic base.

The Copperbelt mining operations are by far the most important in British Central Africa. Sir Ronald Prain, Chairman of the RST companies, commenting upon the importance of the Copperbelt to the Federation, estimated that the industry's direct contribution to the economy in 1955 was 29 per cent of net domestic output, 23 per cent of net national income, 63 per cent of exports, and 37 per cent

[16] "Adventure in Copper," *The Economist* (November 26, 1955), p. 765.
[17] *Investment in Federation of Rhodesia and Nyasaland*, cited, p. 21.

of taxes.[18] The indirect contributions were estimated at $151 million and 44 per cent of net domestic output. The total direct and indirect contributions to the Federation economy were placed at $431 million. In December 1956, there were 7,158 Europeans and 39,153 African mine employees in the Copperbelt. The total population in the mining communities and in adjacent towns catering to them was 31,048 Europeans, 195,560 Africans, and 560 Asians.

Now producing about 13 to 16 per cent of the free world's copper ore, the Copperbelt has reserves adequate for a greatly enlarged production and for sustained high-level production well into the next century. The total reserves are undoubtedly much greater than the published figure of 700 million long tons. Geologists believe that there is more copper in Northern Rhodesia and that the chances for finding it are better than in any other part of the world. Aerial prospecting shows much promise for the vast, unprospected structures of the country. Intensive prospecting is now taking place about 150 miles southwest of Kitwe. With several new mines coming into production, output may increase from the 1956 level of 383,484 tons of blister and electrolytic copper to 550,000 tons by 1960. The proportion of electrolytic copper produced, about three-fifths of the total in 1956, will increase when a new refinery at Ndola starts production in 1958 and reaches full-scale output in 1960. Production of cobalt, derived from several of the copper mines, enables the Federation to rank second to the Congo among world producers. A new cobalt plant is included in the refinery being erected at Ndola. In 1956 cobalt accounted for 1.85 per cent of the value of minerals produced in Northern Rhodesia.

The other important minerals produced in Northern Rhodesia are lead and zinc, mined at Broken Hill, south of the Copperbelt. Reserves are adequate for many years production, while there are several known ore bodies in the general area that have not as yet been touched. In 1956, Broken Hill treated 121,044 tons of ore yielding 15,200

[18] *African World* (July 1956), p. 8.

tons of lead, 28,925 tons of zinc, and 52 tons of cadmium, with a total value of about $13 million or about 3.56 per cent of the value of all minerals produced in Northern Rhodesia. One manganese mine has been opened in the Fort Rosebery area west of Lake Bangweulu; it produced 39,438 tons of ore in 1956.

In Southern Rhodesia, gold played an important part in the early history of the country, being the lure that brought the first large immigration. Production was important for many years, yielding about half of the national income, and although it was still the first ranking mineral by value in 1954, it is now of decreasing relative value. Most of the ore bodies are small, heavily faulted, and widely scattered. A large number of small workings have closed down in post-war years. The value of gold production in 1956 was $18.6 million.

Asbestos, mined since 1908, is now exported in greater value than gold. Southern Rhodesia is the leading world producer of top-grade asbestos but third in total production. There is a large-scale operation at Shabani and a smaller one at Mashaba, 35 miles distant. Chrome ore has ranked third among Southern Rhodesian minerals but is increasing rapidly in importance. It occurs at numerous places along the Great Dike, the chief mining center being at Selukwe. Sales of both asbestos and chrome have been restricted in postwar years by lack of available transport. The new rail line to Lourenço Marques has greatly eased the situation, however, and in the year ended March 31, 1957, movements of chrome increased 45 per cent over the previous year. Totaling 713,000 tons in that period, they may reach a million tons yearly before 1960.

Minerals of increasing importance in Southern Rhodesia are: petalite, a lithium ore, now mined at the rate of 10,000 short tons a month, chiefly at Bikita, 40 miles from the railhead at Fort Victoria; magnesite; and copper, from Mangula, 40 miles north of Sinoia. An extensive nickel reef has been found 40 miles west of Gatooma, and a pilot plant at the Empress Mine was completed in 1957.[19] If pilot operations are successful, a mine comparable to one of the large copper mines may be opened. Corundum has been located at Concession, 40 miles from Salisbury, and a large deposit of molybdenum has been found near Selukwe. In recent years, about 2,300 Europeans and 60,000 Africans have been employed in mining in Southern Rhodesia. More than three-fourths of the Africans come from outside Southern Rhodesia, especially from Nyasaland and Mozambique.

In Nyasaland there is a 60 million ton reserve of bauxite with 42.7 per cent alumina content on Mt. Mlanje, which has suggested the possibility of refining aluminum, using power from the proposed Shire Project. Other minerals known to exist in Nyasaland are asbestos, graphite, ilmenite, kyanite, mica, apatite, and galena. In 1955 a large vermiculite deposit was reported discovered in the middle of the Shire Valley.

Although the output of non-ferrous metallic minerals in the Rhodesias is extremely important to the economy of the Federation, greater importance may attach in the long run to reserves of coal and iron ore, basic to development of a fully integrated economy. Southern Rhodesia, in particular, would appear to be one of the few African areas that has substantial reserves of both these minerals.

The extent and quality of coal deposits have been described above. So far as iron is concerned, a rich hematite body occurs near Que Que in Southern Rhodesia and is worked at that locality, though production is now only about 35,000 metric tons a year. Other deposits are known around Lusaka and at Sabi and Bukwe Hill, only a few miles from the new Pafuri Link. The Bukwe Hill body is believed to be one of the greatest in the world. Total reserves of the Federation are adequate not only to supply a large domestic consumption but to support substantial exports of iron ore or pig iron.

[19] "The New Nickel Venture," *The Central African Examiner*, v. 1 (June 7, 1957), p. 36.

is scheduled for Umtali. The embryonic electrical engineering industry has a factory at Bulawayo capable of producing 100 five-horsepower motors monthly.

The building and construction industry is credited with about 30 per cent of the total output of secondary industry in Southern Rhodesia, though it cannot be considered so significant among manufacturing industries. It includes cement plants at Salisbury, Bulawayo, and Colleen Bawn. Other cement plants exist at Chilanga in Northern Rhodesia and at Blantyre-Limbe in Nyasaland. Concrete building materials are produced at Umtali, and a large asbestos cement plant was scheduled to open in the Bulawayo area in 1957.

The food and beverage industries account for about a quarter of industrial output in Southern Rhodesia, and new plants in this sector are constantly being erected.

The textile and clothing industry is expanding with considerable force and even boasts an export of goods, chiefly to the Union of South Africa. The Gatooma cotton textile factory was erected when ocean shipping was scarce. A half dozen weaving plants followed, and over 60 clothing factories. A new weaving mill was opened in 1955 at Umtali, which now has about 2,100 people employed in the textile industry, including the production of jute bags.

The chemical industry is represented by plants producing fertilizer, oil and soap, paints and polishes, and matches. Large new explosives and sulphuric acid plants are under construction; the Dunlop Rubber Company plans a new tire factory; and the first pharmaceutical plant opened in July 1957.

With regard to the location of industry, primary processing of mineral and agricultural raw materials are typically placed close to the producing areas. Other manufacturing is heavily concentrated in Salisbury and Bulawayo with lesser representation in the Midlands of Southern Rhodesia. The Midlands has the iron and steel industry plus an important part of the textile industry at such centers as Gatooma and Hartley. Lusaka in Northern Rhodesia has received a number of manufacturing plants in postwar years, while Blantyre-Limbe is the focus of the small industrial development in Nyasaland.

The future growth of manufacturing in the Federation will depend upon the availability of markets, labor, power, raw materials, and capital. A brief assessment of each of these factors will show some of the strengths and weaknesses of the area with regard to industry.

The weakness of the market would appear to set definite limits on the size of the industrial establishment. Even if the European population, with a high average standard, triples or quadruples in the next quarter-century it will still be too small to support certain types of industrial enterprises. This provides a strong argument for raising the African standard of living, for it is only the indigenous populace that can supply a potentially large domestic market.

The advantages of the Federation market include the high purchasing power of many Europeans, the demand stimulated by large and small development and construction projects, the fact that almost a sixth of the Africans of Rhodesia and Nyasaland are wage earners, and the very considerable geographic concentration of the two richest market regions on the high veld of Southern Rhodesia and the Copperbelt of Northern Rhodesia. The yearly wage of a European miner on the Copperbelt was $5,102 in 1954 and $6,160 in 1955, representing in the latter year about one-half basic wage and one-half cash bonus based on profits made by the companies at current copper prices. The average earnings of European employees in the Federation in 1956 came to $3,156. In 1952 the average cash income of African wage earners in Central Africa was believed to range from $126 to $140 a year, while the average annual wage for 560,000 employed Africans in Southern Rhodesia was estimated to be $123 in 1957. The Prime Minister of Southern Rhodesia reported in 1957 that the spending power of Africans in that territory was about $120 million per year.[26] The African market is obviously inadequate to absorb luxury items,

[26] Barclays Bank D.C.O., *Overseas Review* (May 1957), p. 29.

but it does call for substantial quantities of basic food and clothing.

It does not now appear that opportunities for export of manufactured products are great, except for items semi-processed from domestically produced agricultural and mineral raw materials. Some textiles and clothing items are exported to the Union, but that country's desire to foster its own industry does not suggest that the Federation will be permitted to secure a very large slice of the Union market. The Federation of Rhodesian Industry has suggested that some items may be produced at lower cost in the Federation than in the Union because of the less restrictive policies of the former with regard to employment of natives in manufacturing, and that these items might, therefore, secure a market in the Union. Yet if the Union is prepared to enforce a strict color bar in its own industries, it is not likely that it will welcome competition from areas that do not apply the same restrictions. Adjacent Portuguese areas may absorb some produce, but the Congo and East Africa have plans for their own industrial development, while sales to overseas markets are hampered by the interior continental position of the Federation. On the other hand, because of the favorable raw material position of its iron and steel industry, the Federation may find it possible to market simple mechanical and fabricated metal items in adjacent territories and to export pig iron and steel overseas.

Regarding labor, the rapidly increasing population should provide an adequate supply, but only if the present prodigal use is abandoned. There are constant complaints in the territories of a shortage of unskilled and semi-skilled African labor, but a large part of this shortage is more apparent than real. With greater rationalization of farming, construction, and industry, and with a reduction in the excessive number of domestic servants (22 per cent of the Africans in the Salisbury municipal area), there would be much less of a problem. If approached with the proper perspective, the so-called shortage could be of tremendous value to the area, for it means that there is opportunity to upgrade the African and to set a goal higher than that of a largely self-subsistent peasantry. The Federation, of course, need not depend solely upon its own manpower resources, and the high degree of mobility from one territory to another is also a factor important in the supply of labor for industry. Southern Rhodesia, for example, gets about 80,000 natives a year from Nyasaland, 45,000 from Northern Rhodesia, 72,000 from Mozambique, and 4,500 from Bechuanaland. However, this also entails a migratory labor supply, the disadvantages of which have already been noted.[27]

The system of land ownership prevailing in Southern Rhodesia has forced the industrialist to adapt his operations to the employment of migratory labor because the African worker, not permitted to settle in European areas, is obliged to keep one foot in the reserve. It is not surprising that labor turnover rates are high and productivity low. It is possible for a manufacturer to stabilize his labor force by providing his own township for African employees, but this is likely to increase capital requirements by about 25 per cent. Very recently there has been a policy change enabling a few Africans to acquire houses in urban areas. The greater stability of settled workers has been revealed on numerous occasions: the average married worker at Wankie who is accompanied by his wife works ten times longer than the unmarried worker, and some settled African employees on the Copperbelt have completed 25 years of service. The complaint is still common, however, that the industrial employer must cope with "almost raw African labourers . . . who leave their jobs almost as soon as they have acquired some measure of skill." [28] Yet the index of physical output per employee increased from 100 in 1938 to 184 in 1952,[29] and it is generally recognized that the turnover is slowing, particularly among married workers.

Shortages of artisans, skilled workers, and managers are

---

[27] See Peter Scott, "Migrant Labor in Southern Rhodesia," *The Geographical Review,* v. 44 (January 1954), pp. 29-48, and "The Role of Northern Rhodesia in African Labor Migration," same (July 1954), pp. 432-434.
[28] *Survey of Rhodesian Industry,* cited, p. 10.
[29] Same, p. 12.

likely to be more restrictive in the future than shortages of unskilled and semi-skilled labor, though the Rhodesians do not have the same limitations in this regard that usually exist in underdeveloped areas. A relaxation of the color bar would help this situation, both by permitting the rise of Africans who are willing and able to absorb the necessary training, and by freeing Europeans from less important jobs so they could make a greater contribution to the economy. A less restrictive immigration policy would also be beneficial, for it would probably be easier to secure certain classes of skilled craftsmen and machine operators from non-British areas. In Northern Rhodesia, the relatively high wages received by mining employees may temporarily delay the location of industry on the Copperbelt, for new establishments might find it difficult to match the wages paid by the mining companies.

The greatest single problem involving labor, and potentially the most serious in the entire economy, is the existence of the "color bar," which effectively restricts Africans from rising beyond a given level in industry, mining, and other pursuits. Maintaining such a barrier indefinitely is impossible and there is no moral or economic justification for its existence today.[30] The case for African advancement throughout the Federation was strengthened by recent agreements on the Copperbelt,[31] but there is still great necessity for improvement. It is increasingly evident that the African is dissatisfied with the position he has been allocated and is increasingly capable of expressing his dissatisfaction.

Labor unrest is not, of course, connected only with the color bar. African unions are youthful, lacking in adequate leadership, and inclined, therefore, to irresponsibility. Strikes are estimated to have cost about 115,000 tons of copper output in 1954 and 135,000 tons in 1955, while a wave of strikes in 1956 caused a state of emergency on the

[30] Alan Paton, "African Advancement: A Problem of Both Copperbelt and Federation," *Optima*, v. 5 (December 1955), pp. 105-109.
[31] Harold K. Hochschild, "Labor Relations in Northern Rhodesia," *The Annals of the American Academy of Political and Social Science*, v. 306 (July 1956), pp. 43-49.

Copperbelt. Manufacturing industry has not had similar difficulties, but it is not unrealistic to expect that it may.

Turning to the raw material, fuel, and power position of the Federation as it may affect industrial development, the excellent coal and hydroelectric resources of the area should be recalled. They permit envisaging the development of a more rounded industrial economy than may be possible in most African areas. The exceptionally low cost of coal must also be noted, only $2.73 a ton at pit head in 1957.

The area is well endowed from the standpoint of industrial raw materials. In agriculture, the production of cotton, vegetable oils, tobacco, food crops, and livestock may be expanded, while physical characteristics permit the introduction of other crops providing industrial raw materials. In forestry, the Rhodesian teak forests of the Livingstone-Sesheke districts support one of the largest hardwood sawmilling plants south of the equator, but the bulk of the forested area of all three countries is in poor quality, open savanna woodlands, and large imports of timber must be expected to continue. Exotic trees such as eucalyptus, cypress, pine, and poplar grow very rapidly in some areas, however, and increased attention to planting forest reserves would reduce the need for importing this bulky item. Mineral raw materials are tremendous and varied, but, for many years, greater importance will attach to them as exports than as raw materials for Federation industry.

From the standpoint of availability of capital, the Federation has been one of the most attractive African areas for foreign investment in postwar years, though the greater part of the funds has gone into transportation, power, and mining rather than to secondary industry. The ratio of investment to gross national product is very large. For example, in 1955 the ratio reached 29 per cent, which compares with 6 to 8 per cent in countries like India and Pakistan, 18 per cent in Western Europe, and 14 to 15 per cent in the United Kingdom. Since 1951 the investment has been nearly $280 million per year. The whole picture of economic development is dominated by the fact that investment will be high, both in the private and public sectors, which means that the danger of inflation will be skirted constantly.

The United Kingdom has traditionally been the chief source of outside capital. In addition to large private investment the Colonial Development Corporation allotted to the two protectorates, up to 1957, $62 million of its total world-wide capital outlay of $208 million. The Union of South Africa has also been important, while Americans have played a significant role in mining investments and, among the foreign governments lending to the Federation, the United States has played the leading role. The World Bank has made several loans for transportation and power, including an $80 million loan for the Kariba Project in 1956, the largest single project loan that it had ever made.

The financing of the Kariba Dam is an interesting example of investment in the Federation. In addition to the $80 million World Bank loan, $56 million is being loaned at low interest rates by the copper companies, which have also agreed to accept a surcharge on the power they receive from Kariba during 1961–1967 to yield a further $28 million. Other loans for Kariba are $42 million from the C.D.C., $11.2 million from the British South Africa Company, $8.4 million from the Commonwealth Development Finance Company, and $5.6 million each from Barclays Bank and the Standard Bank of South Africa.[32]

The position of the Federation, then, is comparatively favorable from the standpoint of investment. High returns from copper have given buoyancy to government revenues; there is a decidedly favorable trade balance, and, in contrast to most underdeveloped countries, substantial funds are available from within the territory. Furthermore, the economy of Central Africa is perhaps somewhat more comprehensible to the middle-latitude investor than that of other African areas. There will, however, be shortages of capital; uneven development may create temporary distortions, and there may have to be short-run controls in specific spheres. Some of these difficulties must be considered

[32] "World Bank and Kariba," *The Economist* (June 23, 1956), p. 1211.

inevitable in an economy expanding with the rapidity of the Central African Federation, but they should not be permitted to detract from long-term prospects.

There are, of course, other impediments to foreign investments. A recent analysis of dollar investment in the Federation finds the most serious deterrent in the pattern of race relations, particularly in Southern Rhodesia, where "paternalistic relationships" do not "produce the type of environment in which a market economy can best flourish." [33] He further notes that, as a by-product of this system, the foreign investor is "faced with a maze of regulations which cover virtually every aspect of an employer's dealings with his African employees—regulations not only comprehensive in coverage, but also difficult to ascertain." Nonetheless, the general attitude seems to be favorable to investment in the Federation.

In conclusion, it may be said that the Federation of Rhodesia and Nyasaland has excellent potentialities for economic expansion. The weakest physical link is the agricultural base. The remarkable metallogenetic zone of the Copperbelt and other substantial mineral reserves can readily be further exploited to yield exchange and provide industrial raw materials. Finally, there is room for expansion in many secondary industries, and there is a power, fuel, and raw material base adequate to justify a fully integrated manufacturing economy. If continued progress is made toward evolving a more enlightened and more practical attitude toward African advancement, there is justification for real optimism.

[33] William J. Barber, "Dollar Investment in Central Africa," *New Commonwealth*, v. 31 (April 30, 1956), p. 212.

Chapter 6

THE REPORT OF THE EAST AFRICA
ROYAL COMMISSION

READING about the Mau Mau revolt, the aborted Tanganyika Groundnuts Scheme, the exile and return of the Kabaka of Buganda, and recognizing the familiar ring of such names as Kilimanjaro, Ruwenzori, and Lake Victoria, many Americans probably have the feeling that they know British East Africa somewhat better than other areas of the continent. Yet these territories, about a fifth the size of the United States and with a population of 20 million, are perhaps as difficult to understand as any African area. For British East Africa is marked by tremendous physical, cultural, and economic diversity.

Coastal mangrove swamps, arid sun-baked grasslands, tropical marshes, sandy and volcanic deserts, thornbush savanna, tropical deciduous forests, and eternally snow-capped peaks suggest the great variety of physical landscapes. Often there is marked change within very limited distances, as from the base to the summits of the mighty volcanic peaks or across a section of the great rift systems. The human contrasts are equally impressive. There are the evolved Ganda and Chagga on the one hand and the intransigent Masai on the other; there are pastoralists and settled farmers; there are areas of oppressive density and others that are nearly empty. So far as the position of the European is concerned, Uganda is fairly comparable to West Africa; Kenya has a dominant white settler group; Tanganyika is somewhere in between. Lastly, there is an important Asian element, and, on the coasts, a sizable Arab and Goan population.

The heterogeneity of economies and cultures frequently results in a crazy-quilt pattern of land use. Any pattern may be bounded by any other, often with little or no physical explanation for the sharp distinctions. The boundaries of individual tribes and clans, as well as those of the Europeans, are rigidly fixed, and this tends to split the territories into a large number of units in which the contact with other units varies to a high degree but is usually very limited. Each unit appears to be functioning to some extent without regard to its neighbors and each unit is advancing at a different pace.

The publication of the Report of the East Africa Royal Commission and of the comments of the East African administrative officers on it [1] provides the means of looking at East Africa in an entirely different way from that in which British Central Africa was approached in the last chapter. The first part of this chapter summarizes the physical and human conditions in East Africa. The second part sets out the more important proposals made by the Commission, together with the supporting arguments, and some of the more significant reactions to them, particularly the disagreements of the East African administrative officers.

The Royal Commission Report is 482 pages long and the responding dispatches total 196 pages. A brief account such as the following obviously must omit much. Quotation marks are eliminated in the following summaries, but it should be emphasized that most of the material is taken directly or paraphrased from the Report. The organization of this chapter, however, is entirely different from that of the Royal Commission Report. The second portion, in particular, brings together material from various parts of the Report that helps indicate several of the Commission's major themes.

The East Africa Royal Commission was established after

[1] *East Africa Royal Commission 1953–1955 Report*, Cmd. 9475 (London: HMSO, 1955), and *Despatches from the Governors of Kenya, Uganda and Tanganyika and from the Administrator, East Africa High Commission, Commenting on the East Africa Commission 1953–1955 Report*, Cmd. 9801 (London: HMSO, 1956). The reporting officials were Sir Evelyn Baring, Governor of Kenya, Sir Andrew B. Cohen, Governor of Uganda, Sir Edward F. Twining, Governor of Tanganyika, and Sir Alexander M. Bruce Hutt, Administrator, East Africa High Commission.

Sir Philip Mitchell, then Governor of Kenya, sent to London a dispatch called *Land and Population in East Africa* [2] which recommended a searching study. The Commission was composed of seven members.[3] Sir Hugh Dow, the chairman, had had wide experience in India; other members were experts in agricultural, economic, and financial matters, and there was one African member. Although there is no indication in the Report, it is understood that Dr. Frankel, a leading South African economist, now teaching at Oxford, was perhaps the most influential member of the Commission and that he was chiefly responsible for many of the ideas presented.

The Royal Warrant appointing the Commission set forth its mission: having regard to the rapid rate of increase of the African population and the congestion of population in certain localities, the Commission was to examine the measures needed to achieve an improved standard of living, including the introduction of capital to enable peasant farming to develop and expand production. It was charged with framing recommendations with particular reference to the introduction of better farming methods, adaptations of traditional tribal systems of tenure, the opening of land not fully used, the development of industrial activities, conditions of employment with special reference to social conditions and the growth of large urban populations, and the social problems which arise from the growth of permanent urban and industrial populations. The Commission was also asked, where necessary, to comment upon policy in such related fields as education and public health, to consider probable trends of population, and to take account of existing obligations in relation to the security of land reserved for the different races and groups in various parts of the territories concerned. The Commission interpreted the terms of reference very broadly, and extended its in-

[2] *Land and Population in East Africa,* Col. 290 (London: HMSO, 1952), 33 p.
[3] Sir Hugh Dow, Chairman, Sally Herbert Frankel, Arthur Gaitskell, Rowland S. Hudson, Daniel T. Jack, Frank Sykes, Sir Frederick Seaford, and Chief Kidah Makwaia.

quiries over a somewhat wider field than had been specifically indicated. Of particular importance was its conclusion that "taking account of existing obligations in relation to the security of land" did not debar it from making recommendations regarding them. Had it decided otherwise, the Report would have lost much of its interest and logic.

I. THE BACKGROUND OF EAST AFRICAN PROBLEMS

Although much of the general approach that is reflected in the recommendations of the Commission could apply to many underdeveloped areas, the proposals refer specifically to East Africa. They can neither be fully meaningful nor fully comprehended except in terms of the area and its physical, economic, and social characteristics. This section, therefore—using material taken largely from the Report—gives a brief regional survey and summarizes the situation regarding population, the changing position of the African, the status of agricultural, mining, manufacturing, urban, and transport development, and several key socio-economic problems.

PHYSICAL FEATURES

Kenya, Tanganyika, and Uganda, lying between the great lakes of central Africa and the Indian Ocean, form a compact block covering 642,728 square miles of land and 38,901 square miles of water. Almost every variety of physical feature is to be found, from the permanent snows of Mounts Meru and Kilimanjaro to the hot, humid coastal belt, and from the arid deserts of Kenya's Northern Province to the lush parklands of the high plateau.

Climates vary greatly, ranging from tropical rainy to tropical desert and to the moderate climate of the tropical highland areas. Rainfall varies from about 5 inches in parts of Kenya's Northern Province to about 50 inches in the coastal belt and the Lake Victoria Basin, and to as much as 100 inches in some of the mountainous areas. In much of Kenya and Uganda and in part of Tanganyika the rainfall occurs in two distinct seasons each year; in some areas the whole annual fall is in too short a period for many crops to mature; other areas receive their annual quota of rain in a few storms of great intensity.

The Main Physical Regions

East Africa may be divided into four main physical regions: the coastal belt, the coast hinterland plain rising to about 2,000 feet, the main East African plateau, and the Lake Victoria depression. The coastal belt, varying from 10 to 40 miles in width, is an area of fairly high rainfall in the middle, but precipitation tapers off toward the Somaliland border and south of the Rufiji River. Soils vary from the fertile alluvium of the river deltas to infertile coral shag occurring in extensive patches.

The coast hinterland plain, or Nyika area, has an hourglass shape, with the northern bulge covering most of the Northern Province of Kenya and the southern bulge covering the whole of the Southern Province of Tanganyika. The neck is about 100 miles wide inland from Tanga. Rainfall is lowest in the north where desert or steppe conditions prevail and the nomadic inhabitants maintain a precarious existence by following the scanty surface water supplies. Rainfall increases to the south where 20 inches or more of rain may be expected, though there is considerable variation from year to year. Soils are generally light, easily exhausted, and erodable. Concentrations of African cultivators are found on the alluvial soils along such rivers as the Tana, Galana, and Rufiji, but most of the region has scattered settlements living on a bare subsistence level by cultivating small patches of more fertile soils and herding sheep and goats in the scrub bush that characterizes much of the region. Lack of water and presence of the tsetse fly are factors limiting a more extensive use of this plain. The area is broken in places by high outcrops and ranges of hills, some of which enjoy higher rainfall and fertile volcanic soils and hence support dense populations of African cultivators.

The third major region, the main plateau, is part of the tableland extending from Ethiopia to the Cape Province of South Africa. Lying generally between 4,000 and 10,000 feet above sea level, it is split by the two arms of the Rift system. The Rift Valleys are flanked by escarpment walls rising as high as 3,000 feet in places. The northern and southern parts of the Eastern Rift consist of dry, infertile grassland or scrub, with a low and unreliable rainfall. That part which traverses the highlands of Kenya, however, contains some excellent ranching land where the difficulties of providing water can be overcome, and there are small areas enjoying higher rainfall which sustain successful arable farming. The Western Rift, at a much lower elevation, is relatively dry and hot, and the soil is generally infertile. Between the Rifts is the Lake Victoria depression, which forms a separate landform subdivision within the confines of the plateau. The plateau region is broken by mountain masses, the largest of which covers the Kenya Highlands and some of the adjoining districts. In Tanganyika the main mountain areas are Kilimanjaro and Meru, the Usambara, Pare, and Uluguru ranges, and the massif at the head of Lake Nyasa. Mount Elgon stands on the borders of Kenya and Uganda, while in Uganda itself the Ruwenzori Range and the Kigezi Highlands lie along the Congo and Ruanda-Urundi border.

This East African plateau is an area of great ecological variety, for the considerable diversity of height is reflected in wide ranges of rainfall and temperature. Agricultural use ranges from intensive peasant mixed farming as practiced by the Kikuyu, to the communal grazing of stock by nomadic herdsmen such as the Masai. Rainfall may vary from 10 to 100 inches, even the highland area being subject to considerable variations. It has been estimated that only about half of the area of the Kenya Highlands is suitable for arable farming. A large part of the mountainous areas was at one time covered with forest, and it is in such areas of deep, fertile soil and high, reliable rainfall that there is the greatest concentration of agricultural peasants.

These are the main problem areas. Much of the highest mountain area is protected forest reserve or national parks. The Lake Victoria depression includes a large part of Uganda, much of the Nyanza district of Kenya, and part of the Lake Province of Tanganyika. It has high, reliable rainfall around the northern half and somewhat lower rainfall around the south. The drier parts are suitable for extensive ranching; the wetter parts include much elephant-grass country and some considerable forest areas. The Lake Victoria depression contains a substantial part of the high-quality farming land of East Africa.

Physical Difficulties in the Region as a Whole

The East African region as a whole is singularly poorly served with permanent rivers; geological circumstances make boring for water an expensive and uncertain operation; a high evaporation rate and porous soils present particular problems of surface water conservation. The tsetse fly plagues men and domestic animals in almost two-thirds of Tanganyika and Uganda and about a tenth of Kenya. The scattered location of areas of high agricultural potential and of known mineral deposits requires extensive and costly communications. This discouraging background, the Commission notes, brings into relief the overriding importance of making proper use of the limited areas of high productivity.

THE PEOPLE OF EAST AFRICA

Population

The total population of East Africa in mid-1956 was 20,199,000, of whom 97.8 per cent were Africans.[4] The Africans do not form a homogeneous group but are divided into many different tribes, of which the Kikuyu, the

4 East African Statistical Department, East Africa High Commission, *Quarterly Economic and Statistical Bulletin* (Nairobi, December 1956), p. 3. The Commission used figures from the 1948 census, when the population was estimated at 17,842,163.

Sukuma, and the Ganda are the largest. The Europeans still form a numerically small group. Of the total of 93,800 in 1956, 57,700 were in Kenya, 27,700 in Tanganyika, and only 8,400 were in Uganda. Asians are more numerous. In 1956 there were 51,900 Arabs and 282,600 people designated as Indians and Goans—a category which includes Pakistanis. Nearly all of the persons of Asian origin live in the towns and trading centers.

The Changing African

When the European came, the African was for the most part using the land either as a cultivator practicing shifting cultivation or as a pastoralist sharing grazing and water supplies on a community basis and practicing in a very general way an extensive system of pasture management alternating between dry-season and wet-season grazing. For both the pastoralist and the cultivator life was precarious; survival depended on a community approach to the physical and human hazards encountered. A balance between man and his physical environment, enabling the bare survival of the former and preventing serious deterioration of the latter, was maintained by series of epidemics affecting both men and animals, by periodic famine, and by intertribal raids and wars.

Today, the picture is one of a disintegrating African society and of land tenure and land use customs changing in varying degrees. The rate and degree of change differ greatly from area to area. In much of central Tanganyika, northern Uganda, and northern Kenya, changes in the old customary ways of life are almost imperceptible. In contrast, the trained African professional man has become a person of Western culture. Between these limits every gradation of change is discernible.

Summarizing the position of the African today, the Commission writes that a large part of the rural community continues to carry on a traditional shifting cultivation and an extensive pasturing of livestock on a subsistence level which has been little affected by alien influences. Those people, however, who live in the favored agricultural areas —in areas where the fixing of boundaries and the alienation of land has stabilized their agriculture—have found that their traditional farming practices have caused soil erosion and loss of soil fertility. The progressive worsening of conditions in such areas and the awakening of new wants have induced the African to seek new sources of income from work on farms, plantations, and in towns. In these new employments he has found no permanent security for himself and his family. He has lived with one foot in his place of employment and one in the reserve, and the retention of his land, which provides the only security to which he can turn, has become a ruling passion. This attitude of mind has bred suspicion against those attempting to change land use or land tenure for his benefit, and has thus exacerbated a deteriorating situation.

The African peasant farmers and laborers have found that the foundations of life in their community are disintegrating. The moral fiber and independence of thought and action required by the changing conditions have been supplied only in part by Christian teaching. The better educated men, to whom the people naturally turn for leadership, have found their personal position in relation to the other races to be one of great difficulty, which has often resulted in bitterness and sometimes hatred.

On the more positive side, the Africans have been protected from major epidemic diseases and famine; cash crops have brought relative wealth and an improved standard of living to some; the battle against soil erosion has almost been won in many areas; and here and there the seeds of new farming techniques have taken root. Growing numbers of Africans in agriculture, business, industry, and government service are acquiring experience and technical skill that command remuneration at a rate which holds out the possibility of achieving security for themselves and their families. Finally, education and Christianity have helped the African to meet, at least in part, his changing circumstances.

THE ECONOMIES OF THE TERRITORIES

Despite the impressive advances that have been made
toward a modern commercial economy, nearly all the inhabitants are still poor. This poverty largely results from
the fact that so small a proportion of the resources of East
Africa is devoted to the production of goods and services
for the modern money economy. It has been intensified by
the elaborate system of restrictions and inhibitions which
pervades the economy and which is in part a feature of the
tribal order of society and in part a creation of public
policy. Broadly speaking, East Africa exemplifies what is
normally spoken of as a dual economy: the subsistence sector on the one hand and the money sector on the other.

In each of the three territories the money economy is
geared to the world markets for primary agricultural products. About 90 per cent of the value of domestic exports is
made up of a small number of pastoral or agricultural
products. The contribution of other sectors of the economy, although small in comparison, is none the less significant.

Agricultural Use and Potential

Examining the agricultural use and potential of East
Africa, the Commission states that, judged by the amount
and reliability of rainfall, about half the land area must
be considered primarily pastoral, about a quarter is marginal between pastoral and arable, and less than a quarter
arable. Broadly speaking, Kenya possesses few of the potentially most productive areas, Tanganyika has more, and
Uganda many more. In Kenya this land is for the most part
heavily populated except for some parts of the reserved
Highlands.

Apart from rain, the fundamental criterion, there are
many environmental and physical factors, technical and
organizational difficulties, which restrain the agricultural
potential. The total or partial absence of water makes
large expanses uninhabitable, while elsewhere there may

be dangerous concentrations of population and livestock.
Access to markets is inadequate. The productive areas already generally carry a population that is dense in relation
to land productivity. The soils of East Africa are relatively
poor, fragile, and unproductive. Human and animal disease is another restrictive factor. The tsetse fly is present in
10 per cent of Kenya, 60 per cent of Tanganyika, and
about 32 per cent of Uganda, and large-scale recovery of
fly country is doubtful until cost of counterattacks is reduced.

Land is still, for the vast majority in East Africa, a basic
necessity from which each family derives its own food.
Where this can be done with the least effort for the greatest result, people have tended to collect and tend to want
to stay.

The largest part of East Africa is the home of pastoral
tribes whose way of life runs the risk of turning their land
into desert and contributes less than the land's potential
to the growing needs of the community. Not only does the
number of stock now bear no relation to the land's carrying capacity, but socially a certain stagnation results.
While the cultivator neighbor is being increasingly drawn
to economic needs, the pastoral tribesman has tended to
remain outside modern society. The main need in pastoral
areas is to find some satisfactory alternative to the old migratory invasion, which will bring the nomad, where possible, into contact with the growing exchange economy,
and will bring to his aid some system of economic wage
which will save his land.

In the cultivated areas the traditional system is "shifting
agriculture." It was under this system that the land tenure
arrangements have evolved in which the individual has
inheritable rights in his arable lands while he shares with
his fellow tribesmen common rights in grazing lands and
forests. This does not mean that he has individual ownership. Ownership is vested in the community. Though
people cling to many of the features of this system, it is
intrinsically unable to support a high standard of living or

a dense population. Its efficiency depends on the constant availability of extra land to carry extra people and stock as these increase.

Before the Europeans came to East Africa, something of a balance was brought about by the slave trade, epidemic diseases, intertribal wars, and starvation. These restraints have ceased to apply. While population and stock have increased under the umbrella of law and order and health services, the operating area of each tribe's activities has come to be limited to the reserves, within which the supply of productive virgin land has rapidly dwindled. The superimposition of a cash economy on this old subsistence agricultural pattern has worsened the situation by reducing the fallow period, dividing the land excessively, fragmenting the holdings, and creating a landless class.

The resulting overcrowding has followed an extremely irregular pattern, varying not merely from one tribe to another but from clan to clan. The increasing pressure on the land has encouraged strong feelings about retaining it. These have been enshrined in the whole history of land status and alienations, in various treaties, orders-in-council, and statements of policy, all intended to give various tribes, clans, and races a sense of security.

This degenerated situation is not yet general. There remain very large regions where shifting cultivation is still virtually inviolate. Over a very wide area the most urgent problem is not alienated land but the need to discover and apply systems of land usage by the indigenous inhabitants which will be both economically productive and socially satisfying, and that can replace the present totally unsatisfactory customary usage before it is too late to be able to do so.

Development of Mining and Manufacturing

One of the factors which has retarded growth in East Africa has been the inability to discover or exploit mineral resources, which have contributed so greatly to the generation of income in other African territories. Though the

Magadi soda deposits and the Williamson diamond mines are important to Kenya and Tanganyika, the amount of mineral exploitation is relatively small. This is because so large an area of the region has not really been opened up, because the geological survey has only recently got under way, and because the East African governments, although aware of the need for stimulating mining exploration and development, have not succeeded, according to the Commission, in adopting a consistent and long-term approach to it.

Manufacturing is also of minor importance. The net product of the manufacturing industry in Kenya amounted in 1951 to about 12 per cent of the total net geographical product, exclusive of African subsistence agriculture. Of the employed Africans in 1952, those in the manufacturing industry were about 10 per cent of the total in Kenya, 13 per cent in Uganda, and 5 per cent in Tanganyika.

Conditions in Urban Communities

The Commission devoted special attention to the conditions of Africans in the towns, which are very unsatisfactory. The evils which inevitably arise among a poor, overcrowded, and unstable population are all present. Poverty and overcrowding are the principal material results of these conditions. Some of the causes of unsatisfactory conditions are not merely physical but are the result of the momentous changes which are taking place in African society. Africans who have broken away from tribal life often find that they cannot become members of modern society and that the road to wealth and positions of prestige is barred. This produces feelings of frustration and also of antagonism to the society which excludes them.

In the towns Africans are confronted with a new way of life in which they join as isolated individuals who must provide for their own material, mental, and emotional needs. In many towns the facilities for doing so are lacking, which leads to drunkenness and crime.

The Inadequacy of Transportation

The roads and railways fall short of the current requirements of the territories, of the potential development of traffic, and of long-run requirements for opening new areas. The railways are inadequate in length (3,100 miles in 1953), inadequately equipped, and under-maintained. There have been particular problems associated with financing railway improvements, and the costs of operating railways are increased by the lack of local fuel supplies and by the long distances through desert, unhealthy, or undeveloped areas which intervene between the ports and the productive areas which the railways serve.

The importance of developing a modern system of roads was not recognized before the war as clearly as it is now. In Tanganyika there was little capital expenditure on new roads; the position was somewhat better in Kenya and Uganda, but even there it was only after the war that construction on a scale intended to cope with the expanded traffic needs of the economy was inaugurated. In all the territories, and especially in the African areas, the present condition of the roads is a main cause of the high cost of food, of the relatively slow rate of expansion in agricultural production, and of the persistence of subsistence economies. The cost of road transport is unduly high because of excessive wear and tear on vehicles.

African Labor

The productivity of African labor is generally low. The general level of African wages is low. Even where there is minimum-wage legislation, as in Kenya, the basis of the statutory minimum has been taken to be the requirements of a single male adult worker with a very small margin above physical subsistence. The machinery for collective bargaining is almost nonexistent. As a rule there is little difficulty in obtaining ordinary unskilled labor even at the low wages prevailing. Much of the labor which is employed is migrant in the sense that it seeks employment for short periods and returns to the tribal area. The migrant laborer, considering his work temporary, is likely to accept relatively lower wages, so the system has a depressing effect on terms and conditions of labor, while the social evils of migrant labor in the towns become intensified. But the idea of a substitute urban security, with the abandonment of traditional interests in the tribal areas, is still novel to the African and is not fostered by the increasing rigidities of the reserve system. Even if he stays in the city for some years, the African does so with the knowledge that he can always go back to the reserve if conditions become unfavorable.

The level of wages African labor is prepared to accept is governed by the real income which can be obtained in alternative occupations. These alternatives may consist either of the production of cash crops or of subsistence farming. However low the real incomes of those in paid employment, there is strong presumption that the real income derived from subsistence farming is still lower. If this is true, the key to raising the price of labor is to foster an increase in the real incomes of the peasants.

There are particular labor problems of resident African families on non-African farms. As early as 1904 such residence was encouraged, and by 1945 it had probably reached 250,000. As the years have passed, legislation and district orders placing restrictions on these Africans have become more limiting and also more variable from area to area. In many areas, acreages have been reduced and stockholding has been reduced or even forbidden (to prevent stock disease and soil erosion). The effect has often been a declining real income of the resident laborer and his family.

THE DILEMMA OF SECURITY AND RACE RELATIONS

The economic security of an exchange economy differs fundamentally from the security which can be attained in a tribal subsistence economy. There is little margin in subsistence production for social and economic measures which will enable the community to escape from its complete dependence upon the particular area of land it occupies; in tribal society "security" and occupation of new land are synonymous. There has been a strong tendency in East Africa to assume that a guarantee that the local population could not be disturbed in its traditional interests would meet the basic requirements of the situation.

The general approach of the Kenya Land Commission in the early thirties,[5] for example, was to consider tribes as exclusive and located entities, and to shape land policy on this basis. There is now abundant evidence that the goal of giving security to both Africans and Europeans through this concept has not been attained. Kenya, in particular, has been divided up into a number of watertight compartments, none of which is or can be made economically self-sufficient, and the frustrations of the last 20 years have been largely due to the failure to recognize that fact.

The result of the Kenya Land Commission was to project the tribal point of view into the racial sphere. Two facts stand out as resulting from the policy of the exclusive tenure of land in the Highlands by Europeans: firstly, the bitterness which has persisted over extinguishing African rights in the area; secondly, the sense of injustice in African eyes of broad acres reserved for a few individuals alongside an African reserve in which land hunger exists. Even those loyal Kikuyu who risked their lives in the fight against Mau Mau oppose the maintenance of unused land for exclusive European use. Africans questioned by the Commission seldom suggested that any European who was using his land fully should be deprived of it.

The pressure upon fertile land leads to conflict wherever land is scarce. Where rival claims and conflicting attitudes divide Africans from Europeans, there are wider repercussions, affecting confidence between government and people in the region as a whole. The indigenous antipathy to non-African enterprise may obstruct the very expansion which

[5] *Report of the Kenya Land Commission,* Cmd. 4556 (London: HMSO, 1934), 618 p.

is needed and drive away to alternative investment funds and skills which might contribute to raising the standard of living. Expansion of the economy through non-African enterprise is certain to increase racial conflict unless particular care is taken to make its value understood and accepted.

Efforts to try and bridge the gap are made increasingly, but racial rigidities affecting land have brought about a situation of increasing tension, based on fear, in many parts of East Africa. In wide areas of Kenya, conflict and resentment have been promoted by group attitudes, arising from the regard of each race for its supposed security in defined land boundaries. It must be a first duty of statesmanship to seek out possibilities and ways of making adjustments to avoid a clash of culture and race; future policy needs to be associated with an ideal which can command general allegiance and inspire a new confidence in joint endeavor.

Throughout East Africa there is a tendency, least pronounced in Tanganyika, to see the clash of progress and security, inevitable in the process of creating a modern social and economic organization, solely as a clash of color, tribe, or race. The belief that advantages have been attained merely because of membership in a favored racial community runs like a pathological obsession throughout the daily life and work of the community. Thus tensions are simplified in terms of political power, and it is concluded that they can be settled only by changes in political and administrative machinery. But in fact, whatever the political arrangements may come to be, there is no evidence now that any appreciable economic advance can be made without the help, efforts, and presence of non-Africans. From an economic point of view it is remarkable that so much has been achieved under the leadership and stimulus of so few in so short a time. But measured in terms of what might have been achieved, the picture is not so satisfactory.

East Africa is still a region of small islands of modern production in a sea of a relatively stagnant subsistence

economy and unexplored or underdeveloped natural resources. The tribal and racial barriers which characterize
East Africa have prevented the migration of skill, enterprise, and capital, have prevented large-scale development
of mineral and agricultural wealth, have retarded the development of communications, and have restricted markets
for local industrial and specialized agricultural and export
products.

II. THE RECOMMENDATIONS OF THE COMMISSION

Having presented the conditions existing in East Africa
as seen by the Commission, we may now turn to the more
important recommendations and solutions included in the
Report. Some of the suggestions are for changes in the
physical use of resources and of the land. Others deal with
organization, while a number are concerned with human
attitudes and problems. The central theme running through
all of the recommendations is that a more willing acceptance and a greater stimulation of economic forces provide
the keys not only to the economic, but to the human problems besetting the area.

THE CONTROL OF POPULATION AS A SOLUTION

Because the terms of reference of the Commission required it, and because the Commission found considerable
apprehension regarding what was generally believed to be
an unduly rapid rate of population growth, it devoted attention to possible control of population increases as a
solution to the problems of East Africa. It found a tendency to assume that the relatively large population densities which were to be found in some areas, as well as the
apparent overcrowding which existed in others, were the
simple and inevitable results of a too rapid growth of numbers. It was also proposed to the Commission that "shortages" of land, lack of employment opportunities at higher
wages, and the migration to the towns could be similarly

ascribed to an excessive expansion of the population as a whole.

The Commission did not agree with these analyses. In fact, its report states that, broadly speaking, East Africa is sparsely populated and that the full economic exploitation of its resources demands not a stationary or a reduced population but an expanding one. The very sparsity of the population in the past has, according to the Commission, contributed to arresting economic development and limiting standards of life. Nor has the permanent immigration in Kenya done much to alter the overwhelming preponderance of the African population, while the effect of new permanent immigration in Tanganyika and Uganda has been extremely small.

While the growth of population presents no serious overall problem, the Commission recognized that particular areas are now carrying so large a population that agricultural production is retarded, their resources are being destroyed, families are unable to find new land, and land which should be fallow is being used. In these areas, outworn systems of land use must be reduced.

The problem of population as seen by the Commission is not, then, one of total numbers. It sees no justification for drastic public measures to encourage birth control or for rigid control of immigration. It recognizes, however, that there is a problem associated with the *attitudes* toward immigration. The African fears that more immigrants will occupy good-quality land and that immigrant-sponsored developments will be those most likely to exclude African participation; the European fears that new immigrants will only encroach upon existing economic activity; and the Indian is concerned lest increasing numbers will add to his present difficulties. The recommended solution to these problems falls under a later category, not under that of population control.

The territorial representatives agreed in general with the conclusions of the Commission regarding population. The Kenya Governor acknowledged that some fears regarding a rising population had been exaggerated, though he submitted that these fears were at least partly justified for certain areas.

The poverty of East Africa, says the Commission, rests on the absence of adequate commercialized and wage-earning activities for the indigenous population. A change to commercialization creates new problems of adaptation, but it also increases the resources with which to deal with these problems. The better technical use of natural resources cannot emerge unless production shifts from a subsistence basis to an exchange basis.

The size of the net product in East Africa is still so small that it must condition all plans for development. As a corollary, every effort should be made to use to the full the assets of land, labor, capital, and enterprise available to the region. It must be recognized by all races that they cannot afford the luxury of dissipating the resources of the region. As the assets of East Africa are still poorly known, a systematic examination and inventory of all natural resources is urgently needed. Improved liaison between technicians and between territories in these fields is also recommended.

The proposed solutions of the Commission in this broad field may best be understood by examining their analyses of the possibilities in agriculture, manufacturing, and mining, and then their views regarding the fundamental stimuli of transportation and education.

Recommended Changes in Agriculture

The customary agricultural systems, according to the Commission, now face a twofold challenge. On the one hand, they are already becoming untenable in crowded areas owing to lack of new land to meet the requirements of the increasing population. On the other hand, they are failing to yield the income now increasingly demanded by people. What is required is a complete economic reorientation. The mere expansion of production for the market is not in itself sufficient; that would lead to soil exhaustion without adoption of a proper fallow, suitable crop rotation, or economic methods restoring nutrients to the soil artificially.

But discovery and development of balanced patterns of production present difficult problems: there must be access to the market, the individual must have adequate land, in overcrowded areas there will be displacement, and suitable systems of agriculture must be discovered. Progress must necessarily be slow. The Commission made specific recommendations with respect to the two major agricultural systems: pastoralism and cultivation.

With regard to pastoral communities, the Commission noted the main characteristics of proper ranching as: carrying capacity, water supplies, pasture management, sufficiency of land, and a market. Breeding policy is hardly relevant until these needs are established. The main fault in the old system is the combination of communal range with unrestricted individual ownership; the community and the individual take no account of the effects of their actions on the land. A solution can be found either communally or individually. The small monetary needs of the pastoral tribes reduce the pressure for improvement, but there are signs of more willing reception of efforts to advance commercialization, which is a vital step in stabilizing stock numbers. An example is seen in the large sale of milk by Masai to the cultivators on Kilimanjaro in recent years. The most practical system of pasture management will no doubt vary in different environments and may well evolve only gradually from a simple two-course rotation to the separate, fenced, and watered paddocks of a good European ranch. One of the difficulties bound to be encountered in any area already overcrowded with stock is the lack of sufficient land. In many parts additional land is needed even to get a modern system going. In enormous stretches of East Africa the high cost of tsetse eradication is still the major stumbling block as far as ranching is concerned. Game preserves did not seem to the Commission to be an important deterrent to progress, as there is plenty of land in East Africa which man has not yet learned to turn to productive use and which can be left to the game to enjoy. A series of experimental ranches is desirable to prevent interference with tribal life everywhere at once. But evidence indicates that with European methods of ranching, Masai areas, for example, could produce five times their present output.

Marketing of stock occupies a paramount position in the problem of land usage in pastoral areas, for without regular sale of cattle, most improvement of land usage is thwarted. The most important measures to improve the marketing of stock are: the active stimulation and supply of the local market; continuance of private trading; use of the veterinary department to establish the confidence that is so important in stimulating sales, to help get rid of the poor stock in large enough quantities, and to overhaul the whole machinery of quarantines and stock routes with the deliberate purpose of speeding the safe delivery of stock to consumer markets.

With regard to the cultivating communities, the Commission thought it easier to see what is wrong with the present state of affairs than to be confident about the success of alternatives. The known major faults of present land usage are: erosion, the lack of integration between the number of animals and the carrying capacity of the land, the insufficiency of the resting period in the cultivation cycle, and fragmentation. The problem of land tenure affects all these technical agricultural faults, and there is an additional drawback in the limitation of the present system to the labor of the woman and the hoe.

Measures to control soil erosion have been introduced and there are general policies for the retention of a certain percentage of land under forests. Attacking the other faults, really the crux of the matter, is far more difficult because it entails radical alterations of the customary system. It is only in Kenya that this attack is now being vigorously launched. The most generally advocated alternative to the old system is a small consolidated holding with a ley and a small area of cash crop. Planned holdings on these lines (the Swynnerton Plan) facilitate the attack on three major faults of the present system: with family herds restricted to their own grazing land there is incentive to improve both land and stock; there is a chance to begin thinking of income and savings without irresponsibility about land; a permanently stable resting period and manuring replace the lack of fallow and manuring in the old system. Commenting on the Commission's Report, the Governor of Kenya said that remarkable progress has been made, especially in the Kikuyu area, and that the demand for consolidation had grown with great rapidity.

The Commission realized, however, that there are a great number of difficulties which affect the establishment of small mixed-farm holdings. One is the ley itself: there is the difficulty of making it profitable, the difficulty of selecting the most suitable grass, and the uncertainty of determining the optimum stock management. Not all the cultivators may be capable of, or willing to meet, the higher sense of management or longer hours needed. Requirements for independent water supplies, fencing, etc., will demand unusual capital outlay. The introduction of planned small-holdings is bound to be slow. Also, the system may not after all be an economic success. The Governor of Tanganyika noted that it cannot yet be said with any confidence by what means the long bush fallow can be obviated.

Particular attention, the Commission recommended, should be paid to the problem of displacement (in many districts of Kenya the most prominent problem), the increased use of fertilizers, the stimulation of interracial cooperation, the individualization of the new system (which opens the door to mobility and private initiative on which a great sector of economic progress tends to depend), the use of mechanization, the development of cooperatives, measures to encourage the progressive individual, promotion of research and collection of basic information, the formation of land development boards to ensure a territorial rather than a district approach to development and to ensure the effective evolution of policy toward a consistent objective.

The Commission urged that special attention be given to the high-productivity areas and to the possibilities of irrigation. It stated, in fact, that the proper use of the limited areas of high productivity transcends in importance all other problems in East Africa, and that water development leading to productive employment over a wide area should be placed in the same category of basic development as railways and roads.

The Commission's views regarding overcrowded areas not only round out its discussion of agriculture but introduce its recommendations concerning manufacturing and mining. Throughout the inquiry the Commission was impressed by the recurring evidence that particular areas are now carrying so large a population that agricultural production in them is being retarded, that the natural resources themselves are being destroyed, that families are unable to find access to new land, and that land which should have been lying fallow is being encroached on. Such areas illustrate in an acute form one of the main causes of poverty in East Africa, namely, that too large a proportion of the population is still engaged in subsistence food production because agricultural methods are employed which yield too small a return on the time and effort expended. In these areas the excessive number of persons engaged in agricultural production on the basis of outworn systems of land use must be reduced, not only to save the land from serious deterioration but to make possible the introduction of new techniques to raise agricultural productivity and to enable a smaller proportion of the population to produce the area's food.

Manufacturing as a Possible Solution

An obvious way to alleviate the situation in overcrowded areas is to stimulate manufacturing that will provide alternative sources of income and absorb redundant population. The Commission felt that the latter reason was improper on the grounds that industrialization should not be thought of as relief work. The East African area presents numerous handicaps to the development of manufacturing: fuel and power are relatively expensive; the supply of suitable labor is frequently inadequate; costs of labor may be high even though wages are low; and the cost of training may be excessive. But more important, there is the possible handicap of the small territorial market.

Manufacturing industry must concern itself with supplying either local or outside markets. The Commission felt that some additional processing of raw materials for export was possible, but that spectacular results were improbable. In the absence of new mineral discoveries, therefore, the most likely direction of industrial development would be in production for the territorial market. The more the African economy passes from a subsistence economy to the production of cash crops, the greater will be the local market for manufactured products. Hence, success in promoting manufacturing will hinge upon success in agriculture. Manufacturing for local markets would enjoy some natural advantage from the reduced transport costs of the finished product, but this saving might well be offset by high costs of power and fuel, and by higher costs resulting from small-scale production based upon what is likely to be, at first, a small market.

Manufacturing development in East Africa will continue to be dependent largely on non-African capital and managerial ability. The Commission felt that this dependence is likely to generate suspicion and mistrust among some Africans and hence an atmosphere not conducive to the growth of successful enterprise. The Governor of Tanganyika, on the other hand, felt that it was not political factors which deterred the investor but the economic immaturity of the region—the insufficiency of communications, of housing, of factory service, and of skilled labor.

Disagreement also arose regarding government support of manufacturing development. The Commission took the position that colonial governments are not equipped to establish and operate new industries and that it is improper for proceeds of forced savings to be invested in such speculative ventures. The Governor of Uganda suggested that experience in that territory led to the conclusion that there are certain types of investment in which private companies wish to be associated with state enterprise. He noted that the Kilembe copper mines and the textile manufacturing at Jinja are conclusive evidence that this association is the best means of doing what the Commission thought important—attracting capital. It is clear that the Commission did not believe that development of industry provided an easy or short-run solution to the economic problems of East Africa.

The Development of Mining

The Report looked more optimistically at possibilities for the expansion of mineral production. The Commission stated that there is probably no single source from which surplus income, of which East Africa is greatly in need, could be so readily obtained as from successful mineral exploitation. They felt, therefore, that the overriding consideration must be to make the conditions as attractive as possible by providing every possible assistance in the form of geological and mining services and by removing legal and fiscal obstacles increasing the cost or risk of mining. In the attempt to attract mining investment, the Commission wrote, the territories should bear in mind the fact that they are competing with the rest of the world and with highly mineralized areas in Africa itself. In this instance, as in others, East Africa needs the enterprise and capital of the outside world more than the outside world needs East Africa.

The Commission recommended that a unified Mining Board be set up to work toward these general objectives, but each of the governors rejected this proposal. They argued that mineral exploitation is too closely allied to fiscal policy to be removed from the jurisdiction of the individual territories; putting it under a separate authority would lead to administrative complications and be politically unacceptable.

The Importance of Transport Development

East Africa cannot hope to develop a modern exchange economy, in the opinion of the Commission, if potentially productive areas remain cut off from local and export markets. Without improved transport facilities the continuance of the existing system of subsistence production is unavoidable because goods can be moved only over very short distances. Transport facilities should be provided to anticipate and stimulate the economic development of traffic and should not be permitted to lag behind such development.

Development expenditure on communications, therefore, should be given priority. This principle has not always been observed, the Commission noted, though the Governor of Uganda claimed that much of the transport in that territory was far in advance of economic needs, while the Governor of Kenya noted that the shortage of money made it impossible to attain the aims of the Commission regarding transport. The Governor of Tanganyika felt that the great need for improved transport touched Tanganyika more closely than any of the other themes of the Commission.

The Commission called specifically for the improved financing of railways by the removal of the cumbersome and rigid procedures now used, by reconstituting the Railway Administration so as to make the governments partners in the undertaking rather than holders or merely guarantors of fixed interest-bearing capital in it, by eliminating the no-profits principle under which the railways operate, and by adopting a more flexible and properly balanced system of rates.

The expansion of the East African road system and its improvement to modern standards also calls for special organizational arrangements according to the Commission. Territorial road authorities, comparable to the Road Authority in Kenya, are recommended for the other territories. The construction of a proper system of roads is not merely a question of serving the convenience of the inhabitants but of providing the very arteries of economic expansion. The Commission concludes that nothing would benefit the development of the three territories more than the establishment of an independent, financially viable, and economically sound transport system.

Health and Education

The Commission's members did not include specialists in disease, nutrition, or health. The Report recognizes the burden of poor health on East African development, but its recommendations are confined to suggesting the appointment of an expert body to examine the many urgent problems such as endemic control measures, the proper balance between preventive and curative medicine, medical education, and nutrition.

The need for improved and expanded education is stressed in several portions of the Report, in connection with the improvement of labor conditions, in the stimulation of manufacturing, and in the development of agriculture. In agrarian matters, the Commission states, the administration of each territory is confronted squarely with the problem of teaching people not only to appreciate the need for change, but also how to bring about changes themselves. With the help of training institutions, cooperatives, specialized agencies, and experts, governments should set out to teach the Africans to lead their own agrarian revolution.

The Commission accepted free universal education as a goal but admitted that it would be unrealistic to propose it at this time. Its particular recommendations were to expand intermediate education, to increase the number of candidates for teacher training, to stop teaching Swahili as a second language to children whose early education has been in other vernaculars, which the Commission called a complete waste since English is preferred as a *lingua franca*, to eliminate grading by race in secondary education, to increase the opportunities for technical education, and to give more attention to the education of girls.

The Need for Capital

The Commission admitted that adoption of many of its proposals would require very considerable capital expenditure. It noted that new capital must come either from savings accumulated within East Africa, or from private and public lending or other investment from outside. The Commission doubted the efficacy of encouraging voluntary savings, rejected forced saving as being more costly than raising a comparable external loan, and considered the use of price stabilization schemes to provide capital as an unreasonable burden on the producer. The African population, furthermore, possesses neither the resources nor the knowledge which could replace the capital and knowledge which have been responsible for the economic development that has taken place. The maintenance and promotion of that development, therefore, will continue to depend on the availability of external capital and enterprise.

Again the Commission notes that the economic importance of overseas capital and enterprise to East Africa is greater than the importance of East Africa to the capital and enterprise available. The smallness of the East African economy and the meagerness of its resources do not provide large and effective inducements. The rationale behind the Commission's arguments regarding railway finance, the provision of basic services, the importance of a thorough resource inventory, stimulation of the mining economy, and avoidance of excessive expenditure on uneconomic projects, is clarified by this interpretation of the capital position of East Africa.

No effort was made in the Report to estimate the capital requirements if the Commission's suggestions were adopted. The Kenya Governor estimated that an expenditure of $700 million would be needed in five years and all the governors' dispatches emphasize that economic expansion on the scale envisaged would require far greater financial resources than the territorial governments possess. This weakness of the Report was mentioned by several reviewers,[6] though *The Economist* asks if the detailed costing of the program is put forward by the governors "to help frighten public opinion off bold and constructive proposals just because they frighten governments?" [7]

DEVELOPING NEW CONCEPTS OF LAND RIGHTS

The Commission's position regarding land tenure is of such importance that it requires special attention. The test of land needs must be replaced by a test of land use, according to the Commission. That is to say, the right to own land should be justified not by the fact that one needs it for subsistence, but that one can use it effectively; the main concern should be to maximize the productivity of the land. The breaking down of tribal and racial boundaries should be encouraged. Where individual titles to land exist they should be confirmed and where they do not their acquisition should not be encouraged.

If living standards are to rise, states the Commission, economic security must no longer rest on a subsistence wrung from the environment by individuals in isolation, but on a combination of the specialized efforts of a community. Tribal and racial rigidities have brought about a situation of increasing tension, the basis of which is fear.

[6] See "East African Development," *African Affairs*, v. 55 (October 1956), pp. 250-251; "Go Slow in East Africa," *The Economist* (July 28, 1956), pp. 305-306; "Adam Smith in East Africa," same (June 18, 1955), pp. 1017-1019.

[7] "Go Slow in East Africa," cited, p. 306.

When tribal authorities restrict the use of land, either by members of their own tribe or by outsiders, in accordance with criteria other than those of the highest productivity of the land, they are diminishing rather than increasing their real "security." For the security which rests on tribal exclusiveness, or on customs which prevent dealings with land as a negotiable asset, is the illusory security of the subsistence economy within which no economic advance is possible. The claim to exclusive tribal rights is a claim to rights without corresponding obligations and so runs counter to the principles on which the policy of any modern state must be based.

As land becomes one of the factors of production, the Commission claims, two fundamental changes occur: the land becomes valuable as a specialized factor of production, and an increasing proportion of the population becomes less directly dependent upon the land and is able to find new income-earning opportunities. A tribal community which is economically isolated from the market cannot introduce these changes.

Policy concerning the tenure and disposition of land, then, should aim at the individualization of land ownership, and at a degree of mobility in the transfer and disposition of land which, without ignoring existing property rights, will make possible access to land for its economic use. The fact that customary tenure is deep-rooted in African society, and resistant to radical change, must be taken into account in devising and applying new land tenure laws. It would be quite wrong to conclude, the Commission warns, that the mere removal of traditional encumbrances would release a flood of enterprise.

Adjudication and registration of land interests was recommended as a first step. In the interests of Africans, the Commission thought that restrictions should be imposed upon the mortgaging of land and upon recovery of debt through the sale of land. The registration law might also prohibit future subdivisions below a certain size; some form of share-in-ownership might conform with established inheritance laws. Land transfers between members of different races should be controlled, the Commission felt, by permitting only registered interests to be transferred, making transfers by lease only—the reversionary rights remaining with the seller—and by making leases subject to the governor's approval, which should be freely given. Legislation should also be introduced to restrict lending on the security of land to specified agencies which would make loans on a conservative assessment of land values.

These are sweeping proposals. Their adoption would basically alter the present pattern of land tenure by Africans. As the Commission pointed out, it is recommending the antithesis of a land reservation policy such as has long been followed. The Commission considers these radical changes to be essential to economic progress in East Africa. Previous commissions and special inquiries, it argues, failed to realize that increased African production required a new concept of land rights and tenure and that it was difficult to reconcile the principle of not disturbing customary land tenure with the need to increase African production.

The proposals regarding land tenure were rejected by the territorial governors. The Governor of Uganda, noting that the recommendations were the most important part of the whole Report, cited the deep concern of all Africans for their land, which would require that any changes be preceded by lengthy and careful discussion in all areas. The Governor of Kenya stated that the policy could not be successful without the support of a large section of opinion in the community involved; though the economic ideal would be for reservations to disappear, present-day political, cultural, and social influences prevent it. He also believed that the Commission had overemphasized economic considerations and overlooked the advantages of recognizing tribal laws as the only practicable basis of administration, at least in the early stages. The change, he wrote, cannot only be one of economics. The African must be given a sense of economic security in the new system. The power freely to transfer land does not itself enhance development.

The Economist also questioned whether "the more rapid introduction of individual land tenures really [would] act as a flywheel to the agricultural economy. . . . The Baganda . . . have developed individual ownership, yet the commission agrees that they are obsessed by fears of land alienation and oppose industrialisation lest it bring in too many whites." [8] *The Times* noted that "an important omission in the report [is] . . . its failure to take due account of the surviving strength of tribalism in African society." [9]

THE REMOVAL OF RESTRICTIONS AND INHIBITIONS

One of the fundamental themes of the High Commission Report is the need to move against the great body of restrictionism that exists in East Africa. If this elaborate system can be removed and if conditions more favorable to the utilization of resources can be created, an important measure of economic expansion may be contemplated and shared by all the inhabitants of East Africa, the Commission contended.

Distribution, for example, reflects the dual economic organization of the area. African trading is mostly a local affair, pursuing traditional paths. The non-African trading system is efficient, attuned to changes in world demand and supply, and generally competitive and enterprising. But it would be more competitive if it could be released from the many restrictions to which it has been subjected, some of them resulting from government policies intended to promote stability. In the aggregate, the various forms of marketing restriction and control which exist in East Africa build up into a very complex structure, the full effects of which are not easily perceived. This complex structure of marketing controls, taken in conjunction with an African subsistence economy, has imposed a degree of

[8] "Adam Smith in East Africa," cited, p. 1018.
[9] "Realistic Replies," *The Times* (London), July 26, 1956.

inflexibility which inhibits the economic advancement which is desired.

The Commission found little sympathy with its proposals in this connection. The Governor of Kenya expressed the view that agricultural development and stability was all-important and was not encouraged by the entirely free operation of the market. The Governor of Uganda felt that organized marketing could not be dispensed with, that it did not inhibit economic advance, and that the Commission had overemphasized the extent of restrictive regulations in Uganda for the protection of Africans.

Restrictionism in other fields was similarly criticized by the Commission—in transportation, in agriculture, in land use, in urban communities, etc. Its position in this regard is linked closely to its positive program for developing the area as an integrated unit.

THE INTEGRATION OF EAST AFRICA

Perhaps the most encompassing plea the Commission made is that East Africa be considered as a social and economic unit and developed as one. Economic and social policies, says the Commission, must be based on the realization that the development of East Africa fundamentally depends on the extent to which the indigenous population can, with the help of necessarily small numbers of immigrant peoples, be integrated into the world economy and draw from it capital and the complementary resources of skill and enterprise. In the long run, the Commission implies, the well-being and security of immigrant peoples depends on the success with which they can further this development and fulfill their special functions in it, just as the development of the indigenous population depends on the clear realization that their own well-being and security depends on the success with which they can attract those who can bring to them the scarce economic

resources—capital, skill, and enterprise—which they so
sorely lack.

In Transport

The Commission holds, for example, that sectional
interests have prevented an objective and proper assessment of the transport needs of African areas. If a particular
section, or certain producers or consumers, are favored by
railway rates that are not warranted by the economic requirements of the railway system as a whole and the development of new traffic, then other users of the railway,
either now or later, must bear the cost. Attempts to subsidize
one section at the expense of others through manipulation
of rates and charges necessarily weakens the economic
viability of the railway and makes it less able to quote
proper development rates for new traffic, thus retarding the
development of all territories.

In Labor

The goal of labor policy should be to enable the laborer
to earn the maximum income which the productivity of
his labor warrants, in conditions of security, and under
supervision designed to raise his efficiency. Certain programs are recommended: the extension of training and
apprenticeship schemes; efforts to reduce the wasteful
aspects of migration; the creation of Wages Councils to
fix minimum wages; and the simplification of procedures
for settling industrial disputes.

The goal of reducing migration implies that the laborer
should be able to reside and to offer his services where he
will, without being tied to sometimes distant and restricted tribal areas. In the White Highlands, therefore,
where this problem is particularly acute, the government
should purchase or acquire land where farm workers
could rent village dwelling plots on long leases. The Governor of Kenya rejected the idea of village dwelling plots,
claiming that among its disadvantages were: the loss of
personal connection between employer and worker, low-

ered efficiency, increased distance which the laborer would often have to travel, the need for large stock farms to have resident labor, the loss of farming land acquired for the villages, and the cost of building and administering the villages.

In the urban areas there is a similar problem of integration. The Africans who have broken away from tribal life often find they cannot become members of modern society and that the road to wealth and positions of prestige is barred. The Commission's proposed solution to this problem was to organize the urban areas to permit a gradual move toward positions and conditions of equality. The urban areas, it stated, should be divided into three or more zones. In the first zone, constructional standards should be those at present imposed; in the second zone, these should be modified to make cheaper building possible; in the third zone, there should be no regulations other than those made essential by considerations of health, fire precaution, and so on. The Governor of Kenya accepted this proposal as a desirable goal, but the Governor of Tanganyika felt that fostering a community of outlook among isolated groups would not be furthered by setting up separate administrative organizations inside and surrounding the towns.

Removing the Isolation of the Races

Time and again the Commission returns to the position that tribal and racial considerations have stultified and inhibited the economic growth of East Africa. One principle is fundamental, they state, namely that if modern economic institutions are to evolve they must be freed to the fullest possible extent from the political authority of the tribe where it is obstructive.

The Indians, for example, are subject to economic restrictions that impinge on their productivity and undermine their capacity to work and to save. These restrictions also mean that with a rapidly growing Indian population largely confined to the urban areas, any marked degree of industrial development will tend to provide greater opportunities for the Indian than for the African population which, as yet, is less well endowed with industrial skills and commercial aptitudes.

In regard to land, the Commission states that improved opportunities can only be provided by the government's taking a country-wide view and adopting a policy emphasizing the use to which land is put and not on protection of the interests of particular communities. Failure to adopt a unitary approach, they predict, will inevitably retard development just when it is imperative to accelerate the process.

The retention of land in the Kenya Highlands for purely European use, it follows, has serious limitations. It makes the Europeans appear as a tribe hanging onto tribal territory. It inhibits interpenetration of lands, which is essential to economic production. And it depicts the Europeans as a political bloc, undermining confidence between the African and European throughout the whole region.

The isolation of the races in East Africa must, therefore, be overcome, otherwise the poverty of the area will continue. It must be clearly and unequivocally recognized that race or color cannot be regarded as a ground for any discrimination or restriction which the community is not prepared to accept on other grounds. But no member has a right to expect to be guaranteed equality of attainment in experience, efficiency, status, or reward. All attempts to impose artificial equalities, the Commission maintains, result in increasing the poverty of the poor rather than in reducing it.

It may readily be understood that the fundamental changes recommended by the Commission, involving the breaking down of tribal and racial boundaries, should meet with a sharply mixed reception. Numerous orders-in-council, treaties, ordinances, and solemn declarations have long placed the emphasis on the opposite principle. Many Africans and Europeans would find it extremely difficult to adjust their thinking to the new concepts outlined by the Commission.

The Governor of Kenya, for example, while accepting the theme of removing the isolation of the races, stated that the government could in most cases take no direct action, as in the last resort economic and social cooperation was a matter of individual behavior. Furthermore, the government could not allow the restrictions to be removed at a faster pace than the social and administrative structure of the colony would sustain. The Governor of Uganda also agreed with the Commission's objectives but felt that too little emphasis had been placed on tribal loyalties and that further economic progress must be based on cooperation with the Africans through their tribal institutions. Comment among the settler community was reported as cautious and reserved, responsible and reflective.[10] No Europeans felt that Africans would regard the opportunity to lease land in the Highlands as adequate compensation for the loss of their exclusive position in the reserves.

The Commission's views received more sympathetic support in the British press. *The Economist* wrote that the "suggestion [of the governors] that the barriers to economic expansion cannot be removed by policy changes is a counsel of despair; how else can they be removed?" [11] Though "the governors have the weight of much practical experience on their side in . . . rejecting . . . the drive for a free market, this . . . simply means that they defend the *status quo,* the political, or sectional, solution of their problems, which has already been found wanting, and whose failure led to the appointment of the Royal Commission." [12] Others predicted that the Report, despite its lukewarm reception, would "overshadow every decision of importance taken by the three Governments in the next 20 years," [13] and that the Re-

---

10 "Land Issue in East Africa," *The Times* (London), June 14, 1956.
11 "Go Slow in East Africa," cited, p. 306.
12 "East African Governors Say No," *The Economist* (September 8, 1956), p. 804.
13 Bryan F. Macdona, "The Development of Africa," *African World* (January 1957), p. 10.

port would be assigned "a place in its possible significance alongside the great state papers of the Empire." [14]

It is appropriate, I believe, to give the last word to the Commission. It believes that the several races in East Africa have in common a wholly restricted conception of the future economic development of the region, paying more regard to the sharing of the market than to increasing it. The Commission's opposing view is that the region must look beyond its borders as the only source of new capital, enterprise, and skill, that the problem, therefore, is not one of a fundamental clash between the interests of the indigenous populations and those of other races. Indeed, in the absence of outside aid in the form of capital, enterprise, and skill, the difficulties which are associated with the growth of the African population are likely to become more intractable. But the enthusiasm of the Africans is more likely to be stimulated by a sense of giving service rather than blindly obeying an order. There is, then, the great difficulty of finding confidence and security for one side, self-respect and efficiency for the other side, and success and contentment in the outcome. It demands a policy which can replace mutual fear by mutual hope.

It may appear from some of the criticisms of the Royal Commission Report that it will be shelved and forgotten as rapidly as possible. But it is difficult to see how the many problems and tensions of East Africa will be solved unless some of the major proposals of the Commission are adopted, and it may be predicted that succeeding commissions will be forced to reiterate with greater force and urgency the recommendations of the 1953–1955 Report. The emphasis on economic freedom, it should also be noted, has applicability to many other underdeveloped areas, where physical and cultural conditions may be far different from those of East Africa. The Report may be considered a classic in the theory of developing backward areas.

[14] T. P. Soper, "East Africa's Economic Problems," *African World* (February 1957), p. 11.

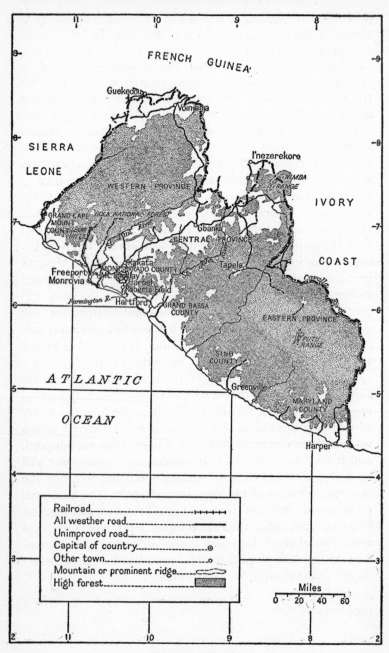

Map 6. Liberia

Chapter 7

LIBERIA: AMERICAN INVESTMENT AND AFRICAN DEVELOPMENT

The Liberian representative here declared this week that his country lagged materially behind the new nation of Ghana because it had always been independent and had never reaped the advantages of colonialism. . . . *The New York Times,* March 24, 1957.

In 1939 Liberian exports totaled $2.8 million and imports $2 million. Government revenue was under $1 million. Economic development was pinpointed in the Firestone plantations and in Monrovia. This capital city had "a few dilapidated mansions vaguely reminiscent of the old South of the United States, many houses of corrugated iron and any number of tar-paper hovels amid the tropical vegetation. There was no telephone system, no piped water supply or sewage disposal." [1] There was no modern port, no rail line, no road system. As late as 1948 there was not one indigenous physician and there were only ten foreign doctors in the entire country. The government allocated $70,000 to its medical program in that year.

The vast bulk of the country was occupied by loosely knit tribes adhering closely to their time-honored cultures, and practicing a primitive subsistence shifting agriculture in the great forests of the area.

For years the country had been subject to virulent criticism, particularly from citizens of colonial powers, and it was frequently the butt of ridicule and scorn. Liberia was given as the object lesson proving that Africans were incapable of self-government.

Americans, whether they realized it or not, were frequently held responsible for the neglected state of the

[1] *The New York Times,* December 26, 1953.

Liberian economy. This country had periodically expressed its "special interest" in Liberia, but this interest was not revealed in any important material way for many decades.

The second World War finally brought the turning point for Liberia. The strategic position of the country made it important in ferrying aircraft across the South Atlantic; air bases were granted to the United States for the duration of the war. From then on American interest and influence have steadily grown. This chapter is concerned with American investment and aid to Liberia.

PRIVATE AMERICAN INVESTMENT

Firestone Plantations

The Firestone interests in Liberia, dating from the midtwenties, were the only significant American investment before the second World War. The Firestone plantations have long been, and continue to be, the largest employer, importer, exporter, and trainer of human skills in the country.[2]

Firestone was one of the first American companies to invest in sub-Saharan Africa, and one of the very few concerned with large-scale, plantation production. The company's decision to produce natural rubber in Liberia resulted largely from a desire to offset the Stevenson Plan of 1922–1928, which regulated rubber exports from British producing areas with the intention of sustaining the world price. Under the original lease, dating from 1924, Firestone acquired an abandoned, 2,000-acre rubber plantation which it used as a pilot plant and nursery for its larger operation at Harbel. There was great difficulty in concluding an agreement enlarging the concession area, but in late 1926 Firestone was given the right to rent up to one million acres for 99 years. During the period of negotiation, Liberia was in a very precarious financial state, and Presi-

---

[2] See Wayne Chatfield Taylor, *The Firestone Operations in Liberia* (Washington: National Planning Association, 1956). Much of the material regarding Firestone is summarized from Taylor's excellent study.

dent King apparently was interested in the Firestone trans-
action only because he felt that a large investment would
help in securing the financial assistance so desperately
needed and because he believed that the presence of a large
American company would strengthen the United States's
resolution to protect Liberian independence. Efforts to secure loans from the American government and from New
York bankers having failed, Liberia and Firestone reluc-
tantly agreed that the required loan would be made by a
second Firestone corporation, independent of the Plantations Company. Firestone also agreed to construct a deepwater harbor at Monrovia under a loan not to exceed
$300,000. After protracted negotiations, the plantations,
the loan, and the harbor agreements were ratified by the
Liberian legislature in November 1926.

The Planting Agreement called for an annual rental fee
of 6 cents an acre, but a more important source of income
for the Liberian government, after production began, was
a tax of 1 per cent on the gross value of all produce exported by the company. In 1950 this was replaced by an
income tax, which the company has since paid at the maximum rate of 25 per cent. The Firestone Company assisted
the Liberian government in drafting the income tax law
and voluntarily waived the exemptions contained in the
original Planting Agreement. The company also pays certain taxes for its Liberian employees while they are in its
service.

Planting proceeded rapidly from 1927 to 1932, when the
low market price for rubber (3 cents in June 1932) not only
discouraged further extensions but made it unprofitable to
tap the trees that were coming to productive age. This
period was the most difficult one in Firestone-Liberian relations, for it coincided with troubles over Liberia's failure
to adhere to the 1926 Loan Agreement and with the League
of Nations censure of Liberia for improper labor practices.

Planting was resumed after 1934 and regular tapping
began. By 1940, 72,500 acres had been planted, 54 per cent
of which were yielding. The importance of the plantations

increased enormously after Japanese conquest of the major rubber-producing countries of southeast Asia, which left only Ceylon and Liberia as important sources of natural rubber for the Allies. The plantations were worked beyond their optimum capacity in the following years, and output almost trebled from 1940 to 1945, when production reached 20,000 tons.

Overtapping was discontinued after the war, causing a temporary decline in production, but a major planting program was undertaken to 1950. In 1954, the plantations adopted a 25-30 year program of replanting with selected seeds which will result in much higher yields per tree than from the older stock. The Harbel Plantation now has over eight million rubber trees on about 90,000 acres; the Cavalla Plantation has over two million trees on about 10,000 acres. In 1955 and 1956 the company produced about 38,000 tons of concentrated liquid latex and coagulated sheet rubber.

The Harbel Plantation is said to be the finest and most modern rubber plantation in the world. Its average yield per acre in 1955, 1,048 lbs., was the highest in the world; yields in the newer divisions were as much as 1,600 lbs. per acre. The plantation has 275 miles of all-weather roads plus 660 miles of "jeepable" roads, the largest latex processing plant in the world, a hydroelectric plant to provide power and light, and a shipping point on the Farmington River about 12 miles from the sea. The employees number 25,000 Liberians, including 3,000 classified as skilled or semi-skilled workers, and 180 Americans and Europeans.

There is no question that Firestone has made and is still making the greatest contribution of any foreign investor to the Liberian economy. In 1955, over 39 per cent of the government's total revenue was derived from tax and rental payments made by Firestone. It accounts for about 90 per cent of the rubber produced in the country. In 1939, rubber was 81.9 per cent of Liberian exports by value; a peak was reached in 1950, when rubber accounted for 96.8 per cent of exports; and it still makes up between two-thirds and three-quarters of total exports by value. The company has also been the pace setter in Liberia in wages and in labor relations generally.

Subsidiary Activities of Firestone Companies

Firestone, like many companies working in underdeveloped areas, found very early that it was impossible to be concerned only with the physical operations of growing, tapping, and shipping rubber. Its 1926 agreements, in fact, immediately involved the parent company in several additional functions. Other activities have developed on the periphery of the plantation operations. These include: a sawmill; a brick and tile factory; a small workshop making latex cups, soap, and rubber sandals; a poultry farm; a 1,000-acre oil palm plantation; the United States-Liberia Radio Corporation providing trans-Atlantic radio service from Harbel; and the United States Trading Company, a wholly owned subsidiary. The USTC conducts a general importing and wholesaling business in Monrovia and operates retail stores on the plantations. It is responsible for 35 to 40 per cent of total imports to the country and exercises a major influence on retail prices, particularly of rice, the main food product. For example, in 1955 the USTC imported about 10,000 tons of rice to help hold down its internal price. Food is sold to Liberian employees of the company at subsidized prices, rice being sold to them in 1955 at 2.5 cents per pound, though its general price was 8.5 cents.

In addition to these economic activities, Firestone has a well-developed program of medical, health, educational, and recreational work. The educational program includes, in addition to regular schools, an adult literacy program, technical training for clerks and tradesmen, and a scholarship program for training and education in more advanced institutions.

The Firestone Plantations Company encourages production of rubber by Liberians by providing seedlings and technical advice free of charge. In 1956 there were 922 independent rubber farmers producing about 10 per cent of the country's total. Yields on these farms average only 300 lbs. per acre. The company also offers to purchase all rubber offered by independent producers according to a scale of prices based on the previous month's prices in New York. In 1955 it disbursed over $2 million for rubber marketed through its facilities. Native-owned rubber plantings continue to expand and may soon be equal in acreage to the Firestone plantations. Some of the largest holdings are owned by Liberians prominent in the government, which means that they are operated on an absentee basis and may have other undesirable features in the long run.

Another subsidiary activity was the formation of the Liberian Construction Company during the second World War to build and maintain roads for the Liberian government. This company, which lost money, became inactive as other contractors came on the scene. Another construction activity, the 1926 Harbor Agreement to build a deepwater port at Monrovia, was canceled after it became apparent that the sum agreed upon was entirely inadequate to the task. The $115,000 that had been spent prior to cancellation was absorbed as a loss by the Firestone company.

Two other subsidiary activities, not connected directly with plantation operations, proved to be sources of considerable embarrassment to the company and items of contention with Liberians and the Liberian government. These were the 1926 Loan Agreement and the Bank of Monrovia, organized by the company in 1938. The latter is discussed on pages 229-230.

Securing a loan for Liberia was probably essential to concluding the Planting Agreement. The Loan Agreement provided for American financial advisers and auditors who were given extensive powers over the whole Liberian financial establishment. The previous record of Liberia with regard to financial commitments appeared at the time to justify and require these safeguards, but the Liberians bitterly opposed them as infringements upon their national sovereignty and freedom of decision. Without reviewing the history of this agreement, which is well summarized by Taylor,[3] it will suffice to say that all parties were extremely relieved when final payment terminated it in 1952.

The Liberia Mining Company

The second most important American investor in Liberia is the Liberia Mining Company. Its formation was largely due to Mr. Lansdell K. Christie of New York, who became interested in the possibilities of mining ore in Liberia during the last war. Contract negotiations began in 1945, but after considerable progress had been made they were interrupted by the cabling of an offer by a competitive group. Mr. Christie was unable to match this offer, which contained a number of extravagant promises, including one to build a new capital in a more favorable location. In the light of this offer President Tubman suspended discussion with Mr. Christie's representative, but it soon became apparent that the competing offer was without adequate foundation, and negotiations were resumed leading to conclusion of a contract which became effective in January 1946. This contract called for a basic royalty of 5 cents per ton of iron ore shipped and an "excess royalty" to become effective if the price of pig iron in the United States increased a certain amount over the average price of the previous ten years.

The Liberia Mining Company was then formed by Mr. Christie, Mr. William H. Mueller of the Netherlands, and the Liberia Company. Funds were still insufficient to cover the required capital expenses, and the American steel industry, which had not yet extended its horizons to Africa, showed little interest in the venture. The Liberia Mining Company, however, used the funds available to finance the necessary preparatory operations, such as construction of roads and houses. President Tubman had expressed particular interest in these and similar features of the operation, which he believed would be its most beneficial aspects as far as Liberia was concerned. Probably none of the parties

[3] Same, pp. 53-57.

envisaged the much greater contribution that the mining company is now making to the Liberian economy.

The necessary capital was finally secured in 1949 through participation of the Republic Steel Corporation and a $4 million loan from the Export-Import Bank. Repayment, which was to be over ten years starting at the end of 1951, was actually completed in 22 months from that time. The first shipment of ore was made in 1951, when 186,000 tons were moved; by 1953, 1,295,000 tons were exported, and in 1956 some 2,016,050 tons were shipped.

Though the 5 cents a ton figure in the original contract, even with the addition of the "excess royalty," now appears extremely low, at the time it had been calculated that ore would bring only $4 per ton delivered at port. Soon after shipments began, however, the price of ore reached $15 per ton, and the company found itself in the position of paying only 5 cents per ton on a profit of $7-10 per ton. With this embarrassment of riches, the 5-cent figure appeared absurdly low. This development was first discussed informally with the government, both parties acknowledging that the arrangement had become inequitable. After formal meetings had been called by President Tubman, a new formula was devised whereby the Liberian government would receive 25 per cent of the company's profits for five years, 35 per cent for the succeeding ten years, and 50 per cent thereafter. It is estimated that the Liberian government is now realizing $4-5 million yearly from the operations of the Liberia Mining Company. Some 2,500 Liberian workers and about 140 Americans and Europeans are employed.

Mining operations are located at Bomi Hills, some 42 miles north of Monrovia. The reserve is stated to have 40 million tons of high-grade ore (c. 68 per cent iron content) and over 200 million tons of milling-grade ore (c. 52 per cent). Operations are conducted at the surface and are highly mechanized; ore is transported by the company rail line to Monrovia, and loaded aboard ship by a mechanical belt conveyor. So far, only high-grade ore has been tapped, but a $10 million beneficiation plant is now being constructed which will concentrate the lower-grade ores to 62 per cent iron content before shipment. Output is expected to level off at about three million tons starting in 1958.

Arrangements are also far advanced for the exploitation of another ore body, 36 miles inland from Bomi Hills. Although another season of geological work is required, the prospects of a large and rich body appear very favorable. It is contemplated that this body will be worked by a company owned 50 per cent by the Liberian government, 35 per cent by Liberian citizens, and 15 per cent by the Liberia Mining Company. The American participants believe that this arrangement will provide a sound base for the future and will help in extending knowledge of the free enterprise system in Liberia. If the Liberian government decides to apply this unusually favorable formula more widely, however, it may result in discouraging new investors in the country.

Like the Firestone Company, the Liberia Mining Company has become involved in subsidiary operations. In addition to the railway and facilities at the port, it constructed a small lumber mill to supply its own needs. In 1955 it signed a contract with the government providing for cutting timber in the Gola Forest Reserve. The mill, which has been moved to a point six miles from the mining area, is expected to cut approximately four million board feet of lumber annually. The government, which encouraged this new enterprise because of the need for lumber in the local economy, will benefit by a stumpage fee of $3 per 1,000 board feet logged.

The Liberia Company

This company was formed with capital resources of about $1 million by Mr. Edward R. Stettinius, Jr., after he left the Department of State. Although he was motivated very strongly by a desire to make a significant contribution to developing Liberia, the contract negotiated was much on the order of an "old-line concession." The agreement gave exclusive rights to the company over many minerals which might be discovered, in addition to land for development of plantations. The concessions were to be owned 55 per cent by the Liberia Company, 35 per cent by the government, and 10 per cent by a general purpose foundation.

It cannot be said that the Liberia Company has as yet made a very important contribution to the country, nor has it been a very successful undertaking. The untimely death of Mr. Stettinius robbed it of its driving spirit, but it has also suffered from lack of experienced personnel and from a somewhat impractical approach. Too much money was spent in the first years on travel and exploration, and the Liberia Foundation, the third intended beneficiary of company operations, began to survey possible philanthropic projects even before the company started operations. No one on the managerial staff had had practical experience in economic development work.

After Stettinius's death the Liberia Company contract was changed to a 12-year concession, and the number of resources over which the company was given control was reduced. Perhaps the company's most successful investment has been a 7 per cent interest in the Liberia Mining Company. Its principal activity, however, is the development of a 25,000-acre cocoa, coffee, and rubber plantation in the Central Province near Ganta. Activity started in 1950 and there are now about 3,200 acres planted. The company has built 30 miles of first-class roads; it maintains a small airfield, a modern garage, and a small diesel electric plant; it has provided school and recreational facilities. Processing facilities are scheduled for completion in 1960, one year after the first commercial crop is expected. In 1957 the company had 1,500 Liberian and 12 foreign employees in the country.

With the Liberia Company we again see the acquiring of subsidiary functions. It shares in the port management company, supervises the Division of Light and Power and the Division of Water and Sewers for the Liberian government, and acts as agent in Liberia for several American companies.

The Bank of Monrovia

American entry into banking in Liberia came as a necessity after the British Bank of West Africa withdrew in the early 1930s because it was dissatisfied with the government's financial policies. At first the Firestone subsidiary, United States Trading Company, handled such banking business as was required by the Firestone Plantations, but its operations in this field gradually expanded until 1938 when they were placed under another wholly owned subsidiary, the Bank of Monrovia. A small bank having no affiliation with a bank of greater resources, it was never able to provide all the commercial banking facilities the country required. Liberians never understood these limitations and felt that much more money should have been loaned at lower interest rates. The bank felt that it could not meet the demands of the Liberians and remain solvent. It thus became a source of friction in Firestone-Liberian relations, and the company began to look for ways of divesting itself of this activity.

In 1946 an arrangement was concluded whereby the new Liberia Company would take over the bank, but this went into abeyance with the death of Mr. Stettinius. Finally in September 1955 Firestone sold its bank to the First National City Bank of New York. From 1955 to mid-1957 the bank's assets quadrupled and its business expanded greatly. The Bank of Monrovia serves as depository for the Liberian government and supplies the United States currency which circulates in Liberia. Additional supplies have to be flown in at frequent intervals because of the rapid disappearance of the currency. To cover the cost of air freight and insurance a charge is levied on cash withdrawals by customers.

The great increase in ship registrations in Liberia has attracted a great deal of money which moves through the Bank of Monrovia. Many of these transactions have nothing to do basically with the Liberian economy.

The Shipping Industry

In recent years there has been a tremendous increase in the number of ships flying the Liberian flag, which has surpassed the Panamanian as a "flag of convenience." This type of interest in Liberia is not confined to Americans, nor is it in the same category as investments, but it brings considerable revenue to the Liberian government, and it owes its success to American initiative. In 1954, 142 ships with a total of 1.22 million gross tons were registered in Liberia, yielding a revenue to the government of $561,990. In 1955 Liberia became the fourth largest country of registration in the world, with about 4 million gross tons under registry. By 1957 tankers using the Liberian flag totaled 7.5 million deadweight tons. At the standard rates the Liberian government would collect $3,600,000 in registration fees and receive $300,000 of annual income from tonnage taxes. In addition to providing the tax and other advantages that draw ship operators to flags of convenience generally, Liberian registry is popular because of the favorable registration laws, which were proposed to the Liberian government by an American shipping company. The registration fee ($1.20) and the tonnage tax ($0.10 per net ton) are low, and there is a guarantee that they will not be changed for a period of 20 years from the date of initial registration. Additional explanations include the efficiency with which the government's maritime administration carries out its registration responsibility, the ability to use English throughout, the fact that the currency is the U.S. dollar, and the absence of detailed control over the operation of ships flying the Liberian flag.

The Farrell Lines Inc. have a direct investment in Liberia totaling a little under $1 million. This includes four small ships, a floating drydock, and miscellaneous dock and shipyard equipment. Two of the ships are latex vessels which make daily trips to the Firestone plantation at Harbel; the other two are dry cargo vessels which serve not only Harbel, but Cape Palmas at three-week intervals.

Other Private American Interests

A variety of other American companies have investments in Liberia. Some are small in scale and restricted in scope, others may some day rival the larger enterprises listed above.

In agriculture there are Letourneau of Liberia, Ltd. and the B. F. Goodrich Company. Letourneau obtained a concession in 1952 to operate a plantation of 500,000 acres at Baffu Bay. While full information is lacking, some evidence suggests that the company suffered from inexperience and an unrealistic approach. The plantation is now apparently dormant. Goodrich concluded an agreement with the Liberian government to establish a rubber plantation in 1954. Operations began in 1955 at Zui, about 20 miles from Bomi Hills in the Western Province and by the end of that year 400 acres had been planted. If adequate labor can be obtained, this plantation may become a major Liberian producer, for it hopes to achieve its initial goal of 10,000 acres by 1960.

In the mineral field, Americans have a small interest in the Liberian-American-Swedish Minerals Company (LAMCO), which is planning to exploit iron ore in the Eastern Province. Several ore bodies have been found, including one at Putu that is reported to be of very good quality (c. 62 per cent metal content) and probably larger than the Bomi Hills deposit, and one in the Nimba Mountains which is now the prime focus of interest. Reserves in the Nimba area have been estimated at 200 million tons of ore with a 60-70 per cent metal content. In 1957 LAMCO was engaged in a preliminary survey of a deepwater port near the mouth of the St. John River in Grand Bassa County some 200 miles from the ore body. The company also indicated its intention to initiate in 1958 a $150 million investment program including the exploitation of two mining properties, the construction of a rail line to the

Nimba Mountains, and construction of a port which will have a capacity superior to that of Monrovia.[4]

The Pan American World Airways System operates and maintains Robertsfield Airport, including its communications and meteorological services. It also runs four weekly flights between New York and South Africa that stop at Liberia. The United Press is considering initiation of its news service in Liberia. International Telephone and Telegraph is studying the integration of the now separate communications facilities of the country. Lastly, there is the inevitable Coca-Cola bottling works.

UNITED STATES GOVERNMENT AID TO LIBERIA

Before the second World War, United States government aid to Liberia was confined to occasional loans designed to bolster the shaky finances of the country. During the war, Pan American was asked to build Robertsfield and subcontracted with Firestone for its construction. More important was the construction of a deepwater port at Monrovia under Lend-Lease arrangements in 1945–1948 at a cost of $20-22 million. Under the terms of the loan the Liberian government agreed to engage an American firm to operate the port during the amortization period; it is now run by the Monrovia Port Management Company, Ltd., which includes on its board of directors representatives of the large American interests in the country. Port operations have yielded about $250,000 a year, which is applied toward amortization of the original loan. But there is some concern regarding the slowness with which this loan is being repaid, while the need for additional facilities suggests that new investments must soon be undertaken to expand the port's capacity. Monrovia is operated as a free port, the only one in West Africa.

In 1944 and 1946 the United States sent public health and economic missions to assist in the development of

---

[4] William H. Rusch, "Growth in Liberian Economy Continues," *Foreign Commerce Weekly*, December 9, 1957, p. 15.

Liberia, and in 1950 an agreement was signed whereby Liberia was able to benefit from American technical assistance. The two missions were merged in the United States Operations Mission in 1951, when the country embarked on a five-year economic and social development plan to cost $32.5 million. A joint Liberian-United States Commission was made responsible for planning and coordinating, and the Liberian government agreed to allocate 20 per cent of its annual revenue to the plan. In 1953, a four-year extension was incorporated in a revised Nine Year Development Program.

Among specific agricultural projects that have been aided by American money and technicians are an extension program designed to introduce improved farming methods, a swamp rice production program, introduction of a number of palm oil extracting presses, and a program to increase coffee production among native farmers. The swamp rice program, started in 1953 in the Gbedin Swamp of the Sanokwelle District, has been labeled a success,[5] though operations are in their infancy and initial costs were relatively high. Increased rice production is important, however, because of the country's food deficit, and because production in swamps is higher-yielding and conserves the high forest areas from excessive use. The introduction of hand presses, which was successful in other West African areas, should increase the extraction rate of palm oil from the 20 to 30 per cent prevailing under primitive methods to 65 to 85 per cent. American technicians have also helped the Liberian government to initiate a modern forest protection program,[6] though efforts to attract large-scale exploitation have not as yet been successful.

Other aid projects have included the photogrammetric surveying of about 87 per cent of the country, magneto-

[5] U. S. Foreign Operations Administration, *Liberian Swamp Rice Production a Success* (Washington: Author, 1955).
[6] See Torkel Holsoe, *Forestry Progress and Timbering Opportunities in the Republic of Liberia* (Washington: International Cooperation Administration, 1956).

metric surveys over small areas, and a jointly operated Road and Highways Bureau manned by American engineers. The Liberian National Airways is a government-owned corporation operated by United States flight and ground personnel.

The United States Public Health Service Mission instituted a nation-wide, anti-malaria campaign with gratifying results, and much has been done to bring other diseases under control. Several new hospitals and scores of new clinics have been constructed since 1946. Attention has also been given to the serious nutrition problem. WHO, UNICEF, and private mission groups have also aided in the health and social fields.

Opinions differ widely regarding the success of American government aid to Liberia. Some label it a dismal failure, others feel that it has done a sound job under very difficult conditions. The shortage of qualified personnel and inability to fill technical posts have been severe handicaps. It must also be noted that some of the problems tackled are among the most difficult the country faces, and that they do not permit the concentrated effort possible in a plantation or mining venture.

PROBLEMS FACING AMERICAN INVESTORS

It is quite obvious that Liberia has been less attractive for investment than other African areas, at least until very recently. It is often stated, in fact, that the poverty of the area helps to account for the nation's success in remaining independent. The explanations for the reluctance of investors to go to Liberia run the gamut from political and economic to social, cultural, and physical. Many of the problems that existed in the past remain today; some have been aggravated by the increased tempo of development. But great progress has been made, and the country is now far more attractive than it was ten or twenty years ago. For this, much credit must be given to President W. V. S. Tubman, who saw more clearly than his predecessors the value, indeed the necessity, of foreign capital if his country were to be developed.

Human Problems

The human problems facing the investor in Liberia cannot be understood except in their historical setting. The history of Liberia begins with the attempts of the American Colonization Society and others to settle ex-slaves in West Africa, following the example of the British in and around Freetown in Sierra Leone. The first permanent settlement was made in 1822 on Providence Island at Monrovia. For years, this and successive settlements on the coast had no political status in the eyes of other countries, which led to serious incidents with foreign traders. Finally, in 1847, the independent state of Liberia was proclaimed, and was soon after recognized by leading European nations. Ironically, the United States did not recognize the country until 1862.

The settlers, whose descendants are known as Americo-Liberians, "did not have an easy time of it. They had grown up in America—to many of them Africa was frightening and alien, even though it had been the place from which their ancestors had originally come." [7] Although some of the first settlers had sufficient skill to build respectable homes and to start various enterprises, they did not impart these skills to their children. The Americo-Liberians came to devote more and more time to politics and to an elaborate social life patterned on that of the plantation aristocracy of the American South. Over the years a wide gulf existed between this group and the much larger number of tribesmen in the hinterland who were among the most primitive peoples in Africa. The Americo-Liberians adopted the master-slave pattern which they had known in America in their relations with the indigenous inhabitants.

For years a small group of men played musical chairs with the available government offices, receiving the only

[7] Republic of Liberia, Department of State, *Liberia* (1952?), p. 5.

income in Liberia. The country had no brokers, no traders with experience, no skilled workers, no capital to invest. Economic stagnation prevailed from 1870 until the 1930s. During this period the government was chronically in financial difficulties, and occasionally in more serious trouble. In the early 1930s the nadir was reached when an international commission concluded that laborers were being shipped, with the connivance of government officials, from Liberia to Fernando Po and French Gabon under conditions of compulsion scarcely distinguishable from slave raiding and trading.

One great achievement stands out in this history, the maintenance of an independent nation, a rather remarkable accomplishment in the face of the recurrent threats and the often passive attitude of the United States.

The legacies of this history remain. There are still many Americo-Liberians who oppose integration with the tribal peoples of the country. There is still a predilection for the law as a career. There is still suspicion of foreign countries and foreign traders, who took advantage of Liberians all too often in the past. But important changes are in progress. The open-door policy and vastly increased American aid and investment have opened a new world to Liberians. Real efforts are being made to bring the Americo-Liberians and the indigenous peoples together, to open up and develop the hinterland which could not even be considered pacified until recent decades. The moving force in integration efforts is again President Tubman, the first president to have any real interest in the matter or the wherewithal to back it up. He is aided by the feeling among some Americo-Liberians that there has been too much inbreeding in this small group, and by the march of economic events which calls for more and more recruits from the static tribal areas.

At present, there are an estimated 15,000-20,000 Americo-Liberians living almost exclusively in coastal towns or on plantations along the St. Paul River. There are about 50,000 westernized Africans and a total of about 150,000

who are involved in the money economy. No one knows
what the total population of the country is; current estimates vary from 600,000 to 2,500,000, with those falling
between 1 and 1.5 million being most common. All but
100,000-150,000 still retain their tribal customs; there are
five principal ethnological groups speaking 28 dialects. Although a Negro republic, Liberia is in the paradoxical
position of having a native policy very similar to that of
a colonial power, with district commissioners operating
under a system of indirect rule.

In this situation, it is obvious that Liberia has both
quantitative and qualitative labor problems. From the beginning Firestone has had a problem in recruiting labor.
The company has met it partially by offering comparatively
high wages, providing numerous amenities, paying the
workers' direct taxes while employed, establishing health
and educational facilities, selling food at below-cost prices,
and, more recently, inaugurating co-financed retirement
pensions, paid vacations, and service awards. Nonetheless,
it was forced to develop a system for stimulating recruitment by compensating chiefs for the labor and services lost
when their tribesmen accepted employment with the company. In 1955, a total of $90,000 was paid to chiefs under
this system, while there was also a regular scale of non-
monetary gifts to paramount, clan, and, occasionally town
chiefs.

With the coming of other large labor employers the
labor shortage has been aggravated, particularly for activities such as the German-owned African Fruit Company
located in the less densely peopled sections of the country. The Department of Commerce reported in 1955 that

One of the most provocative questions in the field of labor . . .
concerned the adequacy of Liberia's labor force to meet the
demands placed upon it by foreign concessionaires and, at the
same time, to produce enough subsistence crops. . . . To encourage recruitment the concessionaires offered certain incentives including grants of money to tribal and town authorities,
free medical attention, housing, education, and subsidies for

certain necessities, but these incentives appear not to have been successful.[8]

In 1957, a diamond rush threatened to produce severe labor shortages by drawing workers from the mines and plantations, but the producing area was promptly closed and conditions were reported as normal in late 1957.[9] Wage rates increased about 10 per cent in 1957 and are expected to continue to rise. The average wage of Liberian workers, outside of government employment, was estimated to be $15 per month in 1957.

The problem of labor turnover, common in many African areas even where there is an adequate supply, is also present in Liberia. Taylor writes:

... Firestone has persistently faced one basic difficulty which has improved only slowly over the years. This is the problem of labor turnover, greatest among the unskilled workers but by no means negligible among its classified employees. The turnover in field labor is now about 30 percent per year, but was formerly even larger. ... Only about one-third of the unskilled labor and about two-thirds of the classified employees are permanently settled on the plantations.[10]

The shortcomings in quality of labor stem largely from the lack of trained and educated Liberians. Nor has there been the interest in entrepreneurship manifested by many West African tribes, so even this avenue of experience is not developed. Almost the entire labor force is unskilled, though a small and increasing number of semi-skilled and skilled workers is available. The need for improved and expanded educational facilities is apparent. In 1954, there were five government high schools, one college, the Booker T. Washington Institute (a trade and vocational school located at Kakata), and numerous mission and concession schools. About one out of every ten children of school age

[8] U. S. Department of Commerce, *Economic Development in Liberia 1955,* World Trade Information Service, Part 1, no. 56-56 (Washington: GPO, 1956), p. 4.
[9] Rusch, cited, p. 15.
[10] Taylor, cited, pp. 69-70.

were believed to be attending school, but only 20 per cent of their teachers had more than an eighth-grade education. Several of the companies have made significant contributions to the training of Liberian workers, and ICA is cooperating in a 25-year program to strengthen the vocational training facilities at the Booker T. Washington Institute.

The recruitment of foreign employees has also become increasingly difficult, particularly in the lower executive and technical grades. There are now about 7,000 non-Liberians in Liberia, but 4,000 of these are other West Africans, mainly Fanti fishermen from Ghana and Africans from French Guinea and Sierra Leone. Some 2,000 are Lebanese who, in handling the commercial life of the country, are represented in almost every village. Only about 1,000 are Europeans and Americans. Shortages of qualified Americans and Europeans have slowed development all along the line; the examples of the Liberia Company and Letourneau have already been cited. In early 1957, there were 24 vacancies on the Technical Assistance Mission staff, while the road-building program was delayed by difficulty in recruiting engineers. The Firestone Plantations have turned increasingly to Western Europe for recruitment of technicians and report considerable success.

PROBLEMS ASSOCIATED WITH UNDERDEVELOPMENT

Other difficulties for investment in Liberia come from the underdeveloped nature of the country. Roads, ports, power facilities, water supply, communications, and other features basic to economic progress have been sadly deficient. Much work and time will be required before these shortcomings are removed.

In 1930 there was only one 27-mile road in Liberia, from Monrovia to Careysburg. Firestone extended this road 29 miles to Kakata, at that time the interior outpost of the country. Today there are about 1,200 miles of public and private roads, about half of which are in a good state; it is hoped that there will be 2,000 miles by 1958. In the interior, headloading is still the dominant means of conveyance. Under the United States aid program, two loans totaling $20 million have been extended to improve roads, so Liberia should have the rudiments of a road "system" by 1960. The highway program envisages five main roads penetrating from the coast and two connecting roads, one near the coast and the other in the interior.

The rivers of Liberia do not contribute importantly to the country's transport, being interrupted by rapids close to the coast and usually obstructed by bars at their mouths. The Cavalla is navigable for 30 miles and the St. Paul for 15 miles from Monrovia to White Plains. The only rail line in the country is the Liberia Mining Company line to Bomi Hills. It is reported that the African Fruit Company plans to construct a 30- to 40-mile line from its banana plantation to its port at Greenville, while a third line will be needed by the Liberian-American-Swedish Company.

The Liberian National Airways, with two DC-3's and a De Havilland Rapide, links Robertsfield with Monrovia, from which regular services are flown to five coastal and three inland towns. Its passenger traffic was 11,050 in 1955.

Before construction of the artificial port at Monrovia, there was no good harbor on the 350-mile Liberian coast. Monrovia now boasts some of the finest facilities in Africa, and there is no question that this port has been a major stimulus to Liberian development. Protected by two long moles, the port has one 2,000-foot quay, capable of berthing four vessels, and there is ample room for additional wharves. Port installations include modern warehouses, a petroleum tank farm, two power plants, latex tanks, and a 1,000-foot conveyor for loading iron ore. Although critics suggested that the port would be excessive for Liberia's traffic, it has been common in the past few years to have one to five vessels awaiting berth space. In 1955, total traffic was 2.01 million tons, including 1.82 million tons of iron ore and bunker fuel.

Additional port facilities are planned at several locations. The African Fruit Company expects to complete a $5 million deepwater port with accommodations for one vessel in 1958 at Giriwakro Bay, Greenville. The proposed mineral port in the St. John River has already been noted, and a $2 million causeway and wharf is planned for Harper.

The position with regard to power is less encouraging. The total capacity of installed plants is only about 7,000 kw., and power is typically high cost. The continued development of the country will require greatly increased power facilities; attention should probably be given to possible hydroelectric sites. It has recently been reported that a power survey will be initiated by the ICA.

Physical Deficiencies

Had the physical wealth of the country been sufficiently attractive in the past it is likely that ways would have been found to meet some of the human problems, but Liberia was considered as one of the unhealthiest stretches of coast in Africa, the agricultural possibilities appeared less favorable than elsewhere, and no mineral deposits were known.

Liberia has all the disadvantages of a humid tropical area: it is uncomfortably hot and humid most of the year; it is plagued by insects, many of which are carriers of animal and human diseases; there are no well-developed valleys or flood plains, alluvial soils cover only about 2.1 per cent of the country; highly leached, porous latosols, poorly adapted for production of annual food crops, cover 75 per cent of the country; [11] the rainforest vegetation is itself a hindrance to penetration. Lastly, the country is only beginning to be mapped and scientifically explored. Large parts of the interior are very poorly known.

FUTURE POTENTIALITIES

Despite the many handicaps that face Liberian development there are very considerable potentialities. From the

[11] William E. Reed, *Reconnaissance Soil Survey of Liberia,* U. S. Office of Foreign Agricultural Relations and U. S. Technical Cooperation Administration, Agricultural Information Bulletin no. 66 (Washington: GPO, 1951), pp. 10, 25.

standpoint of the forest industries, the country is very fortunate in having an estimated one-third of its area covered by virgin timber. It has been calculated that the forests are capable of yielding two billion board feet of lumber annually, worth $100 million. Commercial absorption of the trees now wasted in bush clearing could yield $50 million yearly.[12] Improved transport facilities are basic to increased forest production. The Liberia Mining Company's mill is close to the company railway; construction of a port at Greenville will permit exploitation of a large and completely untouched timber area in the Eastern Province, and it is hoped that the LAMCO line will stimulate forest activity in the belt through which it passes. Holsoe concludes that Liberia could develop into "one of the prime tropical timber exporting countries in the world." [13]

Liberia's greatest natural agricultural resource is the ability to grow tree crops. Tree crops are well adapted to the climatic and soil conditions, and do not result in the soil deterioration that accompanies production of annual crops. Experts recommend particularly the expansion of oil palm production, which would not only improve local food supplies but which could become the country's most valuable export. Other tree crops of interest include coffee, cocoa, kola nuts, bananas, and grapefruit, though it is not certain that cocoa will be entirely suitable because of the short dry season and the rapid onset of heavy rains. That the most important tree crop, rubber, will increase in importance is indicated by the fact that, of the 144,000 acres in rubber in 1957, 40,000 had trees which were not yet old enough to be yielding. Probably the best agricultural areas of the country are the valley floors and seasonal swamps totaling perhaps two million acres, which are suitable for the intensive production of rice, cassava, maize, and other vegetables.

In the mineral realm, the greatest opportunities now appear to be in expanded production of iron ore. Alluvial

[12] Holsoe, cited, p. 10.
[13] Same, p. 65.

gold has been washed for many years from small deposits along the lesser streams, but production has been declining steadily in recent years. An extension of the Sierra Leone diamond-producing area is found in Liberia and there has lately been considerable exploitation. Because of trouble with smuggling, illicit sales, and disruption of the labor market, the government withdrew digging licenses in April 1957 and made it an offense to purchase diamonds outside Monrovia. Other minerals have been reported, including magnetite, quartz, corundum, pyrite, lead, columbium, manganese, and bauxite, but much more intensive prospecting will be required before their value can be more accurately estimated.

THE CONTRIBUTION OF AMERICAN INVESTMENT

Large-scale and diversified American investment has been too recent in Liberia to permit more than a very preliminary assessment of its contribution to the development of that country. Only the Firestone plantations and the Liberia Mining Company are mature operations; other enterprises are still in the early stages of growth, and some have not yet started production.

The past record of the United States's interest in Liberia sheds little credit on this country. Although a "special interest" in Liberia was intermittently expressed, the Liberians could never tell exactly what this interest was. For the most part, we played a passive role. With the beginning of more intensive development, there was frequently a somewhat excessive emphasis on Yankee trading, while, as the Reverend Emory Ross puts it, some investors who went out to Liberia "with a very good front turned out to have no behind."

However, without belittling the very real contributions of Liberian leaders, it is quite apparent that the considerable progress made in the last two decades is largely a consequence of American initiative. In 1940, government revenues were under $1 million; from 1951 to 1956 they ranged between $10 and $15 million. Total foreign trade has increased from $4.82 million in 1939 to $71.8 million in 1956. American enterprises accounted for the vast bulk of exports and supplied most of the government revenue in this period. Total American investment in the country is now estimated at $75 million.

Perhaps greatest credit attaches to the willingness of American companies to change with evolving conditions, and particularly to make voluntary contract alterations calculated to benefit Liberia. An indirect contribution is seen in the stimulus given to other foreign investors to enter the country, and important investments have been made by German, Swiss, Spanish, Italian, and other companies. Rusch suggests that if the present trends continue European investment may soon equal that of the United States in Liberia.[14] In the field of government aid the basic surveys of Liberian resources, the construction of roads and of a first-class port, and assistance in establishing modern governmental procedures have set the stage for future growth.

Very much remains to be done. Economic development is now largely confined to the narrow coastal belt. The bulk of the country is still largely primitive. One of the greatest needs is for improved training and educational facilities. Unlike the more advanced West African nations, the demand for education has not become an obsession, some facilities being not fully used at the present time. Special attention must be given to the development of managerial talent among Liberians, who are likely to demand a greater part in directing the build-up of their country. Care must be taken to maintain a balanced economy: bidding against each other for available labor carries a strong inflationary danger; removal of excessive numbers of able-bodied males from tribal areas threatens the country's food production capacity unless more productive techniques are introduced.

The United States and American companies have bene-

[14] Rusch, cited, p. 15.

fited from opportunities in Liberia. Most of the investments have been financially rewarding. The wartime production of rubber was of great strategic importance, as was the granting of bases for military transport. Experience in Liberia has had an unmeasurable educative value. It has helped to make this country aware of the problems and opportunities in the development of underdeveloped areas, whether they be independent or colonial.

Liberia is, then, on the road to material advancement. It has gained relatively in the past decade with regard to other tropical areas. But starting from a lower level, it will take some years before the legacy of neglect is overcome, and before this independent republic will compare favorably with a number of African colonial territories from the standpoint of economic development.

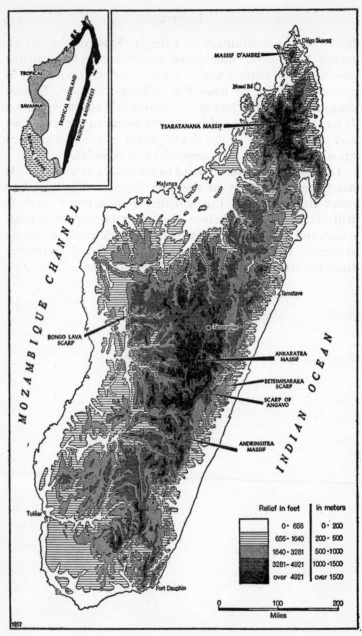

Map 7. Madagascar

Chapter 8

MADAGASCAR AND TROPICAL AFRICA— SIMILARITIES AND CONTRASTS

THE position of Madagascar, somewhat off the beaten track, and the dearth of material about it in English, have made it one of the least known parts of Africa for many people. A comparison of the island with the better known continental parts of tropical Africa seems therefore to be a logical approach. The question immediately arises—is such a comparison justified? Some authors have claimed that Madagascar is not African at all, while others see in it an area where the problems of Africa are collected in a confined space convenient for study. Recent opinion perceives a far greater association between the island and the continent of which it is an appurtenance than has been generally accepted in the past.

THE INDIGENOUS PEOPLE OF MADAGASCAR

As it is the people of Madagascar who are said to be so unlike the Africans, we may properly begin by examining the question of their origins. Most writings have followed the Grandidier theory [1] that "the bulk of the population is descended from immigrants from the East who crossed the Indian Ocean in the early centuries of the Christian era, bringing with them the language which later developed into Malgache, rice, and many culture traits which are still common to Madagascar and Indonesia." [2] The Grandidiers held that the scarcity of Hindu elements in the lan-

[1] Alfred and Guillaume Grandidier, *Ethnographie de Madagascar* (Paris: Imprimerie Nationale, 1908–1929), 4 v.
[2] Robert F. Gray, *Anthropological Problems of Madagascar: A Bibliographical Introduction* (Department of Anthropology, University of Chicago, 1954), p. 7 (mimeographed).

guage and culture of Madagascar indicated "that the main migrations took place before the Hindu expansion into southeast Asia and Indonesia," [3] and that there may have been primitive Negritos on the island when the Easterners arrived but that their influence has been of little significance. To account for the Negroid characteristics of most of the Malgache, the Grandidiers identified them with the Negroes of Melanesia.

A second main theory of long standing is that Madagascar was populated by Africans long before the arrival of the Indonesians, and that the latter imposed their language and many culture traits after subjugating the Negroes. The inclusion of many Bantu words in the Malgache language is cited as supporting evidence. Less widely accepted theories include that of Dubois,[4] who suggests that the Negroes of Madagascar came neither from Africa nor Oceania but represent an independent migration from Asia, and of Linton,[5] who theorized that Indonesian-Polynesian migrants came via Somaliland bringing African natives with them.

The latest summary regarding origins of the Malgache is presented briefly by Louis Michel.[6] He notes the general agreement regarding the eastern origins of the Merina people, who presumably arrived Kon-Tiki style, though he believes that there has been a considerable mixture since their arrival. He concludes, however, that the Malgache Negroids, who make up most of the other tribes, are without doubt of Bantu-Swahili type and that they arrived from East Africa, probably using the islands of the Comores Archipelago as stepping stones. He notes that the somatological types of the Malgache Negroes are entirely unlike

[3] Same, pp. 7-8.
[4] A. M. Dubois, "Les Origines des Malgaches," *Anthropos*, v. 21 (1926), pp. 72-126, and v. 22 (1927), pp. 80-124.
[5] Ralph Linton, "Culture Sequences in Madagascar," *Papers of the Peabody Museum of American Archaeology and Ethnology*, v. 22 (Cambridge, Mass., 1943), pp. 72-80.
[6] Louis Michel, "L'Origine des Malgaches," *Revue de Madagascar*, no. 25 (1955), pp. 8-18.

those of Melanesian Negroes. Even the Betsileo, who are often called the Southern Hova (an incorrect term for the Merina, as it applies only to one of their four main castes), are considered to be largely Negroid, their resemblance to the Merina presumably representing a more thorough mixture of African and Indonesian than is characteristic of the other tribes.

It now seems most logical, in summary, to believe that most of the population is of African origin. There is no question that the language and that some of the practices, including the cultivation of paddy rice as the major staple of the diet, were brought by the immigrants from the east, but many of the customs of the coastal tribes, especially the attitudes of pastoral tribes toward their cattle, appear closely related to those of African graziers. From the standpoint of its people, then, Madagascar is probably more like Africa than has generally been accepted in the past.

Closely associated with the problem of their origins is the question of the degree of unity among the Malgache people. Deschamps states that there is remarkable unity,[7] and, after some backing and filling, Linton concluded that the native patterns of social organization and religion were everywhere fundamentally the same. On the other hand, he stated that the uniformity of Malgache *culture* was a myth, while the *Encyclopédie de L'Afrique Française* says that the Malgache differ as widely as the Russians and Spaniards or the Scots and the Greeks.[8]

Obviously, much further study is required before many of the interesting ethnological questions that the island poses are adequately answered. However, certain points that are pertinent to this chapter may be noted. The most notable similarities with Africa from the human standpoint are in the origins of the bulk of the people and in the great number of tribal groups represented. Even the Merina must have a strong African element, for a study made in

[7] Hubert Deschamps, *Madagascar* (Paris: Berger-Levrault, 1951), p. 6.
[8] Encyclopédie de L'Afrique Française, *Madagascar*, v. 1 (Paris: Encyclopédie Coloniale et Maritime, 1947), p. 2.

1913 revealed that of the 850,000 claiming to be Merina only 300,000 really belonged to the Merina race, the others being more or less mixed with other tribes. Only about one-fifth of the total population is of relatively pure descent from the earlier eastern migrants.

The most important contrasts with Africa would include the greater unifying influences in Madagascar of a more or less common language, Malgache, and the spirit of Malgache nationalism. There are some tribal animosities, and the less-developed tribes probably have little concept of belonging to a larger whole, yet one is impressed with a certain unity of outlook, a sense that many natives consider themselves Malgache as well as Merina, Betsimisaraka, or Bezanozano. This sense of unity could be of great benefit in the future development of Madagascar. It is in strong contrast with the resurgence of tribalism that appears to be a feature of movements toward self-government in such territories as Uganda, Nigeria, Ghana, and the Sudan.

An additional contrast of note between Madagascar and most of Africa is the relatively developed status of the Merina people. Before the Europeans arrived the Merina were practicing a highly organized, intensive agriculture which had either been copied by or been imposed upon many of the other tribes. They had a detailed history, advanced governmental forms, and a well-developed exchange economy. Their standards of dress and housing are superior to those of any African tribe with which I am familiar. Today, the Merina have the highest literacy rate and the largest number of educated people of the Malgache tribes. They are the clerks, the technicians, and the artisans of the island. Some of them occupy positions of responsibility not only in their traditional region around Tananarive but in all parts of the island. The Malgachization of the civil service, which is part of the French political program for the island, is in the main a Merinization. The French must be considered fortunate in having these people to work with in the development of the island.[9]

THE NON-INDIGENOUS POPULATION

Malgache comprised 97.9 per cent of the total population of 4,887,166 in 1956,[10] but the non-indigenous people occupy a place out of all proportion to their numbers, as is characteristic of African territories. The division of non-Malgache peoples in 1956 is shown in Table 9. The posi-

Table 9

THE NON-INDIGENOUS POPULATION, 1956

French	
By birth	52,777
Sainte-Mariens	11,984
French citizens of Malgache origin	10,420
Naturalized French	4,229
Total French	79,410
Foreign	
Greek	422
Other non-Asian	3,130
Chinese	6,841
Indians	12,807
Other Asians	1,739
Total Foreign	24,939
Total non-indigenous	104,349

Source: Service de Statistique Générale, Madagascar, *Bulletin de Statistique*, no. 22 (July 1957), p. 1.

[9] On the other hand, the presence of one tribe which is far more evolved than most of the others presents certain problems, not only for the present government, but for the time when self-rule is attained. There are, for example, the dangers that other tribes will increasingly resent the superior status of the Merina, and that the Merina might eventually attempt to impose their will upon the other tribes as they did before the island became a colony.

[10] Service de Statistique Générale, Madagascar, *Bulletin de Statistique*, no. 22 (July 1957), p. 1.

tion of Madagascar with respect to its non-native population is not exactly comparable with that of any African area. Its Asian population makes it more like East Africa than West Africa; it has elements of the settler problem that characterizes Kenya, Nyasaland, or perhaps Angola because of the presence of small-holders; yet it is the native who has the great predominance in numbers and who accounts for the great part of the output, thus making the island more like West Africa.[11]

In assessing the contribution of "Europeans" to Madagascar it is important to note that about 24,000 French are Creoles from Réunion or Mauritius or inhabitants of Ste. Marie, a small island off the coast, whose people were given citizenship years ago, while about 1,400 of the naturalized French are citizens of Hindu or Chinese origin. Many of the Creoles are small colonists, concentrated to some extent in the coffee areas of the east coast; others are foremen, operators of mechanical equipment, and small merchants. They do not pull the same weight, man for man, as the Frenchmen from France. Chevalier states that the Creoles have limited ambitions and are satisfied to use what there is rather than to create anything new.[12] He further states that permanent European settlement on Madagascar, in which Creoles dominate, has, unlike other French territories, been "exploitative" and characterized by small scale of operation, small capital investment or risk, and by little benefit to the commercial interests of the island.[13] He and Isnard [14] find particular fault with the prevalence of métayage, a system of share cropping which permits operating with a minimum of investment. Both authors suggest that resentment by local tribes of the practices of the small *colons* was among the major dissatisfactions leading to the 1947–1948 revolt.

[11] See H. Isnard, "La Colonisation Agricole à Madagascar," *Revue de Géographie Alpine,* v. 39, fasc. 1 (1951), p. 102.
[12] Louis Chevalier, *Madagascar, Population et Ressources* (Paris: Presses Universitaires de France, 1952), p. 84.
[13] Same, pp. 96, 98.
[14] Isnard, cited, p. 102.

A study of the French government approach to Madagascar before and after that war further suggests that the presence of a fair number of "French" settlers was one of the reasons for the relative neglect of the natives' development before the war. Post-1948 programs have given far greater attention to the needs of the Malgache, displaying at the same time a new firmness toward settler demands which are not considered to be in the best interests of the Malgache.

The original Chinese on Madagascar were mostly Cantonese brought in to work on the Tananarive Côte Est Railway in the first decade of the present century. A large number of them are now small merchants, located especially on the east coast and in the central highlands. The fact that only 13 per cent of the total Chinese are women, while 55 per cent are men and 32 per cent children, suggests that the Chinese often take Malgache women for their wives.

Many of the Indians, who include both Moslems and Hindus, are also small merchants, but they are more congregated along the west coast. Others are masons, carpenters, iron workers, and jewelers. Of the other non-indigenous people, Arabs are of some importance in the Majunga area, and over 400 Greeks are scattered throughout the island. There are very few Americans, the largest group being Norwegian-Americans in a series of Lutheran missions stretching across the south of the country from Tuléar to Fort Dauphin.

As in other parts of Africa, the Asian peoples are frequently accused of exploitative practices. Chevalier states that they pay illicit prices for collection of native-produced crops and lend money at usurious rates.[15] As the small merchants purchase most of their goods from the three large European trading companies, Compagnie Lyonnaise, Compagnie Marseillaise de Madagascar, and the Société Industrielle et Commerciale Marseillaise, he feels that the hierarchy of merchants is a heavy burden on production and

15 Chevalier, cited, pp. 101-103.

commerce. However, other people have not shown a willingness to perform the same functions as the Asians, and it is not easy to see how some of the remote areas of the island could be served without them. To some they appear as "indispensable intermediaries" rather than usurers.

THE POPULATION DENSITY AND GROWTH

Although it is not possible because of the lack of statistical material to estimate accurately the rate of growth of the population, such evidence as there is shows that the long-run demographic pattern has been like that of Africa, not like that of Asia. The average density of population of 21.5 per square miles in 1956 was about the same as tropical Africa as a whole, or of Mozambique and French Cameroun among individual countries.

The keynotes of the demographic pattern have been low density and slow rate of growth or even stagnation. For long, a high death rate nearly canceled a high birth rate. The high death rate was explained by many of the same factors that prevailed in Africa: malnutrition, disease, unhygienic conditions, and intertribal warfare. Certain cultural features have also contributed to the high death rate. The Malgache are said to have "le fatalisme des bantous africains," [16] and "une civilisation de la mort," in which religious rites and superstitions reveal that submission to death is "perhaps the most profound aspect of the civilisation," [17] the attitude being one of complete resignation.

But recent years have seen the same rapid change in population growth that presages a population explosion in many African areas. Improved health measures and disease control have contributed to an increased birth rate and a lowered death rate. The yearly increase in population has grown from 10,978 in 1946 to 102,627 in 1955 and 137,000 in 1956. This demographic boom is one of the most pro-

16 Gustave Julien, "Les Malgaches, Leur Valeur Morale et Intellectuelle," *Revue d'Ethnographie et Traditions Populaires*, v. 8 (1927), pp. 145-146.
17 Chevalier, cited, p. 63.

found forces that will affect Africa and Madagascar in the years ahead.

THE PHYSICAL CONDITIONERS

Having briefly looked at the peoples of Madagascar and seen that there is justification for essaying comparisons with tropical Africa, we may next look at the physical attributes and deficiencies of the island to determine the extent of similarity in these matters.

Location, Size, and Shape

The location of Madagascar, 250 to 500 miles off the coast of southeast Africa, has made for contrast rather than similarity with Africa. This "continent of the Indian Ocean," [18] in fact, owes its distinctiveness in considerable part to the isolating influences of its location and to its island character. These explain the development of independent species of flora and fauna, the absence of other species common to Africa, and the widening gaps in cultural practices.

Some islands are located in the stream of world movements and their interests are more universal than insular, but Madagascar's location has tended to minimize its contact with the outside world. Contributing to this isolation have been the inhospitable nature of much of the coast and the fact that the most highly developed group, the Merina, who might have been expected to develop trade, purposely isolated themselves in the center of the island and long discouraged contact with surrounding peoples.

There were a few early attempts at settlement and at establishing commercial posts. The French Société de l'Orient tried to start a colony at Sainte Luce, 25 miles north of Fort Dauphin, in 1642, but after 27 of the party of 89 were lost in the first month, the colony was moved to the healthier Fort Dauphin. After a long series of misfortunes, violence among the settlers, wars against the natives, pillage, and reciprocal massacres, it was abandoned in 1674. At the end

18 Deschamps, cited, p. 5.

of that century, a French pirate founded the colony of Libertalia at Diégo Suarez, and about 1720 Ile Sainte Marie off the east coast was acquired by the son of an English freebooter and a local chief's daughter. Their daughter, Bety, ceded this island to France in 1750, and a decade earlier the little island of Nossi-Bé on the northwest had become a protectorate.

But most ships sailing to the orient passed by Madagascar, whose participation in world trade was insignificant. Opening of the Suez Canal made the island even less important, though the French did establish their prime naval base in the Indian Ocean in the magnificent harbor of Diégo Suarez.[19] The island's location acquired greater significance in the last war with the closing of the Mediterranean route. After the local government had sided with Vichy upon the fall of France, the British felt it necessary to invade the island to prevent its falling into the hands of the Japanese. An enemy submarine base at Diégo Suarez would have provided a formidable threat to the Middle East supply lines around the Cape.

The generally isolating influence of its location has removed Madagascar to some extent from the flood of journalists, officials, tourists, and businessmen who have invaded Africa in recent years, and even from us academicians who have laid our heavy hands upon numerous parts of the adjacent continent. The government has enjoyed an amazing degree of privacy in Madagascar. The revolt in 1947-1948 went almost uncovered in the world press, though it resulted in far more deaths than the Mau Mau uprising in Kenya.

In size, Madagascar has about the same area as Kenya and is larger than France and Belgium combined. Its 227,-736 square miles are fairly compact in shape, the coastline being little more than half that of the island of Great Britain. The east coast from Foulpointe almost to Fort Dauphin, a distance of about 600 miles, is remarkably

19 Vice Admiral Pierre Barjot, "Madagascar, Pivot Austral de la Stratégie Périphérique," Panorama (Paris, Spring 1954), pp. 60-61.

straight, the absence of indentations and protected bays forcing the use of inadequate and often dangerous open roadsteads.

Geology and Landforms

Geologically, the island has several clear resemblances to Africa. There are two main zones running roughly north-south on the island: the eastern and central zone of Archaen rock comparable to the basement rocks of the African plateau; and the western zone, whose oldest formations are associated with the Karroo series of South Africa, made up of almost undisturbed sedimentary rocks dipping gently toward the Mozambique Channel. The theory that Madagascar was at one time part of the greater continent of Lemuria connected with Asia across the Indian Ocean is not widely accepted. Most recent books follow the hypothesis that, as part of the former continent of Gondwanaland, Madagascar split off and drifted away from Africa. Many American geologists no longer accept this theory, and J. Millot, Director of the Institute of Scientific Research of Madagascar, has recently attempted to quash any connecting of the island with Lemuria or Gondwanaland.[20] He accounts for the presence of African faunal species on Madagascar by the existence of land bridges to Africa in the Primary and Secondary Eras.

There are also similarities in landform features between Africa and Madagascar. The eastern part of the island, in particular, is markedly comparable to the continent; there is a narrow eastern coastal plain, 10 to 25 miles wide, followed by a steep scarp or scarps leading to an upland area usually called "the central plateau." The term plateau is a gross misnomer, however, for the 720- by 240-mile central region is composed largely of hills and mountains and is predominantly in slopeland. The average elevations of 3,900 to 4,600 feet may be reminiscent of Africa, but the features are actually very different from the sometimes mo-

[20] J. Millot, "La Faune Malgache et le Mythe Gondwanien," *Mémoires de l'Institut Scientifique de Madagascar*, v. 7 (1952), pp. 1-36.

notonously level surface of the African plateau. This region of high-based hill lands can perhaps be best compared to the dissected uplands of Ruanda-Urundi.

From the standpoint of human use, the Madagascan uplands are a more difficult landform region than the African plateau. There are the same difficulties of approach, the same fringing scarps, and the same lack of navigable streams that long repelled the opening up of Africa. But even when the heights are attained, the inhibiting influence of the landform continues. Roads are constructed with difficulty; with the aim of reducing expenditure on bridges they meander endlessly along the fairly even crests of the dissected hills. Soil erosion occurs more readily, and is more difficult to control; use of the sloping surfaces for agriculture is not attractive. On the other hand, there is perhaps an advantage in the more rapid accumulation of water in the valleys which may then be controlled for the intensive cultivation of paddy rice.

The west coast topographic region, a belt of plains and low plateaus 60 to 120 miles wide, shelves off gradually toward the Mozambique Channel. This zone of gently dipping sediments is quite unlike the typical African coastal zone and more like that of the continents facing the North Atlantic.

The smaller features of the coastal areas of Madagascar have many of the same inhibiting features of the African coasts. On the east, there are only two sizable indentations: Diégo Suarez in the extreme north and Antongil Bay. Diégo's usefulness is greatly reduced by its location at the narrower extremity of the island and by its small hinterland, restricted by difficult landforms to the south. Antongil Bay is open to the prevailing winds.

The only respectable east coast port, Tamatave, is partly artificial. Its protection is inadequate, however, and a seiche, or rhythmical motion, develops in the harbor even with winds of moderate intensity. River mouths along this coast are offset, and clogged with shifting bars; they are used by lighters but ocean-going vessels must stand offshore in a characteristically heavy sea. Offshore coral reefs further endanger loading and unloading operations.

The west coast is considerably more attractive, but even here the larger river mouths and deltas are unreliable because of rapid silting. Efforts to construct a deepwater port at Majunga, for example, have been frustrated by silting behind a kilometer-long dike which reduced depths from 36 feet to as little as 3 feet in a 10-year period. Madagascar is certainly more favorably oriented toward the sea than many African territories, but its difficult coasts present great problems in directing transport and in developing the economy of the island, just as do the coasts of tropical Africa as a whole.

The topographic features of both coasts and of the interior of Madagascar have been largely responsible for dividing the island into many economic sub-regions whose contact with one another is often very tenuous. The central highlands are tied to the east coast by two rail lines and by a number of mediocre roads, while the unusual Canal des Pangalanes, connecting a series of littoral lagoons, unites some areas of the east coast. But long stretches on both sides of the island function more like island archipelagoes than as parts of the same land mass. One sees, as a consequence and on a miniature scale, the same sort of concentration of economic activity in coastal and highland "islands" that is discernible in tropical Africa.

Climate and Soils

Madagascar is entirely tropical, as is the area with which it is being compared, but it is the position of the island in the prevailing easterlies of the Southern Hemisphere that is the most important controlling factor, while Africa's position astride the equator establishes the general climatic regions of the continent. As a result, the climate regions of the island run mostly north-south while the predominant zones of Africa extend largely east-west.

There are four main climatic regions on Madagascar. First, the tropical rainy climate zone runs almost the full

length of the east coast and is found along the northwest
coast as well (due to the "Mozambique monsoon" as well
as to a returning current of the easterlies). Constantly hot
and humid, this area has a climate analogous to that of
the Congo Basin or the Guinea Coast. Second, the central
highlands have a tropical highland climate, whose temperatures are modified by elevation. It would be comparable
climatically with upland parts of Kenya, Uganda, or the eastern Congo. Third, a tropical savanna climate region extends along the west and across the northern tip of the
island with a well-marked dry period in the winter, but
with precipitation in most months of the year. This would
be comparable to the belts fringing the tropical rainy region of the Congo or to the savanna belt not far inland
along the Guinea Coast. Lastly, a tropical steppe climate
prevails in the south and southwest, much like that of the
great Sudan belt stretching across Africa from Dakar to the
Ethiopian Massif. This belt is characterized by a long dry
period and by great irregularity of precipitation. Famines
are not uncommon, causing great human suffering and loss
of livestock.

As would be expected, the climate regime of Madagascar
permits production of the same tropical crops that are produced in Africa, though the emphases have been quite different. Palm products, the great staple agricultural exports
of the Congo and Nigeria, are almost absent; cocoa is produced in only very small quantities; and interest in cotton
is just beginning. But almost all the other crops of tropical
Africa are included in the list of exports, while the island
enjoys a nearly unique position in production of vanilla
and certain essential oils.

One additional feature of the climate must be mentioned,
the frequency of hurricanes, one or more of which visit the
island each year.[21] The east coast is most severely and reg-

21 Pierre Platon, "Madagascar: Service Météorologique," *Encyclopédie Mensuelle d'Outremer*, v. 3, fasc. 41 (January 1954), pp. 27-29; H. Pelleray,
"Quelques Données de Base en Vue de l'Étude des Régimes Hydrologiques
de Madagascar," *Mémoires de l'Institut Scientifique de Madagascar*, Series D,
v. 6 (1954), p. 44.

ularly hit, but west coast and highland areas are by no means immune. The prevalence of hurricanes and, indeed, of generally high winds, is another of the many disadvantages of the east coast ports. They account for the absence of Arab dhows in the coastal and international traffic of the east coast, while a large number of these vessels engage in the carriage of freight along the west. And it is estimated that bad weather and heavy seas account for over half of the days lost by ships operating in Malgache waters.[22]

The soils of Madagascar are also quite like those of the continent. Laterites, the curse of the tropics, cover not only the bulk of the rainy tropical east coast, but also most of the highlands and part of the savanna area, where somewhat better soils might be expected. These soils, which are usually formed under forests, are adequate for a few years' production, but, the cycle having been broken by removal of the forest, they soon wear out and must be abandoned to permit a lengthy recuperation. This is the explanation for the shifting agriculture which is characteristic of the laterite regions of Africa and which is practiced along the east coast of Madagascar, where it is known as *tavy*.

In view of the deficient soils, it is perhaps fortunate that the prevailing agriculture of the highlands is confined to the usually small valley bottoms, and that it is centered upon cultivation of paddy rice. Here is found the accumulation of the somewhat better top soil, while paddy farming results in far less of a drain on the soil than does the typical subsistence crop farming of Africa. The sedimentary and drier west has somewhat better soils, but even here much of the area is covered with an infertile skin of clayey sand.[23]

As in Africa, the best soils are azonal, that is, they are special soils which for one reason or another do not conform to the regional pattern. They usually occur in limited

[22] "Les Problèmes Portuaires à Madagascar," *Industries et Travaux d'Outremer*, 3rd yr., no. 15 (February 1955), p. 84.
[23] Olivier Hatzfeld, *Madagascar* (Paris: Presses Universitaires de France, 1952), pp. 10-11.

and irregular expanses and do not total more than a small per cent of the whole area of the island, though they will be far more important in the future agricultural development of the island than their small area suggests. Most important are the alluvial soils occurring in the flood plains and deltas of both the shorter east coast rivers and of the larger but more irregular rivers that flow to the Channel. On the east coast, these soils have frequently been utilized for paddies and a considerable portion of the population is found upon them. There is sometimes an almost continuous string of villages along the lower valleys. On the west, development of the valleys and use of their fertile soils is much more haphazard, though some of the greatest postwar projects have been located with primary reference to the soil factor. Another category of azonal soils includes those formed from basic volcanic rock. Examples of these usually rich soils are found in the Lac Itasy area west of Tananarive, around Antsirabe, and on the island of Nossi-Bé.

Soil erosion is a problem of immense proportions on Madagascar, particularly on the central highlands, where bright red gashes scar the landscape wherever one looks. The major cause of erosion in the highlands is not farming of the slopelands, which is uncommon unless rice terraces are laboriously constructed, but the almost complete removal of the natural forest by deliberate firing and subsequent overgrazing of the resultant grasslands. Soil erosion is, of course, a severe problem in many African areas, but there are few regions on the continent where it has gone as far as it has in central Madagascar.

The Flora and Fauna

The vegetation of Madagascar, responding primarily to the climate, shows patterns comparable to those of Africa.[24]

[24] See Edmond François, *Plantes de Madagascar* (Tananarive: Imprimerie Moderne de l'Emyrne, 1937), 74 p.; H. Humbert, "Les Territoires Phytogéographiques de Madagascar: Leur Cartographie," *L'Année Biologique,* 3rd series, v. 31 (Paris, 1955), pp. 439-448.

The rainy tropical area is primarily a rainforest region, while the highland, savanna, and steppe areas are either predominantly grassy or have medium height to low bush vegetation. Many species are unique to Madagascar, some of them having great beauty. There is some forestry carried on along the east coast, but many of the species are even less known in world markets than those of the much more important Guinea Gulf. Much of it has also been cut for the preparation of subsistence plots and the succeeding forest, or *savoka*, is usually somewhat degraded in character. Forests now cover an estimated 10 to 13.5 per cent of the island, approximately the same proportion that prevails in tropical Africa.

Man is accused of downgrading about 70 per cent of the vegetational areas of Madagascar. As noted above, only remnants of the forest which covered the central highlands a few centuries ago are left, and mediocre grasses, lacking in nutritive values, have replaced them.[25] Similar losses have occurred on the continent, Shantz having estimated that the tropical forests now cover only one-third of their original area.[26] One is often surprised to see the grasslands of Africa and of Madagascar come abruptly to the edge of a high forest belt instead of finding an intermediate zone of mixed woodlands as might be expected. The forest losses on Madagascar have apparently been even greater proportionately than those of Africa and have occurred in a shorter period. Efforts to reforest on the highlands, primarily with eucalypts, have only begun to reduce the vast denuded areas.

The fauna of Madagascar show some striking contrasts to the African pattern. There is no big game inhabiting the grasslands of the island—no lion, elephant, buffalo, antelope, giraffe, etc. Only the crocodile is found, plus numerous lemur, whose presence almost gave the name Le-

[25] See J. Bosser, "Les Paturages Naturels de Madagascar," *Mémoires de l'Institut Scientifique de Madagascar*, Series B, v. 5 (1954), pp. 5-77.
[26] Homer Shantz, "An Estimate of the Shrinkage of Africa's Tropical Forests," *Unasylva*, no. 2 (Food and Agriculture Organization, Washington, 1947), p. 67.

muria to the island. There are many snakes, and they seem to be more frequently encountered than in Africa, but none of them are poisonous, though some are constrictors.

Insects are more or less comparable to those of Africa. But there are two important contrasts to note. First, Madagascar is the scene of one of the most successful anti-malaria campaigns in the tropics. Since about 1948, the aim has been to spray every house and hut on the island at least once a year with DDT, and nivaquine has been dispensed free in the schools. *Anopheles funestus* has been almost eliminated from the highlands and *A. gambiae* has been greatly reduced on the coasts, which were formerly considered to be particularly malarious. The governor was able to claim in 1955 that malaria had been practically arrested on the entire island. The effect of this sudden great improvement in health conditions of the island is already apparent in the rate of increase of the population, and study in the next few years of the effects of this program on the physical and mental outlook of the people may be of interest to African continental areas.

The second great contrast is the absence of the tsetse fly in Madagascar, an actual and potential blessing of very great dimensions. In Africa, a huge belt is still ruled by the tsetse fly, prohibiting man from grazing his cattle in savanna grasslands and from introducing in savanna and rainforest areas a mixed agriculture which might solve the problem of maintaining soil fertility. There is the opportunity on Madagascar, then, to work out systems of agriculture which are not now applicable to the continent, but which may be of great benefit when some method of fly control has been discovered. The work of the Ivaloina Agricultural Station in a rainforest area north of Tamatave is interesting in this regard. Experiments thus far carried out suggest that a rather satisfactory system of mixed agriculture is possible.

SYSTEMS OF AGRICULTURE

The systems of farming on Madagascar include: primitive forest gather (represented by only a very few people in the eastern scarp zone), shifting agriculture (in the east coast zone), intensive paddy rice cultivation (primarily in the central highlands but found in all zones), sedentary grazing with associated production of some agricultural crops (western region), nomadic grazing with little or no interest in cropping (south), and European estate farming of varying types.

The most important system of tillage agriculture, paddy cultivation, stands in contrast with typical African systems, while the other farming and grazing systems are quite comparable to those carried out by African farmers and pastoralists. The cultivation of paddy rice, which often requires a considerable degree of community organization, and which sometimes involves fairly difficult systems of irrigation and drainage, is the main concern of the farmer on most of the lowland east coast, in the central highlands, and in many of the west coast valleys. It is quite obviously a contribution of the people who migrated from Indonesia. Whether it is the most appropriate use of the land in view of the relatively low densities of population and the large areas of unused land (less than 2 per cent of the island is cultivated) may be questioned, but it does have advantages from the standpoint of soil preservation.

There are few *large* rice plains, the two most important being the Betsimitatatra Plain around the capital, Tananarive, and the Lac Alaotra Basin on the intermediate level between the two eastern scarps. The former has been completely developed, though there are possibilities for perfecting control of the water and for increasing yields by improving practices. The Lac Alaotra area, which was far less populated, has been selected as one of the key areas for development on the island, the major concern to be the mechanized cultivation of large fields of rice. As the lake is very shallow and is surrounded by swamps, there is opportunity for at least trebling the area now cultivated.

It is interesting to note that the tribes of presumed African origin, who inhabit the scarp zone where opportunity to develop paddies is restricted, still place considerable emphasis on rice, producing it in a shifting "hill rice" system on some excessively steep slopes. Other subsistence crops that are important on Madagascar include manioc, corn, sweet potatoes, bananas, and peanuts, all of them also important in Africa.

In the area around Tananarive, and to a lesser extent near the other towns of the highlands, there is a surprising development of market gardening. The moderate climate permits growth of middle-latitude, subtropical, and tropical crops, and the large *Zoma* at Tananarive is certainly one of the most remarkable of African markets. In addition to the profusion of vegetables and fruit offered for sale at all times of the year, there are chickens, ducks, geese, pigeons, rabbits, and meat of all the larger domesticated animals.

Grazing is the most important agricultural activity from the standpoint of area involved, about three-quarters of the island being used for the extensive raising of cattle and a few goats. There are about six million head of cattle, mostly Zebu, believed to have been introduced from Africa in about the ninth century. Although some cattle are used to pull the ubiquitous two-wheeled carts and others are used to trample rice paddies in preparation for planting, the usual practice on the central highlands is to let the cattle fend for themselves on the grassy slopes, sometimes far removed from the owner's habitation. There is no selective breeding; there are too many males for the best annual production; even the head of the herd is not selected by the usual signs. In the drier south and west, cattle become the prime interest of tribes such as the Bara, Mahafaly, Antandroy, and Antanosy. Although cattle are of great importance in the ceremonial life of these pastoralists, and are considered as the main wealth of the tribe, practices are just as poor as those on the highlands.

The types of European farming are quite varied: some of the small Creole *colons* on the east have little better holdings than the natives; in Nossi-Bé there are small estates producing high-value crops; large owner-managed properties are characteristic of the mechanized rice cultivation in the Lac Alaotra area and of the sisal area in the Mandrare Valley; large corporate holdings or plantations are very rare, the new Sosumav sugar development on the Mahavavy being the most important.

AGRICULTURAL PRODUCTS

Although the cash crops of Madagascar are generally the same as those of Africa, as has already been noted, there is a considerably greater variety both in subsistence and cash crops than is found in most African countries. The variety of Malgache crops is revealed in the following listing:

1. Food crops: rice, corn, manioc, beans, peanuts, potatoes, taro, sorghum, bananas, sugar.
2. Vegetable oils: copra, castor oil, candlenut oil, peanut oil, tung oil.
3. Fibers: sisal, raphia, paka, cotton.
4. Stimulants: coffee, tobacco.
5. Perfumes and spices, etc.: ylang ylang, lemon grass, cloves, pepper, vanilla.

The variety of crops may be shown by another classification based upon the producer and the destination of the product:

1. Crops grown exclusively on European holdings primarily for export: sisal, tung oil, pepper, ylang ylang, lemon grass, cacao.
2. Crops grown exclusively by Malgache of which there is a considerable export: beans, raphia, oil bearing seeds.
3. Crops grown by Europeans and Malgache of which there is a considerable export: coffee, tobacco, cloves, vanilla, sugar, manioc, rice, peanuts.
4. Crops grown principally for food, mainly by Malgache but with some European production: rice, corn, peanuts, potatoes, market garden crops, taro, sorghum, bananas.

The relative importance of crops in the country's exports is shown in Table 10, which lists the major exports of Madagascar by tonnage and by value in 1956.

As Table 11 shows, the exports of Madagascar are spread

Table 10

PRINCIPAL EXPORTS OF MADAGASCAR, 1956

Product	Quantity (tons)	VALUE Mil.fr.CFA	Per cent of Total
Coffee	52,487	7,017	43.1
Rice	36,171	1,341	8.2
Cloves	7,613	986	6.1
Tobacco	3,783	917	5.6
Vanilla	387	766	4.3
Raphia	6,001	499	3.1
Meat and conserves....	2,898	481	3.0
Graphite	15,401	397	2.4
Peanuts	9,043	392	2.4
Essential oils	686	343	2.0
Sisal	9,233	328	2.0
Tapioca	7,518	285	1.7
Peas................	9,020	235	1.4
Pepper	550	189	1.2
Hides	2,678	170	1.0
Mica	641	162	1.0
Manioc	7,350	103	0.6
Wood	366	93	0.6
Crocodile skins	47	80	0.5
Cattle	—	80	0.5
Tung oil	654	67	0.4
Beans	1,226	47	0.3
Rum	—	46	0.3
Corn	2,699	36	0.2
Other	49,956	1,240	8.1
Total	226,408	16,300	100.0

Source: Service de Statistique Générale, Madagascar, *Bulletin Mensuelle de Statistique*, no. 18 (March 1957), p. 1.

Table 11

CONCENTRATION OF EXPORTS OF AFRICAN COUNTRIES, BY VALUE

Country	Year	NUMBER OF COMMODITIES IN FIRST						
		30%	40%	50%	60%	70%	80%	90%
Madagascar	1956	1	1	2	4	6	10	19
Mozambique	1956	2	3	4	5	6	—	—
Tanganyika	1956	2	2	3	3	5	8	—
Nigeria	1956	2	2	2	3	3	4	6
French Cameroun	1956	1	2	2	3	4	6	—
French Equat. Africa	1956	2	2	2	2	4	5	5
Sierra Leone	1956	2	2	2	2	2	3	—
Belgian Congo	1956	1	1	3	4	6	8	—
Uganda	1956	1	1	2	2	2	2	3
Kenya	1956	1	1	1	3	4	7	10
Angola	1956	1	1	2	3	4	5	7
Cent. Af. Fed.	1956	1	1	1	1	2	3	7
Sudan	1956	1	1	1	2	2	4	5
Ghana	1956	1	1	1	1	3	4	—
Liberia	1955	1	1	1	1	1	2	2
Mauritius	1956	1	1	1	1	1	1	1

Sources: Territorial statistical documents; Barclays Bank D.C.O., Overseas Review; Marchés Tropicaux du Monde.

among a greater number of commodities than are those of most tropical African countries. This suggests Madagascar has a somewhat broader and hence sounder economic base. Unfortunately, this is not the case, because there is a heavy imbalance in international trade and because there has been stagnation or even regression in the production of several important exports, while other commodities have not expanded with sufficient strength to replace them.

Until the past few years, for example, the production of coffee had been stagnant, the 1954 production having been practically identical with that of 1938. Most Madagascan coffee is Robusta coffee, grown in the east coast hills from Vohémar to Vangaindrano, where plantations cover the alluvials that line the river banks and where coffee trees surround native villages, benefiting from the availability of local fertilizers.[27] In many cases the trees are very poorly tended, the system being almost one of collection rather than of cultivation. Manuring is not yet general and the majority of plants are old, 80 per cent having been over 20 years old in 1954. A much smaller quantity of better grade Arabica coffee is grown on the highlands, where soils of sufficient fertility are present. Additional explanations for the failure of coffee to follow its prewar trend of rapid expansion include the destruction of plants and plantations in the 1947–1948 revolt, and inflated costs of production.

In 1953, a fund was created to counteract the downward trend in this most important of Malgache exports. As a result, many nurseries have been established to supply new bushes and to stimulate extension of the crop to new areas, and it begins to appear that this program has had success. Exports of 47,437 tons and 52,487 tons of coffee in 1955 and 1956 were both records. Furthermore, the quality has improved substantially, 68.8 per cent of coffee exports having been of superior quality in 1956 compared with 44 per cent in 1954. It is now hoped that production will be

27 Gilbert Cours, "L'Extension de la Production Caféière à Madagascar," *Marchés Coloniaux du Monde,* 11th yr., no. 495 (May 7, 1955), pp. 1195-1199.

increased to 60,000 tons and possibly even to 65,000 tons by 1960.

Efforts are also being made to sell Madagascan coffee in other markets than that of France, which has always been the principal buyer. At first, considerable objection was found in the New York market to Madagascan coffee shipments, including the non-neutral taste which makes mixing difficult, a high humidity content, inclusion of too high a proportion of green beans, and the lack of firm prices and assured delivery dates. In 1955 an office was opened in New York to stimulate the sale of coffee and it has apparently had some success, imports of Malgache coffee to the United States having risen from 50 tons in 1951 to 9,677 tons in 1956.

The export of rice from Madagascar has been highly erratic in recent years, the high level of 1956 exports not being characteristic. Hatzfield stated that the difficulty of exporting rice in postwar years resulted chiefly from inflation, which had pushed the price so far above the world market level that imported rice cost less even after transport to the island.[28] Only the top grade *vary lava* rice, with long, white grains, was readily saleable. The markedly high exports of 1955 and 1956 resulted in considerable part from special reductions in railroad freight rates and in costs of treatment that were made to encourage exports. There are conflicting forces that will affect future exports of this second most important commodity. The rapidly increasing population will probably require more rice, especially if a higher standard is achieved, permitting greater per capita consumption of this favored grain. A continuing inflation would also be a strong deterrent to the export of this relatively low-value crop. But there are opportunities for intensifying and extending production, particularly in the Lac Alaotra Basin and in some of the west coast valleys.

[28] Hatzfeld, *Madagascar*, cited, p. 74. See also "Le Riz," *Entreprises et Produits de Madagascar*, no. 10 (January-March 1952), pp. 7-87; nos. 11-12 (April-September 1952), pp. 7-79.

The export of live animals, of meat, canned meat, and hides and skins has declined markedly from prewar years, a serious trend in view of the great importance of cattle to many of the tribes and their wide dispersion on the island. It has been predicted that if this decline continues, the island, which was once dubbed the "Ile de Boeuf," will be forced to import meat by 1960.[29] In addition to the poor practices which are characteristic, there has been a cattle head tax which agricultural department officials considered as a major discouragement to the build-up of herds. The willingness of the Malgache to sell their cattle contrasts, however, with the reluctance of numerous African pastoralists. With gradual improvement in practices expounded by extension officers, control of cattle thievery and grass firing, and increased drilling of wells in the drier areas, there should be a reversal of the present trend. There is ample opportunity for the increase of herds, as it has been estimated that the island could readily nourish 12 million head.

The production of vanilla is only about one-third of the 1929 level,[30] an unfortunate drop in view of the importance of this commodity as a dollar earner. The chief cause of declining sales has been the substitution of the considerably cheaper synthetic vanillin. The high value of this crop, however, permits it to hold fourth or fifth place among Malgache exports measured by value.

One of the greatest declines in exports has been in manioc, which was the largest tonnage export in 1929 and third largest in 1938. Tapioca, which is made from manioc, has also lost favor in world markets. Other crops which have declined in exports over prewar years include corn, dry vegetables, copra, castor oil, sugar, perfume essences, and raphia.

[29] "L'État du Cheptel Malgache," *Bulletin de Madagascar*, no. 6 (April 1, 1950), pp. 52-53. See also Jean Dieppedale, "Les Problèmes de l'Élevage Bovin," *Marchés Coloniaux du Monde*, 10th year, no. 440 (April 17, 1954), pp. 1105, 1107.
[30] See "La Vanille," *Entreprises et Produits de Madagascar*, no. 9 (October-December 1951), pp. 5-65.

Among the stronger Malgache crops are tobacco, now ranking third or fourth among exports, cloves and clove oil, third to fifth by value, and peanuts, pepper, and sisal. Tobacco enjoyed a steady increase from 1920 to 1954 and has an assured market in the French State Tobacco Monopoly. The major opportunities for expansion, however, may rest more with an increase in domestic consumption than in enlarged sales to the metropolitan market. The sale of Madagascan cloves and clove oil has been aided somewhat by the damaging attacks of "sudden death disease" in Zanzibar, and by the use of clove oil in the fabrication of vanillin.[31]

There has been a large-scale postwar expansion of sisal production in the Mandrare Valley in the south.[32] Stimulated by high postwar selling prices, exports of fiber increased from 2,378 tons in 1948 to 10,297 tons in 1955. Although the substantial drop in price in 1953 was discouraging, there has been a continuing development of new sisal estates. Sugar should become of greater importance in the exports of Madagascar as development in the North Mahavavy continues, while cotton may become the leading export of Tuléar in the southwest.

It would not, of course, be accurate to say that the variety of Malgache crop exports did not strengthen the economy, but one is impressed by the weakness of many Madagascan exports, including some of the most important ones. As has been seen, there are opportunities both for improving and standardizing the quality and for extending the cultivation of these and other crops, but there is no "bright haired boy" among them, and until longer-range programs take hold, Madagascar has a weaker economy than many of its "one product" competitors in Africa.

[31] See "Le Girofle," *Bulletin de Madagascar,* no. 5 (March 16, 1950), pp. 22-27.
[32] See Jean Defos du Rau, "Le Sisal dans le Sud Malgache," *Cahiers d'Outre-Mer,* no. 7 (Bordeaux, 1954), pp. 51-83; "Le Sisal à Madagascar et aux Comores," *Entreprises et Produits de Madagascar,* no. 13 (October-December 1952), pp. 9-14.

THE MINING ECONOMY

Madagascar has not had a modern geological service until recently, so the mineral resources of the island are very incompletely known. The two most important minerals, mica and graphite, accounted for only 3.4 per cent of total exports by value and 7.1 per cent by weight in 1956, the tonnage output being insignificant in relation to some of the great mines of Africa. Minerals have not, then, had the stimulating effect on the economy that is so apparent in central Africa, justifying a substantial system of roads and railroads, demanding large-scale output of power, creating a concentrated local market, and contributing heavily to governmental revenue.

In addition to these two minerals, whose output has not increased over prewar years, there is a small output of beryl, gold, precious stones, garnet, quartz, and cerium. Madagascar is apparently the richest of French territories in thorium sands, and a small but unpublished tonnage of urano-thorianite is now mined in the Behara area on behalf of the French Atomic Energy Commissariat. Reserves of thorium on the beaches from Mandrare to Mananjary are sufficiently large to permit Madagascar to become one of the leading producers of the world, but only small quantities of uranium have been located after some years of extensive research.[33]

For the future, the Sakoa coal basin in the southwest holds some interest, especially in view of the relatively meager reserves of the African continent. But the reserves at Sakoa are relatively small, estimated at about 60 million tons above a depth of 400 meters, and it is a non-coking, high-ash-content, mediocre-quality coal. Efforts to find petroleum in the west have not as yet been successful. Manganese, copper, lead, and nickel deposits have also been reported to be under study.

[33] J.-J. Lecoq, "La Recherche et L'Exploitation des Minerais Radio-Actifs à Madagascar," *France Outremer*, no. 34 (January 1957), pp. 43-45.

THE INDUSTRIAL ECONOMY

Madagascar is comparable with the less-developed territories of Africa in the extent of manufacturing development. Modern industry is poorly represented, by far the most important category being that concerned with the primary processing of raw materials for export. There is a well-developed handicraft industry, especially in the highlands, but modern factories producing articles from domestic raw materials for the domestic market are represented only in the output of soap and vegetable oil, beer, cigarettes and chewing tobacco, beverages, cord and bags, and bricks and tiles. Only a few plants produce finished articles from imported raw materials for the domestic market. These include a textile mill at Antsirabe, printing works, and plants producing metal containers, mirrors, acetylene, and batteries. The usual service industries—power plants, railroad workshops, machine shops, and refrigerating plants—complete the list. There is nothing unusual in the industries that are represented; many underdeveloped areas would have very similar listings.

For the future, Madagascar has advantages for manufacturing in the presence of large-scale hydroelectric reserves, some coal, substantial reserves of radioactive materials, and possibilities of additional minerals, including petroleum. It also has a labor supply which is perhaps somewhat superior to that of many African areas, the Merina having displayed excellent aptitude in modern machine techniques and being more stabilized than many African workers.

The chief disadvantages for increasing industry would appear to be the small size and scattered nature of the market, the somewhat remote location of the island, and the lack of capital. Although there are possibilities for new plants, particularly for producing cement, cotton textiles, and clothing, one cannot expect a rapid increase in manufacturing activity.

TRANSPORT DEVELOPMENT

We have already seen that the physical difficulties besetting development of Malgache transport are similar to
those of Africa. The road network, totaling 15,600 miles,
is rudimentary, consisting of a discontinuous north-south
backbone which would doubtless be called the Great North
Road if the island were British, plus a number of roads extending as ribs to the more important coastal points.[34]

There are only two rail lines: the Tananarive Côte Est
Railway connecting the capital with Tamatave, with
branch lines to Lac Alaotra and Antsirabe; and the Fiana-
rantsoa Côte Est Railway, running from the capital of the
Betsileo country to the lighter-port of Manakara. The rail
lines hauled 44.1 per cent of the total imports of the island
by tonnage in 1955, reflecting in particular the high consumption power of Tananarive. They hauled less than 20
per cent of tonnage exports in the same year, the centers
of export production being widely scattered about the
island. Although totaling only 528 miles, the railways serve
four of the eight leading cities of the island and sizable
portions of the two most populous regions, the central
highlands and the east coast. They are well equipped and
well run, and would compare favorably with any rail line
in tropical Africa in these regards.

One rather unusual feature of Malgache transport,
though it is not entirely unlike the lagoon system of West
Africa, is the Canal des Pangalanes, which connects a series
of littoral lagoons along the east coast for about 400 miles.
Its capacity varies widely, however, from 30-ton barges for
the first 101 miles below Tamatave to 5-ton barges the next
44 miles and only canoes on much of the remaining length.

Madagascar has a surprisingly well-developed air network.
With over 400 airfields and emergency landing strips, of
which about 60 are served by scheduled flights, it has the

[34] See William A. Hance, "Transportation in Madagascar," *The Geographical Review,* v. 48 (January 1958), pp. 45-68.

densest airline net in the whole French overseas area.[35] A few of the more remote productive areas rely almost entirely on air transport for their exports and even for the supply of staple rice. The Andapa basin in the northeast, for example, ships its coffee and vanilla solely by air, while about 850 tons of tobacco move by air each year, especially from Miandrivazo, west of Antsirabe. The island is connected with Europe by four weekly flights, either via Nairobi and Cairo or by Djibouti and Cairo.

The total international port activity of Madagascar is rather feeble, having been only 718,935 tons in 1955, a record year, and 654,012 tons in 1956. The total tonnage, distributed among some 14 ports, is inferior to that of many single ports in tropical Africa. Coastwise trade totaled 319,165 tons in 1955. There is a heavy imbalance in favor of incoming cargo, imports representing 65.4 per cent of total international traffic in 1956.

Tamatave is of outstanding importance among Malgache ports, handling 55 per cent of international traffic and 45.9 per cent of total port traffic in 1955. It is the only really modern port, though its facilities are inadequate for the present traffic. Majunga, on the west, is the only other port with over 100,000 tons a year (153,709 tons in 1955); four ports follow with between 50,000 and 100,000 tons, six with between 10,000 and 50,000, and six with below 10,-000 tons, some of the smaller ports functioning only in cabotage traffic.

The dispersion of traffic among 18 ports (some handling only coastal trade) condemns them as a whole to budgetary and physical mediocrity, so a major goal is to rationalize port activity by concentrating upon fewer ports. Here is certainly a contrast with tropical Africa, where postwar efforts have been directed to building such new ports as Abidjan, Tema, and Mtwara, and where the greater problem is lack of sufficient ports, not an excessive number. The proposed rationalizations affect mainly the

[35] Xavier Adam, "Le Rôle Primordial de l'Aviation à Madagascar," *Marchés Coloniaux du Monde*, 10th yr., no. 440 (April 17, 1954), pp. 1059-1063.

east and north of the island.[36] Fénérive, Vatomandry, and Mahanoro have already been closed to international traffic, their goods being shipped to and from Tamatave via road, rail, or canal. In the north, improved roads from Diégo Suarez may permit closing three or four smaller adjacent ports. Not only is there incentive from the budgetary standpoint to concentrate upon a limited number of ports, but also from the physical standpoint. The general absence of protected harbors, especially at east coast ports, makes operations at them slow and even dangerous.

INTERNATIONAL TRADE

Perhaps the most important feature of the international trade position of Madagascar is the heavy imbalance, imports being substantially greater than exports as is shown in Table 12. If this merely represented a high level of investment for the economic development of the territory it would be less disturbing but, as has been seen, it also reflects stagnation in the production of many products.

Table 12

INTERNATIONAL TRADE OF MADAGASCAR

FOR SELECTED YEARS, 1938–1956

Year	Exports Mil $	Imports Mil $	Exports as % of Imports
1938	23.6	17.4	135.6
1948	50.0	77.7	64.4
1951	77.1	131.4	58.7
1954	91.6	137.4	66.7
1955	81.5	122.4	66.6
1956	93.1	132.0	70.5

Sources: *Statistical Yearbook 1956*, UN Doc., 1956.XVII.5 (New York, 1956), pp. 404-405; *Bulletin de Madagascar*, no. 130 (March 1957), p. 262.

[36] See Louis Pierrein, "La Question Portuaire et l'Économie de Madagascar," *Revue de Géographie Alpine*, v. 39, fasc. 1 (1951), pp. 127-147.

The high level of imports in relation to exports is not entirely unfavorable, however. The prewar "favorable" balance concealed the fact that Madagascar was, to some extent, a "colonie d'exploitation." [37] After the serious 1947–1948 revolt, however, the French attempted to correct many of the elements of their practices most resented by the Malgache, to give greater attention to indigenous agriculture, and to improve the island's social and economic conditions. Some of the programs that have been instituted are long range in nature, and it is probable that the island will not pay its own way for some years to come.

From the standpoint of level of trade, Madagascar's exports compare most closely with French Cameroun, Angola, and French Equatorial Africa among tropical African countries, each of these being among the less developed African territories. The two small islands of Mauritius and Réunion have combined exports about equal to those of Madagascar.

France has always been the predominant supplier and purchaser of Madagascan goods. In 1956 France supplied 72 per cent of imports and took 62 per cent of exports, while other French bloc areas took an additional 11 per cent of exports. The United States took only 4.7 per cent of Malgache exports in 1955, but 14.6 per cent in 1956, purchases of coffee accounting for a large part of the increase. It is not unusual for an African territory to have a trade pattern closely oriented toward the metropolitan power, though many are not so closely tied as Madagascar.

Important in explaining the high per cent of Malgache trade with France and other members of the French Union, in addition to preferential trade arrangements, is the inflation that has affected the franc bloc and that has been particularly serious in Madagascar. As a consequence, the prices of many of the island's major products are above world market prices. Special provisions have even had to be made to sustain the exports to France itself of rice, coffee, and sisal. Inflation has made living in Madagascar

[37] Chevalier, cited, pp. 100-101; Isnard, cited, p. 147.

very costly, and Tananarive is one of the most expensive of African cities, with prices quite typically above those of Paris. The high cost of transport occasioned by the remote position of Madagascar is often given as the main explanation of the high cost of living, but one has only to go to Mauritius at the end of the same trade routes, where prices are far below those of Madagascar, to see that inflation, not transportation, is the villain of the piece.

The economic problems of Madagascar were well summarized by the chief provincial administrator of the Province of Tamatave in his address to the Provincial Assembly on November 5, 1955: "We suffer from a serious imbalance in accounts, from stagnation of certain products, from regression in certain activities, from a disequilibrium between consumption and production, from an increase in operating costs, from costs of production above the level of world prices, from inflation, from the proliferation of intermediaries." [38]

CONCLUSION

In reassessing the appropriateness of comparing Madagascar with tropical Africa it may be concluded, I believe, that the island is really much more a part of Africa than it is of Asia. Only a minority of its people are of Asian origin, though the language and one of the main cultures, the production of paddy rice, were borrowed from or imposed by the immigrants from the east.

The physical milieu has striking similarities with that of Africa: the eastern coast and scarplands, the lateritic soils, and the basic climate and vegetation patterns. Economically, the problems are shared by many underdeveloped areas and are certainly familiar to anyone who has studied Africa.

Yet Madagascar has its own individuality. It is something of an anachronism to see an intensive rice economy in a relatively sparsely populated area; it is unusual to

[38] *Bulletin de Madagascar,* no. 117 (February 1956), p. 151.

see rice so important in essentially lateritic areas; it is unique for Africa to have cattle distributed among all climatic zones; and it is somewhat surprising to have such a range of crops figuring in the exports of a single African territory. It is also true that the Malgache people have acquired their own culture, neither entirely comparable to that of the Malayo-Polynesians, nor that of the Bantu-Swahili.

Chapter 9

POTENTIALITIES AND NEEDS:
A REASSESSMENT

WHAT lessons, what common substance can be distilled from the foregoing chapters? Are there relations between developments in the Federation of Rhodesia and Nyasaland and in Liberia, between the Volta Project and the Gezira Scheme? What generalizations can fairly be made about development problems in tropical Africa?

At least three important features are clear on the mind's-eye map of this economic-geographer: the great variety that is Africa, the high percentage of the area that now has a low level of commercial production, and the high percentage of area that has low productivity under present techniques.

Tremendous variety is apparent in the physical realm —in landforms, climate, soils, vegetation, and animal life. Cultural variety is greater than on any continent except Asia. Contrasts and diversity in the economic field are illustrated well by P. T. Bauer.[1] On the one hand he notes the existence of an African trader in Port Harcourt dealing in six figures under essentially modern conditions, while 30 miles away markets are forbidden to sell meat without hides to insure that there be no sale of human flesh. Or, he points to the Oni of Ife, spiritual head of the Yoruba tribe, who is a member of the Cocoa Marketing Board of Nigeria dealing in millions of pounds yearly, but who is also considered responsible by his fellow tribesmen for the supply of rainfall. Political variety is also striking. Contrast, as examples, the sophistication of Ghanaian leaders with the semi-colonial position of the

[1] P. T. Bauer, *West African Trade* (London: Cambridge University Press, 1954), pp. 2-3.

indigenous Liberian, the widely varying policies of colonial powers toward their African territories, the position of all-African West Africa with British East and Central Africa with their dominant white minorities. There is no such thing as "the African."

Attention was called in the opening chapter to the vast areas of Africa now characterized by low production for commercial return, to the existence of only small islands of intensified activity. This pattern has been illustrated by several of the chapters. In Liberia, three economic points are dominant—the Harbel Plantation, Monrovia, the Bomi Hills—while the vast bulk of the interior is little touched. In Madagascar, producing areas are only a fraction of the total surface. Even in the relatively advanced Federation, most of Northern Rhodesia and the lower parts of Southern Rhodesia are not concerned with commercial production.

The high percentage of area with low productivity under present techniques is explained by two main factors: the physical deficiencies of the area—particularly the permanent or seasonal aridity—and deficiencies of indigenous farming methods. Even if the most modern techniques could be applied, however, the larger part of the continent would still have a low productive capacity.

AFRICAN POTENTIALITIES

These somber conclusions should not result in obscuring the very great potentialities that do exist. Space alone permits expansion of production simply by extension of present indigenous practices and techniques. Application of known non-African techniques also holds forth interesting potentialities: better feeding, breeding, rotational, fertilizing, and other practices, for example. Control projects of one kind or another are likely to be of increasing significance, largely because of poor moisture distribution. In areas of excessive drainage, the use of pipe-laying and trench-digging equipment may permit relatively low-cost drainage; in swampy areas, the mechanical cutting of *sudd* or of mangrove trees should be perfected; while in areas of inadequate precipitation there are many large and small control projects that invite attention. Still other control projects will benefit the area through navigational improvements and provision of hydroelectric power. Two of the foregoing chapters have been concerned with important river schemes, while other chapters have contained dozens of references to the possibilities of better use of the area's water resources.

Thirdly, in the realm of economic potentialities, is the development of new techniques not known at present. It is certainly true that we do not know how to make proper use of many tropical environments today. But in 1800, we knew very little about rotation, seed selection, breeding, milk recording, soil analysis, etc. With intensive application of scientific research and experimentation, we may expect an accelerated response in the answers to African physical and farming problems.

It is well to remember that tropical rainy areas compare favorably with any areas in the world in two of the major requirements for intensive vegetational growth—high moisture supply and year-round high temperatures. With improved knowledge regarding tropical soils and tropical diseases, these areas may one day come into their own. Given a solution to the tsetse fly problem, an area larger than the United States will be opened for production of livestock products.

Unfortunately, however, the development of Africa cannot be expected to move with the same rapidity that characterized the economic growth of Western Europe or the United States. Great as the potentialities are, they are nearly matched by the scope and difficulty of the problems requiring solution. The wealth of Africa, with some conspicuous exceptions, is not that of the ripe fruit waiting to be plucked; it will require careful cultivation and nurturing for a long period before a full harvest may be won. The problems and the limitations affecting development are physical, economic, political, and human. They affect every aspect and phase of the African scene, and the solution of some cannot be expected before considerable slow and tedious scientific work has been accomplished.

AFRICAN NEEDS

In Africa, the force of the physical environment is tremendously important. The physical problems appear to be greater and more intransigent than in the middle latitudes. The need here is for research and more research. The limited extent of scientific study into basic physical problems of tropical areas before the last war is notorious. Fortunately, the situation has been greatly improved in postwar years with all of the territories and all of the metropolitan powers devoting far larger sums to scientific research. But no one would claim that either the funds available or the personnel engaged in this work is adequate to the task.

In the economic field there are numerous and often obvious requirements. The need for improved transportation has been noted in almost all of the preceding chapters. The benefits of more efficient services are well illustrated by the importance of Monrovia to Liberian development, by the stimulus of the Nigerian railways to commercial production in the north, or by the effect of improved facilities on an economy such as that of the Rhodesias. Other requirements basic to continued development include increased power facilities, improved water supply, modern sewage disposal systems, and expanded radio, telephonic, and telegraphic services.

A continuing need will be the promotion of a more balanced economic development. Northern Rhodesia and Liberia are examples of countries where commercial development has outpaced native agriculture. The danger of creating an imbalance between food production and other enterprises was stressed in the study of the Gezira and illustrated, directly or peripherally, in several of the other chapters. In some areas, such as the Kenya Highlands, it is apparent that there is overemphasis on agriculture and that attention needs to be given to promoting alternative pursuits. One of the greatest needs is to stimulate development in the more backward, sometimes quite untouched, portions of the several territories. We think of Ghana as one of the more advanced of African areas, yet its Northern Territories lag far behind Ashanti or the coastal areas. In East Africa the contrast between development on Mt. Kilimanjaro or in Buganda and such areas as the Ufipa Plateau in Tanganyika or the West Nile district of Uganda is greater than the contrast between farming areas of Western Europe and the former regions. Attention needs somehow to be given to the underdeveloped areas within the underdeveloped whole.

A third economic need is for the removal of restrictions of one kind and another—restrictions on the marketing of crops, restrictions on advancement, color bar restrictions, interterritorial barriers, restrictions of tribal boundaries, and so forth. The Report of the Royal East Africa Commission pleads this case with eloquent logic. Whether its recommendations are accepted or not, this study will stand as a landmark to which reference will be made for decades.

Closely allied to this need is the need for increasing cooperation among the many African territories. Despite the great variety of the continent, there are many common problems. Fortunately, there has been a growing willingness to exchange information, to coordinate research, to discuss common difficulties, as witnessed by the great increase in joint conferences in postwar years, or the work of the Conseil Scientifique pour l'Afrique au Sud du Sahara. But the continuing requirements for cooperation are apparent in the fields of transportation and trade, as revealed in the paper on transportation problems, or in the control of major streams such as the Nile.

Tropical Africa will not develop in a vacuum; it is inextricably tied with the rest of the world. It needs markets, capital, and skilled personnel from Europe and

America, and, not least of all, it calls for an increasing awareness of its problems in those areas. The demand and the price of cocoa or copper, for example, may be of minor significance to a country such as the United States, but they have the greatest importance for the economic welfare of Ghana or Northern Rhodesia.

The requirement for capital is apparent in many areas. It has been stressed in connection with the transport needs of East Africa, the development of the Volta Project in Ghana, and elsewhere. The need for skilled personnel is no less great than the need for capital. Developing a continent requires trained men, and in all the world there are not enough trained people available to perform the tasks that should be done in the next few decades. Railroad and mining engineers, geologists, educational experts, labor leaders, doctors, climatologists, and agricultural experts from every field will be required. Britain, France, and Belgium, with long histories of colonial enterprise, find themselves embarrassingly short of qualified personnel. The United States is even worse off, and finds it most difficult to fill existing vacancies let alone the hundreds of positions that will inevitably open in the years ahead. The importance of advanced knowledge has been pointed up, for example, in connection with the Gezira Scheme. The work of plant geneticists has been crucial to the success of that scheme, but there are no Sudanese geneticists, nor can they be quickly trained. The extremely rapid economic growth of the Federation is closely correlated with the existence of a relatively large European population. The contribution of skilled personnel in the recent rise of Liberia is apparent.

The emphasis of this book has been on economic geography, not on political, social, and cultural matters. But almost all African problems are many-faceted; they can be studied from many points of view, and they all center in the final analysis on human factors. The retarded economic development in northern Ghana has important political implications for that country; the existence of a large European group in the Federation creates grave social and political problems there. An economic geographer may, then, conclude by calling attention to political and social needs that appear to him to have great importance.

There is, first, the need for a more effective partnership among the races, for focusing more directly upon the goal professed by most of equality for all. The gravest political problem, though it is not present in all the territories, is that of racial relations. To solve it, there is need for less emotionalism and greater understanding, for less sensationalism and greater scientific reasoning. Other important needs are to channel nationalism more constructively, to open up a broader vista than that of tribalism, to eliminate some of the artificial barriers that divide the nations and peoples of Africa.

A pervasive requirement is to recognize the evolving position of the African. There are still many Africans who value leisure too highly, who do no more than their wives can manage, who are scarcely aware of the opportunities that a higher civilization can offer. But there is a rapidly increasing number of Africans who are quite capable of actively promoting their own development. Their ability and vigor must be welcomed, not constrained.

Next there is the need to relieve the African of the miseries of disease and poor health. But the demographic changes that result from decreased infant mortality, longer life spans, and lowered death rates must also be recognized. It would be tragic if the potential population explosions in several regions were to bring African areas to the pattern of east and southern Asia. As Elspeth Huxley writes: "Doctors, bearers of mercy though they be, must yet be seen as the gravest threat to Africa." [2]

Finally, and most important of all, is the need to relieve Africans from the burden of ignorance. It is fortunate that sufficient progress has been made in some areas to develop an incessant demand for wider educational opportunities.

[2] Elspeth Huxley, *Four Guineas* (London: Chatto and Windus, 1954), p. 32.

This is one of the most optimistic things in the African scene. But it is not only the African who needs greater knowledge, training, and understanding, but the rest of the world, which needs a greater awareness and comprehension of Africa. The paramount need is for education, always and everywhere.

BIBLIOGRAPHY

Chapter 1

Brown, William O., ed. "Contemporary Africa: Trends and Issues," *Annals of the American Academy of Political and Social Science,* v. 298 (March 1955), pp. 1-179.

Food and Agriculture Organization of the United Nations. *The State of Food and Agriculture, 1957.* Rome, 1957. 171 p.

Gourou, Pierre. *The Tropical World.* Translated by E. D. Laborde. London: Longmans, Green, 1943. 156 p.

Hailey, Lord, *An African Survey* (Revised 1956). New York: Oxford University Press, 1957. 1,676 p.

Lee, Douglas H. K. *Climate and Economic Development in the Tropics.* New York: Harper, for the Council on Foreign Relations, 1956. 182 p.

Stamp, L. Dudley. *Africa, A Study in Tropical Development.* New York: John Wiley, 1953. 568 p.

Stillman, C. W., ed. *Africa in the Modern World.* Chicago: University Press, 1955. 341 p.

Trewartha, Glenn T., and Wilbur Zelinsky. "Population Patterns in Tropical Africa," *Annals of the Association of American Geographers,* v. 44 (June 1954), pp. 135-136.

United Nations. Department of Economic Affairs. *Enlargement of the Exchange Economy in Tropical Africa.* 1954.II.C.4. New York, 1954. 59 p.

———. Department of Economic and Social Affairs. *Economic Developments in Africa, 1955–1956.* 1957.II.C.3. New York, 1957. 97 p.

———. ———. *Review of Economic Activity in Africa, 1950 to 1954.* 1955.II.C.3. New York, 1955. 146 p.

———. ———. Statistical Office. *Statistical Yearbook 1956.* 1956.XVII.5. New York, 1956. 646 p.

———. ———. ———. *Statistics of National Income and Expenditure.* Statistical Papers H, no. 10. 1957.XVII.4. New York, 1957. 280 p.

———. Department of Social Affairs. *Processes and Problems of Industrialization in Under-developed Countries.* 1955.II.B.1. New York, 1955. 152 p.

United Nations Educational, Scientific and Cultural Organization. *Social Implications of Industrialization in Africa South of the Sahara.* Tensions and Technology Series. Prepared by the International African Institute, London. Paris, 1956. 743 p.

Chapter 2

Baldwin, K. D. S. *The Niger Agricultural Project: An Experiment in African Development*. Oxford: Basil Blackwell, 1957. 221 p.

Beer, C. W. "The Social and Administrative Effects of Large-scale Planned Agricultural Development," *Journal of African Administration*, v. 5 (July 1953), pp. 112-118.

De Schlippe, Pierre. *Shifting Cultivation in Africa: The Zande System of Agriculture*. London: Routledge and Kegan Paul, 1956. 304 p.

Ferguson, Hugh. "The Gezira Scheme in the Anglo-Egyptian Sudan," *World Crops*, v. 4 (January, February, March 1952), pp. 15-18, 50-56, 98-102.

Gaitskell, Arthur. "The Sudan Gezira Scheme," *African Affairs*, v. 51 (October 1952), pp. 306-313.

————. "Lessons of the Gezira Scheme," *The Times Survey of the British Colonies* (Winter 1950), pp. 7-8.

Great Britain. British Information Services. *The Sudan, 1899–1953.* I.D.1799. London: Author, August 1953. 58 p.

Hance, William A. "The Gezira: An Example in Development," *The Geographical Review*, v. 44 (April 1954), pp. 253-270.

————. "The Zande Scheme in the Anglo-Egyptian Sudan," *Economic Geography*, v. 31 (April 1955), pp. 149-156.

Hewison, R. "Some Factors Affecting the Gezira Irrigation Scheme," *Empire Cotton Growing Review*, v. 12 (January 1953), pp. 25-31.

Sudan Government. *The Gezira from Within*. Khartoum: Government Printer, 1954. 48 p.

Tothill, J. D., ed. *Agriculture in the Sudan*. New York: Oxford University Press, 1948. 974 p.

Chapter 3

Church, R. J. Harrison. *West Africa*. London: Longmans Green, 1957. 547 p.

Gold Coast. *Economic Survey, 1954*. Accra: Government Printer, 1955. 69 p.

Great Britain. Colonial Office. *An Economic Survey of the Colonial Territories, 1951*, v. 3, *The West African Territories*, Col. 281-283. London: HMSO, 1952. 103 p.

Organization for European Economic Cooperation. *The Main Products of the Colonial Territories: Cocoa*. Doc. C(56)60. Paris, 1956. 164 p.

United Africa Company, Ltd. "What Cocoa Means to the Economy of the Gold Coast," *Statistical and Economic Review*, no. 2 (September 1948), pp. 1-28.

The Volta River Project. London: HMSO, for the United Kingdom and Gold Coast Governments, 1956. 3 v.

Ward, W. E. F. *A History of the Gold Coast.* London: G. Allen and Unwin, 1948. 387 p.

The Economist (London).

Gold Coast Weekly Review (issued on behalf of the Gold Coast government).

West Africa (London).

Chapter 4

Buchanan, K. M., and J. C. Pugh. *Land and People in Nigeria.* London: University of London Press, 1955. 252 p.

Church, R. J. Harrison. "Geographical Factors in the Development of Transport in Africa," United Nations *Transport and Communications Review,* v. 2, no. 3 (New York, 1949), pp. 3-11. Also *West Africa,* cited under Chapter 3.

Giraud, M. "Les Problèmes des Transports en A.O.F.," *Industries et Travaux d'Outremer,* 5th yr. (Paris, May 1957), pp. 247-251.

Hance, William A., and Irene S. van Dongen. "The Port of Lobito and the Benguela Railway," *The Geographical Review,* v. 66 (October 1956), pp. 460-487.

———. "Port Development and Rail Lines in Portuguese West Africa," Eighteenth International Geographical Congress, Rio de Janeiro (August 1956), unpublished.

———. "The Port of Matadi (Belgian Congo) and Its Hinterland," *Annals of the Association of American Geographers,* v. 48 (March 1958).

———. "The Port of Dar es Salaam and Its Tributary Area," forthcoming.

———. "Beira, Mozambique Gateway to Central Africa," *Annals of the Association of American Geographers,* v. 47 (December 1957), pp. 307-335.

———. "Lourenço Marques in Delagoa Bay," *Economic Geography,* v. 33 (July 1957), pp. 238-256.

Munger, Edwin S. "Voie Nationale," *Institute of Current World Affairs Newsletter,* no. ESM—27 (1952), 24 p.

United Africa Company, Ltd. *Statistical and Economic Review.*
"The Company's River Fleet and Port, Nigeria," no. 2 (September 1948), pp. 33-48.
"Forcados and Escravos Bars," no. 6 (September 1950), pp. 46-60.
"Port Capacity and Shipping Turnround in West Africa," no. 19 (March 1957), pp. 1-50.

van Dongen, Irene S. *The British East African Transport Complex.* University of Chicago Geography Research Paper, no. 38. Chicago: University Press, 1954. 172 p.

———. "Nacala, Newest Mozambique Gateway to Interior Africa," *Tijdschrift voor Economische en Sociale Geografie,* 48th year (Rotterdam, March 1957), pp. 65-73.

Chapter 5

Debenham, Frank. *Study of an African Swamp*. London: HMSO, 1952. 88 p.

Federation of Rhodesian Industry. *Survey of Rhodesian Industry*. Salisbury: Author, 1954. 139 p. (Multigraphed.)

Great Britain. *Central African Territories: Geographical, Historical and Economic Survey*. Cmd. 8234. London: HMSO, 1951. 47 p.

————. Colonial Office. *An Economic Survey of the Colonial Territories, 1951*, v. 1, *The Central African and High Commission Territories*. Col. 281 (1), 1952. 106 p.

Guernsey, T. D. "A Summary of the Provisional Geological Features of Northern Rhodesia," *Colonial Geological and Mineral Resources*, v. 1, no. 2 (1950), pp. 121-149.

Hance, William A., and Irene S. van Dongen. "Beira, Mozambique Gateway to Central Africa," *Annals of the Association of American Geographers*, v. 47 (December 1957), pp. 307-335.

Hochschild, Harold K. "Labor Relations in Northern Rhodesia," *The Annals of the American Academy of Political and Social Science*, v. 306 (July 1956), pp. 43-49.

Mason, Philip. "Masters or Partners? Race Relations in the African Federation," *Foreign Affairs*, v. 35 (April 1957), pp. 496-506.

Paton, Alan. "African Advancement: A Problem of Both Copperbelt and Federation," *Optima* (quarterly review of the Anglo American Corporation of South Africa Ltd.), v. 5 (December 1955), pp. 105-109.

Prain, R. L. "The Stabilization of Labour in the Rhodesian Copper Belt," *African Affairs*, v. 55 (October 1956), pp. 305-312.

Trapnell, C. G., and J. N. Clothier. *The Soils, Vegetation and Agricultural Systems of North-western Rhodesia*. Lusaka: Government Printer, 1937. 81 p.

Trapnell, C. G. *The Soils, Vegetation and Agriculture of North-eastern Rhodesia*. Lusaka: Government Printer, 1953. 146 p.

U. S. Department of Commerce. *Investment in Federation of Rhodesia and Nyasaland*. Washington: GPO, 1956. 158 p.

Wellington, J. H. *Southern Africa*. Cambridge: University Press, 1955. 2 v.

Woodruff, H. W., and C. W. Thompson. *Economic Development in Rhodesia and Nyasaland*. London: Dennis Hobson, 1955. 205 p.

Whittlesey, Derwent. "Southern Rhodesia: An African Compage," *Annals of the Association of American Geographers*, v. 46 (March 1956), pp. 1-97.

Barclays Bank D.C.O., *Overseas Review* (London).

The Central African Examiner (Salisbury).

The Economist (London).

The Rhodes-Livingstone Journal (Livingstone).

Standard Bank of South Africa Limited. *The Standard Bank Review.*

Chapter 6

Cullen, A. D. *Précis of the East Africa Royal Commission 1953–1955 Report.* Nakuru, Kenya: Nakuru Press, 1955. 65 p.

Great Britain. *East Africa Royal Commission 1953–1955 Report.* Cmd. 9475. London: HMSO, 1955. 482 p.

――――. Colonial Office. *Despatches from the Governors of Kenya, Uganda and Tanganyika and from the Administrator, East Africa High Commission, Commenting on the East Africa Royal Commission 1953–1955 Report.* Cmd. 9801. London: HMSO, 1956. 196 p.

――――. ――――. *Commentary on the Despatches. . . .* Cmd. 9804. London: HMSO, 1956. 6 p.

――――. ――――. *An Economic Survey of the Colonial Territories, 1951,* v. 2, *The East African Territories.* Col. 281-282. London: HMSO, 1954. 204 p.

Mason, Philip. *A New Deal in East Africa: The Basic Arguments and Certain Implications of the Report of the Royal Commission on East Africa.* London: Royal Institute of International Affairs, 1955. 55 p.

Matheson, J. K., and W. E. Bovill, eds. *East African Agriculture.* New York: Oxford University Press, 1950. 332 p.

Chapter 7

Anderson, R. Earle. *Liberia, America's African Friend.* Chapel Hill: University of North Carolina Press, 1953. 305 p.

Brown, George W. *The Economic History of Liberia.* Washington: Associated Publishers, 1941. 366 p.

Buell, R. L. *Liberia: A Century of Survival, 1847–1947.* Philadelphia: University of Pennsylvania Press, 1947. 140 p.

Hanson, E. P. "An Economic Survey of the Western Province of Liberia," *The Geographical Review,* v. 37 (January 1947), pp. 53-69.

Republic of Liberia. Department of State. *Invest-Trade-Prosper-with Liberia.* London: Diplomatic Press, 1957. 40 p.

Taylor, Wayne C. *The Firestone Operations in Liberia.* Washington: National Planning Association, 1956. 115 p.

U. S. Foreign Operations Administration. *Liberian Swamp Rice a Success.* Washington: Author, 1955. 49 p.

――――, and Foreign Agricultural Service. *Agriculture in Liberia,* by Clayton R. Orton. Washington: Authors, 1954. 111 p.

U. S. International Cooperation Administration. *Forestry Progress and Timbering Opportunities in the Republic of Liberia,* by Torkel Holsoe. Washington: Author, 1956. 67 p. and appendices.

U. S. Office of Foreign Agricultural Relations, and Technical Cooperation Administration. *Reconnaissance Soil Survey of Liberia,* by William E. Reed. Agriculture Information Bulletin, no. 66. Washington: GPO, 1951. 107 p.

————. *Forest Resources of Liberia,* by Karl R. Mayer. Agriculture Information Bulletin, no. 67. Washington: GPO, 1951. 69 p.

U. S. Department of Commerce. *Economic Development of Liberia 1955.* World Trade Information Service, Part I, no. 56-56. Washington: GPO, 1956. 8 p.

————. *Basic Data on the Economy of Liberia.* World Trade Information Service, Part I, no. 55-58. Washington: GPO, 1955. 13 p.

Wilson, Charles M. *Liberia.* New York: Sloane, 1947. 226 p.

Chapter 8

Chevalier, Louis. *Madagascar, Population et Ressources.* Paris: Presses Universitaires de France, 1952. 212 p.

Decary, Raymond. *Madagascar et Dépendances.* Paris: Société d'Éditions Géographique, Maritime, et Coloniale, 1952. 225 p.

Deschamps, Hubert. *Madagascar.* Paris: Berger-Levrault, 1951. 192 p.

Encyclopédie de l'Afrique Française. *Madagascar.* Paris: Encyclopédie Coloniale et Maritime, 1947. 2 v.

Hance, William A. "Transportation in Madagascar," *The Geographical Review,* v. 48 (January 1958), pp. 45-68.

————. "The Economic Geography of Madagascar," *Tijdschrift voor Economische en Sociale Geografie,* 48th year (Rotterdam, July-August 1957), pp. 161-172.

Hatzfeld, Olivier. *Madagascar.* Paris: Presses Universitaires de France, 1952. 127 p.

Isnard, Hildebert. *Madagascar.* Paris: Armand Colin, 1955. 219 p.

République Française. *Madagascar.* Paris, 1954. 211 p. (Mimeographed.)

Rotival, Maurice. *Madagascar: Essai de Planification Organique.* Tananarive: Service Géographique de Madagascar, 1952. 58 p.

Bulletin de Madagascar (Tananarive).

Encyclopédie Mensuelle d'Outremer (Paris).

Entreprises et Produits de Madagascar (Tananarive).

Marchés Tropicaux du Monde; Marchés Coloniaux du Monde (Paris).

Revue de Madagascar (Tananarive).

INDEX

This index covers only the text and not footnote references, tables, maps, or the Bibliography.